CRAFTING SHORT SCREENPLAYS THAT CONNECT

SECOND EDITION

CRAFTING SHORT SCREENPLAYS THAT CONNECT

SECOND EDITION

Claudia Hunter Johnson

Amsterdam • Boston • Heidelberg • London
New York • Oxford • Paris • San Diego
San Francisco • Singapore • Sydney • Tokyo

Focal Press is an imprint of Elsevier

30 Corporate Drive, Suite 400, Burlington, MA 01803, USA
Linacre House, Jordan Hill, Oxford OX2 8DP, UK

 Recognizing the importance of preserving what has been written,
Elsevier prints its books on acid-free paper whenever possible.

Library of Congress Cataloging-in-Publication Data
APPLICATION SUBMITTED

British Library Cataloguing-in-Publication Data
A catalogue record for this book is available from the British Library.

ISBN: 0-240-80641-7

For information on all Focal Press publications
visit our Web site at www.focalpress.com or www.books.elsevier.com.

05 06 07 08 09   10 9 8 7 6 5 4 3 2 1

Printed in the United States of America

For my dear friend, mentor, and teacher, Sam Smiley,
who taught me most of what I know about drama.

"Most movies celebrate the ways we connect with each other."

—Jeremy Irons, at the 68th Annual Academy Awards

"Conflict may certainly arise, but I think it's on a secondary or more superficial level; in a sense, it arises when we are frustrated in our efforts to achieve love and affection. It is not part of our most basic, underlying nature."

—His Holiness The Dalai Lama
The Art of Happiness

CONTENTS

PREFACE TO THE SECOND EDITION

This book is the distillation of a decade and a half of teaching screenwriting and dramatic technique at Florida State University—and an epiphany I had halfway through.

During that decade and a half, to my delight, I've seen the American short film (thirty minutes or less) rise in importance from a résumé piece intended to launch a filmmaker's career to an art form in its own right. As interest and access to short films increases, as well as outstanding venues like *homestarrunner.com* and *triggerstreet.com*, the short screenplay/film is becoming the central short narrative form of our time, analogous to the short story in the 1940s, argues Ray Fielding, former Dean of the Florida State University Film School.

"It's a new day for the short film," Fielding said. "It's a phenomenon, a phoenix rising from the ashes. With the gradual perfection of wideband Internet transmission, and the already well-established market for long-play DVD discs, the short film is coming into its own. Not since the golden years of live television, when distinguished original dramatic plays were presented several times a week to national audiences, has the marketplace for short film and video drama looked so bright."

But during my decade and a half of teaching at F.S.U., I found three things sorely missing: A nuts-and-bolts book about crafting short screenplays; access to short films and their screenplays so writers (and teachers and students) can *see* the choices and changes—good, bad, or ugly—that were made in production; and any discussion in screenwriting books that there is more going on in good screenplays than conflict (stay with me; there is). To liquidate this lack over the years—often through trial and error—I designed the practical, hands-on approach to crafting short screenplays that I'm offering here. And, to give you easy access to outstanding short films and their screenplays, I'm including a DVD of the seven short award-winning films made from the screenplays published in Part III of the book.

By craft I mean "the sum total of all means used to draw the audience into deep involvement, to hold that involvement, and ultimately to reward it with a moving and meaningful experience," as Robert McKee writes in *Story*.

In other words, to connect. This book is dedicated to the proposition that connecting—to oneself and to others—is the source of great screenplays, regardless of length.

And craft, I'm convinced, can be taught, though I agree with playwright William Gibson's wry observation, "The rest is art and up to God." Craft *must* be taught to those who want to write effective short films, which require "deft characterization, a compressed narrative style, and something to say that is focused and fresh in voice," as Michael Rabiger reminds us in *Directing the Film: Film Techniques and Aesthetics*. The shorter the film, in fact, the taller the order for craft.

"A good five- to ten-minute film is actually more demanding to make than a passable thirty-minute one," Rabiger says.

Screenwriting is such a complex and difficult craft, I have found it most effective to break it into teachable, learnable pieces that you can tackle one at a time. This approach underlies the design of this book.

I believe in learning by doing, so you will write—and rewrite—five short screenplays of increasing length and complexity that focus on a different essential aspect of dramatic technique and the craft of screenwriting. Each screenplay will build on the skills and techniques you learned in the previous one. Ideally, by the time you've written all five, you will have grappled with most of the issues, small and large, in screenwriting.

My purpose has always been—and still is—to elicit the richest, most resonant work from my students—short screenplays that are, at once, unique and universal. The goal of this book is the same—to offer an experiential approach that will help you—or your students—craft short screenplays that connect. To that end, the book is divided into three sections:

Part I—Preparing to Write the Short Screenplay—explores essential preliminary issues: the importance of connecting to others; connecting to your unique material and vision; connecting to your own creative process; and connecting to what screenplays *are* at their deepest level—patterns of significant human change—and to what they are on the surface level of screenplay format. I have also added a new chapter, "Connecting to Collaboration," about the art of collaboration, both in the workshop and the increasingly popular and productive process of co-writing scripts.

Part II—Five (Not So) Easy Screenplays—guides you through crafting five short screenplays, each focused on a crucial aspect of dramatic technique:

1. The Discovery: A three-page screenplay focused on a character making a discovery that makes a difference to the character.
2. The Decision: A five-page screenplay focused on a character making a decision that makes a difference to the character.
3. The Boxing Match (creating conflict): A five- to seven-page screenplay focused on one character wanting what another character does *not* want to give.

4. The Improbable Connection (creating connection): A seven-page screenplay focused on creating a plausible, but not predictable, pattern of human connection.
5. The Long Short Screenplay: A ten- to fifteen-page screenplay focused on telling the best story you can for the screen, using the techniques you've learned in the first four screenplays.

Part III—Seven Screenplays That Make It Look Easy—offers, for your illumination and, I hope, inspiration, the screenplays of the seven award-winning undergraduate and graduate F.S.U. thesis films on the companion DVD, from the Student-Emmy-Award winners for Best Comedy, *Kosher* and *The Making of "Killer Kite"*, to the Student-Academy-Award winners *Slow Dancin' Down the Aisles of the Quickcheck* and *A Work in Progress*. I've included *A Work in Progress* and two other outstanding and strikingly different short-short screenplays, *Kosher* and *My Josephine*—all under ten minutes and all outstanding examples of how well you can tell a story in a very short time— to inspire anyone faced with writing and making a film on a very small budget. As these three amazing films show, less can truly mean more.

I asked the seven screenwriters to select the version of the screenplay that they wanted published. None is transcribed from the screen like so many published screenplays you'll find. As Bob Gray said when he sent me the screenplay for *The Making of "Killer Kite"*, "I resisted the temptation to rewrite the script and make it fit the edited film. This is the shooting script from which the film was made. It is, I think, a better educational exercise to see how a project can change from the final script to the completed edit."

I agree. And you will have the opportunity to see and study the changes that were made on that arduous journey from script to screen by comparing these seven screenplays to their finished films on the DVD that accompanies this second edition. I strongly urge you to read the screenplays before screening the films and even before reading the rest of the book, as I will refer to them throughout.

In the brief introduction to each screenplay, I've let the writer describe how the screenplay changed in production. Five writers—Aimee Barth, Barry Jenkins, Wes Ball, Lani Sciandra, and Thomas Jackson—directed their films, *Kosher*, *My Josephine*, *A Work in Progress*, *Cool Breeze and Buzz*, and *Slow Dancin' Down the Aisles of the Quickcheck*, respectively. Matt Stevens—who wrote the story for *The Making of "Killer Kite"*—directed the film, but Bob Gray wrote the screenplay. And Rachel Witenstein wrote *Lena's Spaghetti*, but Joe Greco directed. Each introduction also describes where these talented writers are now and what they are doing.

Some, like Matt Stevens, are writing short-short-short films (thirty seconds) for Web sites like Mattel's *myscene.com* and other new media, a burgeoning market for those skilled at writing short scripts. Others are writing features, a testament to the often overlooked truth that the short film—while an art form in its own right—is excellent preparation for writing long screenplays. The dramatic principles explored in this book are found in all good screenplays, long and short. And even if you're writing long screenplays, crafting short scripts will help you hone your skills (after writing five features, I took a whack at a short screenplay—*what a challenge!*—and came away with renewed respect and admiration for the screenwriters published here in the book).

Writing short screenplays that connect requires the craft and concentration of a medieval artist carving scenes in a walnut. And writing in a nutshell, in a nutshell, forces you to be more creative, resourceful. That is why I beg to differ with people who say that writing short scripts is as useful as lips on a chicken. It may well be the toughest screenwriting training you'll get.

And writing short screenplays is the best way to see your work on the screen and have others see it. "Getting seen is the precursor to getting noticed," Michael Rabiger says, "and for actuarial reasons alone short films are always more likely to be shown in festivals than long ones." Feature-length screenplays, alas, are like sperm: There's a one-in-a-million chance they'll get made.

But perhaps most important, this book is the first to explore connection (and not just conflict) as a crucial part of good screenplays and the screenwriting process. Including human connection in the stories they tell has helped my students write richer, more resonant short screenplays that have become award-winning films screened and celebrated at festivals all over the world. In the spirit of their own screenplays, they have competed and they have connected. I hope, with this book, you will, too.

ACKNOWLEDGMENTS

Warmest thanks to . . .

My editor, Elinor Actipis at Focal Press, for shepherding this second edition.

My husband, Ormond Loomis, and our children, Anne and Ross Loomis—three of the best writers I know—for kicking these ideas around with me for the past fifteen years, and for all our trips to the movies and the lively discussions that follow. A special thanks, too, to Ormond, for your patience with a still-low-tech writer and for taking care of the art work.

My writing partner, Matt Stevens, for continuing to listen to my rants about connection, for collaborating with me on our own screenplays and our book *Script Partners*, and for providing so many of the insights included here in the chapter about collaboration.

Meryl Warren and Kathy Barber at the Florida State University School of Motion Picture, Television and Recording Arts, for helping me corral the screenwriters and their awards, and Dean Frank Patterson for letting me use award-winning F.S.U. films for the DVD.

Farrar, Straus & Giroux for granting permission to quote from Seamus Heaney's poem "Station Island."

And last but not least, the seven screenwriters featured here—Aimee Barth, Barry Jenkins, Wes Ball, Rachel Witenstein, Lani Siandra, Bob Gray, and Thomas Jackson—for letting me publish your wonderful screenplays. It's an honor to honor your work in this book.

INTRODUCTION: THE POWER AND IMPORTANCE OF HUMAN CONNECTION

For years I gently browbeat my students. "Dig deeper," I said. "The best stories are about the human heart."

I wasn't quite sure what I meant. I knew I didn't mean that old Hollywood saw—*throw in some love interest!* I meant something closer to Samson Raphaelson's remark about Shakespeare in *The Human Nature of Playwriting*, "[He] is not a realistic writer but he is overwhelmingly real because he reports the hearts of human beings."

I was teaching dramatic technique—first playwriting in the English Department at Florida State, then screenwriting when the Film School began—rounding up the usual suspects, conflict, crisis, and climax—but I had this nagging sensation that these overlooked something important in stories. I couldn't figure out what it was, so I hoped, if sufficiently coaxed, my students could.

WHAT WE TALK ABOUT WHEN WE TALK ABOUT DRAMA

Derived from the Greek *dran*—"to do"—drama means someone strives. Will meets obstacle, and this creates conflict. For two hundred years, perhaps more, we have talked about dramatic stories this way. George Bernard Shaw defined drama as "the conflict between man's will and his environment." Across the channel, Ferdinand Brunetiere said it was "the will of man in conflict." And so it has gone, like a roll call, each person casting a vote for drama's conventional wisdom.

"Since the early nineteenth century the 'conflict theory' of drama has dominated dramatic criticism and, to a considerable degree, the practice of playwrights," Eric Bentley says in *Concepts in Dramatic Theory*. "It is a central assumption of most twentieth-century dramatic theory." In film, where the budgets (and insecurities) run wilder and the flops are more catastrophic, the rule of the game is more rigid.

1

"The basis of all drama is conflict," Syd Field says in almost every one of his books. "Without conflict there is no action; without action there is no character; without character there is no story. And without story there is no screenplay."

Most screenwriting books—about long or short screenplays—essentially say the same thing, though in *Screenwriting Tricks of the Trade*, William Froug is the most emphatic: "Without conflict, you might as well pack it in—you are in the wrong field of endeavor. Without conflict, your reader will fall asleep and you will never have to think about having an audience. The ballgame is over."

Conflict has shaped the way that we think about drama and the way that we think to shape it. In *Writing Great Screenplays for Film and TV*, Dona Cooper offers a new improved metaphor for the screenplay—a roller coaster. It's a rollicking image, more energetic and imaginative than most I have found in screenwriting books, but the author's graphic depiction—action that rises and rises and rises then falls—is merely a remake of a nineteenth century model, Freitag's Pyramid (conflict, crisis, and resolution), which keeps cropping up in all kinds of books about writing, including former editions of Janet Burroway's *Writing Fiction*. But Janet—a colleague—was increasingly uncomfortable, too, with this conflict-bound way of seeing the story.

Other writers, most of them women, were also uneasy. But Ursula K. LeGuin came closest to articulating what I was feeling:

> People are cross-grained, aggressive, and full of trouble, the storytellers tell us; people fight themselves and one another, and their stories are full of their struggles. But to say that that is the story is to use one aspect of existence, conflict, to subsume all other aspects, many of which it does not include and does not comprehend.
>
> *Romeo and Juliet* is the story of the conflict between two families, and its plot involves the conflict of two individuals within those families. Is that all it involves? Isn't *Romeo and Juliet* about something else, and isn't it the something else that makes the otherwise trivial tale of a feud into a tragedy?[1]

Conflict was not incorrect, it was *incomplete*. It didn't get to the heart of the matter, to that level of story that engages most deeply. It was half the story, but I couldn't figure out what the other half was.

RUBY & ME

In January 1994, taking a shower, I saw it—the other half of the story. I don't know what it is about showers and baths that's conducive to insight, but the fact is well documented: Einstein reportedly claimed his greatest ideas occurred in the shower, and everyone knows about Archimedes. I'm a Pisces so I like to think it's the water, but it's more than likely the break from our work. "These insights tend to come suddenly and, characteristically, not when sitting at a desk working," Fritjof Capra writes in the *Tao of Physics*, "but when relaxing, in the bath, during a walk in the woods, on the beach."

I'd taken a break from researching a documentary film about the most famous murder in Florida, the trial of Ruby McCollum, an African-American woman in my small town of Live Oak convicted of shooting and killing the town's Great White Hope, Senator-elect Leroy Adams, her doctor and, allegedly, lover. When she fired the gun—if she, in fact, did it—her life also came to an end: Every major connection was severed; her husband died the next day of heart failure; and she was separated from her children, other family, and friends for more than twenty years.

Immersed in Ruby's story, I wondered why it engaged me so deeply. She and I had nothing in common except for our gender and the small North Florida town where we lived. The surface events of her story were the stuff of soap opera—wealth, corruption, infidelity, murder—and this had no connection to my quiet life. There was something deeper at work. Mulling over what it might be, I saw that it was connection itself. Underlying the conflict of Ruby's story, underlying the events of her life and mine—underlying any good story, fictitious or true—is a deeper pattern of change, a pattern of connection and disconnection. The conflict and surface events are like waves, but underneath is an emotional tide—the ebb and flow of human connection. It's just as essential to story as conflict but it has been essentially overlooked.

I'm no Einstein and I didn't run naked trailing bathwater into the street but I did shout "Eureka, I've found it!" I did. For the first time, I saw drama *whole*. Here was its deepest humanity, structure, and emotional rhythm, the "something else" LeGuin knew was missing.

Everything seemed to fall into place. I understood the emotional power of plays in a way that I hadn't before: What keeps *Romeo and Juliet* from being an "otherwise trivial tale of a feud" is the underlying pattern of connection and disconnection, not just between the two star-crossed lovers, but between them and those others who make up their web of connections—nurse, parents, Mercutio, Tybalt, Friar Lawrence, the Prince; what keeps *Death of a Salesman* from being a trivial tale of a failed businessman is Willy's tragic pattern of connection and disconnection with others, especially Biff.

I saw tragedy and comedy in a new light—comedy ends in connection, tragedy in disconnection. "The tragic side of tragedy," to borrow Aristotle's phrase, is more than the hero's fall from position and power. "Those who have had the misfortune to do or undergo fearful things," are, in the end, disconnected. We may pity the fallen because we fear falling but we fear it less, perhaps, than we fear disconnection. Even death, the ultimate disconnection, is less fearsome for some than life without connection.

"Ha! banishment," Romeo cries. "Be merciful, say 'death,'/For exile hath more terror in his look,/Much more, than death. Do not say 'banishment.'"

Connection is human sustenance, the substance of story. Its gain and loss provides the emotional power, as Aristotle implies in *The Poetics*:

> Let us determine, then, which kinds of happening are felt by the spectator to be fearful, and which pitiable. Now such acts are necessarily the work of persons who are near and dear (close blood kin) to one another, or enemies, or neither. But when an

enemy attacks an enemy there is nothing pathetic about either the intention or the deed, except in the actual pain suffered by the victim; nor when the act is done by "neutrals"; but when the tragic acts come within the limits of close blood relationship, as when brother kills or intends to kill brother or do something else of that kind to him, or son to father or mother to son or son to mother—those are the situations one should look for.[2]

I understood, too, that connection and disconnection provided the emotional power of the films I had seen, even the best of the hard-boiled genres. *The Fugitive*—warmed-over TV show that it is—engages more deeply than most films in its genre because of the grudging but growing connection between the fugitive Kimble and Federal Marshall Gerard, the deeper emotional journey from Gerard's "I don't care," (a line Tommy Lee Jones rehearsed for days) to his closing line, "I care. Don't tell anyone." This unlikely connection is the heart of the story, its pattern of meaning. It fills the emotional void created by Kimble's wife's brutal murder. In story as in life, human nature abhors an emotional vacuum.

I went to see Janet. She said, "This is big—the other half of Aristotle." She pulled books from her shelves that touched on connection—Lewis Hyde's *The Gift* and Jean Baker Miller's *Toward A New Psychology of Women* and Carol Gilligan's *In A Different Voice*. She opened Hyde's book and showed me a passage from Pablo Neruda, a memory about a connection he made when he was a child, an exchange of small gifts—a pine cone and a faded toy sheep—with a boy about his own age, a stranger he did not see again:

> That exchange brought home to me for the first time a precious idea: that all humanity is somehow together. This is the great lesson I learned in my childhood, in the backyard of a lonely house. Maybe it was nothing but a game two boys played who didn't know each other and wanted to pass to the other some good things of life. Yet maybe this small and mysterious exchange of gifts remained inside me also, deep and indestructible, giving my poetry light.[3]

This, I think, is the heart of it all: There are moments of change in our lives and stories that are not comprehended by conflict. These moments of change are connections, human exchanges, however fleeting or small—a faded sheep for a pine cone—or, as Stephen Jay Gould says in "Counters and Cable Cars," "people taking care of each other in small ways of enduring significance." Large or small, they are like gifts—they create ties between us.

Janet asked if she could mention my insight in her new edition of *Writing Fiction*:

> I'm indebted to dramatist Claudia Johnson for this further— and, it seems to me, crucial—insight about [LeGuin's] "something else": whereas the hierarchical or "vertical" nature of narrative, the power struggle, has long been acknowledged,

there also appears in all narrative a "horizontal" pattern of connection and disconnection between characters which is the main source of its emotional effect. In discussing human behavior, psychologists speak in terms of "tower" and "network" patterns, the need to climb and the need for community, the need to win out over others and the need to belong to others; and these two drives also drive fiction.[4]

As a writer who has worked in four genres—plays, fiction, screenplays, and, most recently, memoir—I suspect these two drives drive most stories (I'll leave it to others to explore the exceptions). In *Metaphors of Interrelatedness: Toward a Systems Theory of Psychology*, Linda Olds acknowledges our "vertical strivings for power, achievement, knowledge, and accomplishment," but she adds:

> We no longer inhabit a universe capable of being represented vertically alone; the embeddedness of us all in an intricately interrelating dance of energy and spacetime, of connection and change, has become the inescapable heritage of our time. We must reach out for horizontal metaphors which speak the language of embrace and interconnection, rather than striving and rising above.[5]

The film *Red* does this with its powerful opening image of telephone cables carrying the young model's call at breathtaking speeds across land, under water, and across land again. One of the most compelling films that I've seen, it is a story told with almost no conflict, a film, finally, about connection itself. But *Lost in Translation* may be the most superb example of how moving and successful a screenplay/film about human connection can be.

Still, most stories have both. Rooted in the same Latin prefix (*con*—together), conflict (from the Latin *confligere*—to clash or strike together) and connection (from the Latin *connectere*—to bind or tie together) are complementary forces. The physicist Niels Bohr introduced the concept of "complementarity," but as Capra points out in *The Tao of Physics*, it goes back 2,500 years:

> "The Chinese sages represented this complementarity of opposites by the archetypal poles of *yin* and *yang* and saw their dynamic interplay as the essence of all natural phenomena and all human situations."

Connection and conflict are also dynamic and interrelated. They are woven together like strands of deoxyribonucleic acid, the double helix of drama.

A MODEL OF WHOLENESS

Like the newly pregnant woman who never noticed pregnant women before but now sees them wherever she goes, I noticed connection wherever I looked.

I saw its ebb and flow in the novels I read. Anne Tyler's *Ladder of Years* is a series of emotional movements of connecting and disconnecting and reconnecting as Delia drifts from her family, builds a new life, and returns to her own.

I saw connection and disconnection in films that I screened, even the wild-assed rides in *Pulp Fiction*—"Vincent Vega and Marsellus Wallace's Wife," "The Gold Watch," and "The Bonnie Situation." For all the vintage Tarantino violence and conflict, marvelous connections occur in each of the stories.

In *Apollo 13*, I noticed how painstakingly the story establishes Jim Lovell's web of connections—wife, children, colleagues—and how these become the real stake in the film, as important as survival itself, the reason survival matters to him at all.

Like Forster's once cryptic epigram, "Only connect," this made a new kind of sense. Eight months after my insight, on tour with my book, *Stifled Laughter*, I heard a lecture by Betty Friedan. It was an interesting update of Abraham Maslow who ranked connection (belonging) just below survival in his well-known hierarchy of needs. Friedan cited research that shows connection is no less a need. "Connectedness," as she calls it in *The Fountain of Age*, "has a direct effect on mortality." Epidemiological studies across the country show that men and women without significant human connection are twice as likely to die. Widowers, disconnected from their central and often their only significant connection, are "40 percent more likely to die in the first six months after their spouse's death than other men their age."

That women live longer than men is well known. The conventional wisdom says that men die younger because of too much striving and competition, but Friedan and others show it is also caused by too little connection. Studies on the male midlife crisis have linked men's psychological pain to the realization that they have (like dramatic theorists) neglected connection. This lack of "closeness, relatedness, and intimacy," Friedan says, contributes directly to men's shorter lives. To survive, men and women alike must have "purpose and intimacy," what Tolstoy called "work and love," goals to strive for and what Friedan bluntly calls "the life-and-death importance of connectedness."

I connect, therefore I am.

We cannot live by conflict alone; neither can a good screenplay. The best screenwriters understand this intuitively, but the rest of us will be better screenwriters if we think about both halves of the story—conflict and connection—when we think about the stories we're telling. In this way, we'll "facilitate new ways of seeing" the story and work with "a model of wholeness," to borrow two phrases from Linda Olds. Most important, we'll open the aperture wider, to use a film metaphor, and give our stories more light.

NOTES

1. Ursula K. LeGuin, quoted in Janet Burroway's *Writing Fiction: A Guide to Narrative Craft*, Fourth Edition, HarperCollins, New York, 1996, p. 35.
2. Aristotle, *Poetics*, translated, with an introduction, by Gerald F. Else, Michigan University Press, fifth printing, 1978, pp. 40, 41.
3. Lewis Hyde, *The Gift*, Vintage Books, New York, 1979, pp. 281, 282.
4. Janet Burroway, *Writing Fiction: A Guide to Narrative Craft*, Fourth Edition, HarperCollins, New York, 1996, p. 35.
5. Linda E. Olds, *Metaphors of Interrelatedness: Toward a Systems Theory of Psychology*, State University of New York Press, 1992, p. xii.

PART I

PREPARING TO WRITE THE SHORT SCREENPLAY

CONNECTING TO PURPOSE

ONLY CONNECT

A screenwriter's purpose is to connect.

"Only connect," E.M. Forster tells us in *Howard's End*. He meant it as a rule to live by. I see it as a rule to *write* by. The best screenplays—long or short—are written by those who know how to connect—to themselves (their unique vision, material, process), to what drama *is*, and, most important, to others.

"You must never forget the umbilical cord is to real life, real people," Oliver Stone says in Linda Seger and Edward Jay Whetmore's *From Script to Screen*.

"I think of the medium as a people-to-people medium," Frank Capra says in Eric Sherman's *Directing the Film*, "not cameraman-to-people, not directors-to-people, not writers-to-people, but people-to-people."

"You know," Jean Renoir agrees, "if art doesn't take us as collaborators, art is dull. We must be in communion, the artist and the public. Without the collaboration of the public, to me, we have nothing."

Only connect. Write it down on a Post-It™ note or a three-by-five card and stick it on your computer, desk, forehead. This deceptively simple advice is the heart of the art of writing good screenplays.

It is also the impulse to write. "When talented people write well," Robert McKee says in *Story*, "it is generally for this reason: They're moved by a desire to touch the audience."

Thomas Jackson described this desire when I asked how he came up with *Slow Dancin' Down the Aisles of the Quickcheck*:

> I was driving back [from Bainbridge, Georgia to Tallahassee] and I was thinking about a character, a grocery store manager who had a crush on his head cashier. You know, when I worked in this grocery store I had crushes on all the cashiers, you know, in some way or another, because I was very shy and I didn't speak to them so I always had crushes on them. But I was thinking about this guy and I was thinking that,

> because I'm a songwriter, too, what if he played . . . I could just see this guy playing this woman a song, and it's not something that he normally does, and it's like he's pouring his heart out and it's just so un-him. And I'm describing this into a little tape recorder I keep with me all the time, and I got choked up. You can hear me get choked up on the tape because I'm getting emotional about this. And I say on the tape, I said, "Man, if I can just make people have that feeling, I'd feel like I did something." I thought, If I can get people to feel that way, I would feel like I did something.

You may have a different purpose in mind. If you're anything like the ambitious students I teach, you may well want to write the script for that short film that will open Hollywood's doors. And that can certainly happen—as I write, Thomas is at the Cannes Film Festival with *Slow Dancin'*—but it won't happen unless your screenplay connects. Connecting with others is what you must do to succeed as a screenwriter, and it will also be your greatest success.

Ask any dramatist—playwright or screenwriter. They'll describe the sheer wonder—and joy—of seeing an audience connecting to a story they've written. People lurching with laughter (in the right places) or staring rapt at the screen because they're so moved by the story they're seeing. And the worst times are those when an audience doesn't connect. Groans. Sighs of impatience or boredom. Bad laughs.

Years ago, during the intermission of one of my plays, I overheard two young men in the lobby discussing a dog. I like dog stories, so I sidled over to listen. The dog, I found out, was my play. That's what is so terrifying about writing plays or screenplays: Failure is so damn *public*.

Okay, you've been warned.

But even an evening of *My Play As a Dog* cannot cancel the incomparable pleasures I've had connecting to others, seeing an audience—to my ever-lasting joy and amazement—stand up and *cheer* for a short play I wrote. And, yes, that play opened doors—terrific reviews ("offers hope for humanity"), my first agent, and publication—but I promise you nothing—*nothing*—equaled the sense of achievement I felt when that play connected to others. And, when I keep that in mind, I'm a much better writer. Maybe that's why Fritz Lang says:

> I asked myself—why is the first work of a writer or a screen-writer, or of a playwright almost always a success? Because he still belongs to an audience. The more he goes away from the audience, the more he loses contact, and what I tried to do my whole life long was I tried not to lose contact with the audience.[1]

But even Fritz Lang—for all his magnificent films such as *Metropolis*, *M*, *The Big Heat*—wasn't always successful.

Why? Because connecting to others is one of the hardest things that we do. As Bruno Bettelheim observed in his book *Surviving*, human beings are like porcupines trying to stay warm on a cold winter night: We want to be close to one another for warmth, but we don't want to be too close for comfort. We're distinct—and we're not. We want to remain distinct, unique—and we don't.

Imagine a screening room full of strangers waiting to see the short film you've written—young, old, male, female, different ages, professions—a bag boy, a film buff, a periodontist who's had a bad day, an attorney who's just realized she hates practicing law. Put yourself in their place; this shouldn't be hard; you've been an audience member longer than you've been a writer. Like you and everyone else on this planet, they're preoccupied. Yet, somehow, the story you've written must engage—catch and hold—their attention. If it doesn't, they'll think, "So what? Why are you telling me this? Wasting my time? What the hell does this have to do with my life?" They'll daydream or rattle cellophane wrappers or get up and walk out.

"The first business of the playwright is to keep the audience from walking out," William Gibson says in *Shakespeare's Game*. This goes for screenwriters, too.

Luckily, audiences *want* to connect, though this desire may be unconscious, buried. "It is true that America is a high-tech, speed-driven, 'Gimme-the-fax/facts-and-get-on-with-it' society," Marylou Awiakta says in *Selu*. "Few can escape this dynamic. But it's also true that most of us, deep down, yearn for relationship, connection, and meaning."

Good stories satisfy this deep yearning. Once upon a time, we shared stories around a fire—sometimes we still do—but now we usually share them in movie theaters, and the flickering light on our faces comes from the images up on the screen. The stories we see may take place in a galaxy far away, on a sheep farm in New Zealand, or in a depressed Sheffield, England. The hero may be a rebel fighter or a piglet or an unemployed steelworker, but stories like *Star Wars* and *Babe* and *The Full Monty* not only entertain us, they make us more human. They show us in fresh and wonderful ways that we're not the only fools on the planet struggling with this Godawful difficult business of being alive. They "induce a moment of grace, a communion," Lewis Hyde says in *The Gift*, "a period during which we too know the hidden coherence of our being and feel the fullness of our lives."

As audience members, we spend a good deal of time and money in this culture to feel that sense of communion, to be fully engaged, to feel so tied to a story we're carried away.

"I want to be transported by the screenplay," Actor Peter Strauss says in *From Script To Screen*, "to go to the movie, to be in the dark and have magic happen."

I think it helps us as writers—I know it helps me—to think of a screenplay as a magic carpet ride, to ask these questions: "How does my story lift an audience off the ground? Take them on a journey? Return them to their seats?" And, perhaps most important, "how does the ride make them *feel*?"

"I look for passion, aliveness, hatred, rage, fear, pain, joy, bigness," Strauss continues. "I want to feel big, I want to be angry big, feel sad big."

Look at the language he's using. *I want to feel big. I want to be angry big, feel sad big.* He isn't content to see characters having emotions, *he wants to feel those emotions himself.*

The late great Paddy Chayefsky (*Marty, The Hospital*) put it bluntly, "Drama is concerned only with emotion." And, in interview after interview, even Tarantino insists that a story must work on an emotional level. "A play"—or, in this case, a screenplay—"is the shortest distance from emotions to emotions," George Pierce Baker says in *Dramatic Technique.*

The stories we tell must create shared emotions, those golden threads that connect the audience to the characters up on the screen. Or on paper.

When Alan Arkin came to Tallahassee to direct a short film, I asked what he looked for in a screenplay. "I just want a good story," he said. "I want to be moved."

I just want a good story.

"You can't involve them with gimmicks, with sunsets, with hand-held cameras, zoom shots, or anything else," Frank Capra says in *Directing the Film.* "They couldn't care less about those things. But you can give them something to worry about, some person they can worry about, and care about, and you've got them, you've got them involved." Involved. Engaged. Connected.

At the 59th Annual Academy Awards in 1987, accepting the Thalberg Award for his contributions to the industry, Steven Spielberg admitted he was more culpable than any other director for the popular practice of supplanting story with the camera and special effects. He pledged to inculcate in the next generation a greater interest in writing and to develop that interest himself.

It was this realization, this rededication to story, that led Spielberg back to that same stage to receive an Oscar for a film that connected to audiences worldwide with its wrenching disconnections and one of history's most improbable connections—Oskar Schindler caring for those on his list.

THE SCREENPLAY PARADOX

Joan Didion once said that the reason we write lies in the very vowel sounds of the phrase "Why I Write": *I, I, I.*

It has also been said that the reason audiences go to see what we've written can be summed up in the phrase: *Tell me about me.*

It's a miracle shared emotions happen at all. Still, it's true: We go to *The Full Monty* to see a story about unemployed steelworkers who save relationships and self-respect with a strip-show, but we also go because, on some level, we want to see our own life. But we don't want to *see* our own life up there on the screen because we've seen it already, and that would be boring. We want to see our own life—and we don't.

Porcupines!

This seemingly contradictory statement is nonetheless true: a paradox. The Screenplay Paradox, I like to call it, though it's true for all stories. So the screenwriter's job—the great sleight of hand—is to create a story that satisfies both.

NOT ABOUT ME
ABOUT ME

The burning question is *how?*

There's no formula, gimmick. If there were, Disney or DreamWorks would own the rights to it. And the answer doesn't lie in cheap hooks, manipulation, second guessing, or pandering to what an audience likes.

Because nobody knows.

"Nobody knows anything," William Goldman says about Hollywood.

"By God," John Huston says in *Directing the Film*, "I don't know what my best friend or wife or son or daughter would like. I only know what I like, and I hope that there are enough like me to feel the way I do about it."

Why some stories connect and others do not is, ultimately, a mystery, but we move closer to the solution when we think about what stories that *do* connect have in common.

A few years ago, presenting the Academy Award for the best film in a foreign language, Jeremy Irons said, "Though our language may be different, our desires, our needs, are the same." If we substitute the word "lives" for "language," I think we move closer to understanding why some stories connect: *Though our lives may be different, our desires, our needs are the same.*

DIFFERENT LIVES
SAME DESIRES

I've never poured steel in my life, I've never been unemployed (knock on wood), and I've never danced on stage in a night club. I can't even understand some of the things the characters in *The Full Monty* are *saying . . .*

> GAZ
>
> Dave, they're taking him away. All I need is seven hundred quid and they've got nowt on me.

> DAVE
>
> Gaz. No.

> GAZ
>
> Dave, he's me kid. Suppose they're nicking cars . . .

. . . but I connected like crazy. So did millions of others—bag boys, film buffs, periodontists, attorneys—because under the surface particulars of the story, beneath its unique universe in Sheffield, England, lie the deeper, universal human patterns of striving, failing, and striving again as well as connecting, disconnecting, and reconnecting.

$$\frac{\text{NOT ABOUT ME}}{\text{ABOUT ME}} = \frac{\text{UNIQUE}}{\text{UNIVERSAL}}$$

We strive—some say compete—and we connect. We need to win and we need to belong. That's the human matrix—a vertical pattern of striving and a horizontal pattern of connecting. And these human patterns—recreated in unique ways—are the source of a story's shared emotions.

Art, Shakespeare tells us in *Hamlet*, holds a mirror up to nature. Human nature. And somehow, through the mysterious alchemy of art, we look at characters like Hamlet and Gaz and we see ourselves.

NOTE

1. Eric Sherman, *Directing the Film: Film Directors On Their Art*, Acrobat Books, Los Angeles, 1976, p. 310.

2

CONNECTING
TO SELF

There's a depressing rumor going around that there's nothing new under the sun. Every story's been told. When you go to the movies, it's easy to see how this rumor got started. Few films are fresh. Most are warmed-over versions of what we saw last year. We wander out of the theatre convinced that everything *has* been done. So how, my students ask, can their screenplays be unique?

The answer, I say, is . . .

LE MENU

Le *what?*

Le Menu. A cross-section of their concerns. Self-analysis lite, so to speak, like those low-cal frozen dinners (I jokingly called it *Le Menu* one day in class. The name stuck).

I ask them to take out a pencil or pen and a clean sheet of paper and divide it into ten columns labeled *What I Love, What I Hate, What I Fear, What I Believe, What I Value, What I Want, What I Know About, People Who Made a Difference in My Life, Discoveries That Made a Difference in My Life,* and *Decisions That Made a Difference in My Life.*

When they're finished making the menu, the top row looks something like this:

Le Menu

What I Love	What I Hate	What I Fear	What I Believe	What I Value	What I Want	What I Know About	People Who Made a Difference in My Life	Discoveries That Made a Difference in My Life	Decisions That Made a Difference in My Life

Next, I ask them to fill in each column with their top five answers. Ten, if time allows. (If an answer is private, I ask them to flag it so I don't shoot my mouth off about it in class.) A few roll their eyes, and I have to assure them it's not some pop-psychology gimmick. I'm not trying to find out who's

15

crazy. "In a way, we're all crazy," one of my favorite writers, Joko Beck, says, and I'm content to leave it at that.

The exercise may *seem* a bit crazy—"touchy feely," as we said in the Sixties—but there is method in my madness. I've been giving this matter a great deal of thought since the literary manager of Actors Theatre of Louisville said to me a few years ago, "American dramatists lack passion and perception!" He was referring to playwrights, but the same could be said of screenwriters.

It isn't due to a lack of education or brilliance or vitamin K. It's due to our lack of awareness. We're all passionate and perceptive about certain things—we just have to figure out what they are.

"In order to create art works of any worth, each artist must have something to say, some values, some attitudes, some store of experience—a vision," my former playwriting teacher, Sam Smiley, said in *Playwriting: The Structure of Action*. Each artist must "identify those attitudes before they will ever energize a work of value."

That's what *Le Menu* is all about—identifying those attitudes, values, and experiences that will energize our work as screenwriters, creating a menu of what we know and care deeply about. It's one of the most important things we can do as screenwriters, because our unique material and vision is the source of unique screenplays.

So take a moment or an hour or a half-day to fill out a chart of your own. Work in pencil, if possible; you will probably be erasing a lot; this is a harder task than it may seem at first. Noodle first on scrap paper if you prefer, then, when you're ready, fill in each column. You don't need to rank order your answers (but do if it makes you happy); just fill in the top five or ten.

And keep your answers small and specific. Hating phenomena like global warming is too general, or, as Mark Twain said about glacial epochs, "they are vague, vague." Hating nuclear war is too sweeping; these are *short* screenplays we're talking about. It's hard to tell *Dr. Strangelove* in fifteen minutes. Or seven. Or three.

But if hating nuclear war keeps turning up on your own menu, take a moment to figure out why. Shake it down. See what *specific* connections you have to this passionate feeling. Remember, there are no right or wrong answers. The point is to get down on paper what makes you tick. So dig deeper. Annihilation aside, why do you hate nuclear war? How does this hatred resonate with your own life?

This shaking-down process can be rich and revealing. Digging deeper usually is. Annihilation aside, I hate nuclear war because when I was a child in the Fifties and early Sixties, my South Texas elementary teachers made me and my elementary school colleagues crawl under our flimsy school desks and sit there hunched over, hugging our knees, as if that would do any good if Khrushchev (or later Castro) dropped the Big One.

This drill was supposed to make us feel safe, but it unleashed an unexpected emotional fallout among American schoolchildren—stark terror—not that we were going to die, but that we were going to die *apart from our parents*. Talk about *bomb scare*. I sat crouched under my desk plotting the fastest route home (through the cotton field next to my school). My future husband was in high school in a Connecticut prep school, a thousand plus miles from his parents in Florida, plotting how to steal a Jeep and drive back roads all the way home so he could be with them before they all went *kablooey*. Ask any Boomer. It's a Christmas miracle we're normal at all.

I think you see the point. It's hard to create a short screenplay from hating something as sweeping and vague as nuclear war, but you can begin to see possibilities in a terrified tomboy crouched under her South Texas school desk plotting short cuts through cotton fields or a high-school prep in Connecticut plotting to rip off a Jeep.

The best short screenplays are deeply felt and highly specific.

Don't get me wrong. I'm not talking memoir. I'm not saying you have to write autobiographical screenplays. You may, of course—most of the seven screenplays included in this book have autobiographical elements—but that's not the point. The point is to have a point of authentic connection to the screenplays you write. The best short screenplays I've seen over the years have sprung from a person or image or scene or belief, from *something* in the story that has deep resonance for the writer.

"The idea for *My Josephine* came from an image in my head of two people's feet dangling over a table," Barry Jenkins told me. "I saw them working the night shift at a twenty-four hour Laundromat, young and intimate."

Why did this image resonate with him? It took him fifteen months—and many drafts—to find out.

He wrote the first draft shortly after September 11 and decided to make the characters Arab-American, a difficult process for him, but one that led him to his central point of connection to his characters and story:

> I am not Muslin, nor Arab-American, so it was quite a stretch for me to attempt to draft characters that were truthful. To get a new perspective on it, I took the few specific assessments I'd made about what it must be like to be Arab-American, closed my eyes, and pictured the characters living in a society where the ideal American experience is advertised as a thin physique, Caucasian, English-speaking, carefree, consumerist one. If you're not, at the very least, Caucasian and English-speaking, it can be very frustrating to live in a society where the preceding image is thrown at you every thirty seconds in print, radio, film, and television. And if you're Arab-American in post 9/11 America, it's downright daunting. This is where the pursuit of love gained importance in the script. Once I solidified my opinion of what living in America as an Arab-American was like, I immediately decided that to circumvent the harshness of that reality, the character of Aadid would devote himself to the pursuit of happiness in the love of his coworker Adela. In this way I managed to transplant all my past longings for the love and affection of women who seemed (chose) not to requite my advances but remained so close.

Barry wasn't aware of an even deeper level of connection to his spare, moving story of two Arab-American Laundromat co-workers until the film was screened in Los Angeles, and a black filmmaking friend of his wrote: *I like the film mainly because, while it does not have anything to do specifically with African-Americans, it does touch on issues of ethnicity and language/linguistic inequality within a community as depicted and portrayed through Barry's eyes/experiences as an African-American.*

"While I hadn't consciously opted to include these things," Barry said, "I couldn't help but see myself reflected in them once it was pointed out to me."

Thomas Jackson used to have crushes on all the cashiers; his main character, Earl, sprang from that root emotion. But the connection for him, too, goes even deeper. In *Slow Dancin'*, Earl finally finds the courage to tell Maybelline that he loves her, and courage is a subject close to home for the writer:

> I like to explore courage in ordinary people, extraordinary courage in ordinary people. They're just ordinary people and what they're wanting to do is not like some grandiose thing, but it's just like the moment of courage, taking that step, leaving home. I am these characters in the sense that, you know, I'm still in Bainbridge. I'm afraid to take that step out, and so that's why it's interesting to me because these are characters that are afraid, just like I am, but they actually take that little leap of faith that it takes to make the move.

And Wes Ball also looked to himself when he created the character of Melissa in *A Work In Progress*:

> I really just took bits and pieces of myself. I was always sketching when I was a kid, and I was never really good at sports. I was often left on the sidelines to watch my friends play during recess. And I was always fascinated with a friend's tire swing in her back yard, so I put it in to kind of symbolize my innocent childhood growing up in a really small country town.

I've learned the hard way that the *best* idea in the world can be hell to write if it doesn't resonate with you on some level. *Le Menu* is a very good place to look for ideas that do. It's your secret weapon, a menu of the passions and perceptions that make you—and your screenplays—unique. So finish the menu (though you're never really finished because your answers will change and evolve as you do), and for heaven's sake, don't throw it away. When I teach, I always keep a copy of my students' menus on file.

Inevitably, some of them tell me they don't have an idea. Or they'll try to write an idea that doesn't have real resonance for them. More times than not, the idea doesn't work out. The student comes to me in a panic. One student, Lani Sciandra, worked on such an idea for her thesis script, but it blew up in her face halfway through the semester. She came to my office, dazed and confused. Ready to throw in the towel. I asked her what she wanted to write about. She didn't know. So we did menu stuff (the idea for the menu was beginning to take shape in my mind). I asked her what kinds of things gnawed on her bones, as Faulkner once put it.

She said, "Like what?"

"Oh, like shame, envy, hate, love."

She talked about her relationship with her father. It was troubled. He was rarely around.

"Well," I said, "what about that?"

Lani left my office to think about this. A few weeks later she returned with a screenplay titled *Cool Breeze and Buzz*—a deceptively simple story of a young girl, Paula (a.k.a. Cool Breeze), who is living on a river with her Aunt Barbara when her father, Buzz, drives back into her life in a red Cadillac he won playing poker and invites his daughter to go live in Las Vegas with him.

Lani was living on the Wakulla River south of Tallahassee at the time, and the story sprang from that "magical kingdom—hermetically sealed from forces unnatural to itself," she told me.

> An image echoed in my mind—from the river—gliding downstream with the current—a discovery—a secret revealed—drawing from the part of me that had the most resonance—it had to do with identity and responsibility— my mother, who raised me, was the obvious choice—but as I played off the title it transformed into something less immediate, transparent—a fantasy of the absent father, the true figure in the shadow—I liked the idea of contrasting elements—the image of a man like Buzz in his red Cadillac crashing in on this pristine microcosm—and the dynamics this creates when posed with the question, "to go or not to go"—where do you really belong?—what is home?

Cool Breeze and Buzz may be a simple story on the surface, but like the river that inspired it, there are deeper currents, and they have a profound connection to Lani. As a result, the story is so deeply felt and so rich in detail, emotional honesty, and humanity that it has won more awards than any other undergraduate film produced at the Florida State Film School—first prize at film festivals across the United States and numerous recognitions abroad. And, for the same reason, *Kosher, My Josephine, A Work in Progress, Lena's Spaghetti, The Making of Killer Kite,* and *Slow Dancin'* have won numerous awards, too.

Ultimately, an authentic connection to the screenplays you write will be more important than any gimmick, sunset, hand-held camera, or zoom shot in the film that you or someone else makes. Michael Rabiger puts it this way:

> Setting out to develop a style or an artistic identity, as students often feel they must do in fine art schools, leads to superficialities and attention-demanding gimmickry. Far

more important is to develop your deepest interests and to make the best cinema you can out of the imprint left by your formative experience. Working sincerely and intelligently is what can truly connect your work to an audience.[1]

It's the Screenplay Paradox: The best way to connect with others is through the honest expression of our unique experience of being human.

DEPART THE *DONNÉE*

Your menu will be a goldmine for *germinal ideas,* as Sam Smiley calls them—undeveloped inspirations for stories—but feel free to depart the *donnée*—French for "given"—as Henry James said. Make the leap into making the rest of it up.

For Lani, the world of the river was familiar. "I started with what I knew in order to explore what I didn't, and the seed was planted, so to speak."

So did Rachel Witenstein in *Lena's Spaghetti,* the story of two lonely people—a young girl, Hannah, and a mailman, Herbie—who connect as pen pals:

> Like Hannah, I was the "misfit new kid." I was also a late bloomer. As an adolescent, I used my journal as a time-travel machine; I frequently sought the advice of my "older self," who I knew would one day read what I was writing. I would write out all my questions and thoughts, then concentrate really hard and try to hear my adult voice answering back. I guess this story was a way for me to explore the implications of taking this "older self" into the real world, into a real relationship. The concept of using your imagination to overcome obstacles such as insecurity or loneliness was familiar territory. With Herbie, I tried to create a character who would benefit from the imagination of this girl. Even though she wasn't particularly honest with him, he was better off in the end because of their relationship.

Matt Stevens loved and knew a lot about campy cult horror films and, as an M.F.A. student, the horrors of filmmaking. With these two areas of knowledge as his springboard, he created the wacky unique mockumentary, *The Making of "Killer Kite."*

As Grace Paley so wisely put it, "Write about what you know that you don't know."

Find something you're passionate or perceptive about or something that gnaws on your bones and then ask, "What if?" See where the creative river takes you.

That's what another student, Andy Zare, did after I threw a fit in my screenwriting class because all the ideas were so familiar. Boring. Sleep city. Yawners.

I said, "Okay, next time I want you to bring me the most outrageous idea you can think of." And I walked out of class, leaving my students there, a bit stunned.
Andy went home and brainstormed.

> I was always fascinated by superheroes. *Superfriends* was my favorite cartoon when I was a kid. Superman wasn't my favorite because he could do anything. I was more intrigued by the less-than-mainstream heroes that had odd abilities like Aquaman and the Wonder Twins. It's good that we had Aquaman to fight all that crime that goes on under water.
>
> The Wonder Twins were my favorites because they were so absurd. One could turn into an animal and the other would turn into some form of water. This of course was quite useful.

But the original spark came from Andy's old high school friend, Joe Wagner, the name he gave his main character.

> Joe heads a comedy sketch group in Los Angeles called "Laughingstock." He had this comedy routine about a superhero called "The Tongue" who fought crime with his super sense of taste. His nemesis would force him to brush his teeth so as to dull his taste buds. I took this idea and turned him from a superhero into an "Ordinary Joe." I was basically more interested in the downside of his ability and what type of problems it would create.

So Andy explored what those problems might be.

> I figured that the thing that Joe Wagner would dread more than anything else would be to kiss anyone. So it's really just a simple love story. It's your typical "Boy meets girl; girl wants to kiss boy; boy has super-sensitive tongue and doesn't want to kiss girl" story. There were a lot of areas to explore with Joe's tongue, but I wanted to focus it around his fear of kissing.

Andy came to the next class and pitched *tongue*—one of the freshest ideas I'd heard. And it started with a passion for superheroes and a person he knew.

Whatever your own experiences, relationships, passions, and perceptions, these will be the greatest source of uniqueness in the screenplays you write.

"We bring our life experience into the theatre," Sam Shepard said. The same is true of the movie theatre.

Unfortunately, we don't always trust this. We give into the Tarantino Temptation. Surrounded by success—and hungry for it ourselves (hey, we're just human)—we begin to believe it's easier to imitate someone like Tarantino than develop our own vision and voice. But as Anne Lamott says in *Bird By Bird*:

> The truth of your experience can *only* come through in your own voice. If it is wrapped in someone else's voice, we readers [or viewers] will feel suspicious, as if you are dressed up in someone else's clothes. . . . Sometimes wearing someone else's style is very comforting, warm and pretty and bright, and it can loosen you up, tune you into the joys of language and rhythm and concern. But what you say will be an abstraction because it will not have sprung from direct experience.[2]

Imitating others can be instructive. And it can feel like a shortcut to success—but in the long run it will short-circuit your own talent and creativity. Because your own vision, based on your direct experience, is the *source* of your creativity and the stories you tell, as Ray Bradbury reminds us in his inspiring essay, "How to Keep and Feed a Muse":

> Be certain of this: When honest love speaks, when true admiration begins, when excitement rises, when hate curls like smoke, you need never doubt that creativity will stay with you for a lifetime. The core of your creativity should be the same as the core of your story and of the main character in your story. What does your character want, what is his dream, what shape has it, and how expressed? Given expression, this is the dynamo of his life, and your life, then, as Creator. At the exact moment when truth erupts, the subconscious changes from wastebasket file to angel writing in a book of gold. Look at yourself, then.[3]

If you're in this for the long haul, you'll write many screenplays, short and long. It takes five to ten years to learn your craft, if you're lucky. So don't waste time seeking overnight success (which, by the way, takes fifteen years).

Seek yourself, your experience, your unique vision. In the end, that's the most valuable thing you have to offer.

"All you can give us is what life is about from your point of view," Anne Lamott tells us.

Everything else has been done.

NOTES

1. Michael Rabiger, *Directing: Film Techniques and Aesthetics*, second edition, Focal Press, Boston, 1997, p. 213.
2. Anne Lamott, *Bird By Bird: Some Instructions on Writing and Life*, Pantheon Books, New York, 1994, pp. 199, 200.
3. Ray Bradbury, *Zen in the Art of Writing: Releasing the Creative Genius Within You*, Bantam Books, New York, 1992, p. 47.

3

CONNECTING TO PROCESS

There's another half to the self-knowledge story: You need to know your own writing process. I'm not talking about the specific steps in the process of screenwriting; I'll talk about that in Part II. I'm talking about understanding how you *work* as a writer—your own creative process—and how to create optimum conditions for that to occur.

No one can tell you your process. Every writer's is different. Individual. Idiosyncratic. That's the point. But you need to understand yours.

You may not have been writing long enough to know what it is. That's okay, just start paying attention. And start asking yourself the following questions, which will help you solve what my writing partner, Matt Stevens, and I call . . .

THE SPACE-TIME CONUNDRUM

When do you work best? What are your own creative rhythms? Do you write best at night? In the morning? High noon? If you don't know, try different times until you figure out what works best for you, then *do everything in your power* to work on your screenplays during that time.

"Yeah, right," I hear those of you who are students snicker. "C'mon, I'm in *film school*."

I know what you're talking about. I've seen my students stagger into my classroom after an all-nighter in the editing suite with that stunned look on their faces that cartoon characters get when other characters bash them on the head (I've learned not to take it personally when they nod off in class). Still, I tell them what I'm telling you: *Clear time and space for your writing.* Not just any time and space—the time and space that works best for them. More often than not, they snicker, too.

And I understand. For my first twenty years as a writer, I had to write around raising children, which meant grabbing a couple of hours before they woke up. *Early* mornings. "O'dark thirty," as we say in our family. Or when they were at school. I assumed I worked best in the morning, but recently, while writing this book, I've discovered if I start writing later, I go into a deep and productive creative trance in the late afternoon. So even if you know your creative process, it will probably change with your circumstances, evolving as you evolve as a writer.

Where do you do your best writing? I'm speaking geographically now, as Mihaly Csikszentmihalyi does in *Creativity*:

> At the macro level, the question may be whether you feel you would be happiest if living at the seashore, surrounded by mountains or plains, or in the bustle of a big city. Do you like the change of seasons? Do you hate snow? Some people are physically affected by long sunless periods.[1]

If you're a student or otherwise tied to one place, this discussion might strike you as silly, but it's sillier not to think about it, according to Csikszentmihalyi:

> There can be many reasons why you might feel trapped in the place that you live, without a choice to move. But it's a great waste of time to spend your entire life in uncongenial surroundings. One of the first steps in implementing creativity at the personal level is to review your options of life contexts and then start thinking about strategies for making the best choice come true.[2]

In the long run, this kind of thinking is absolutely essential. A writer's *first concern*, Tennessee Williams once said, must be "to discover that magic place of all places where the work goes better than it has gone before, the way that a gasoline motor picks up when you switch it from regular to high octane. For one of the mysterious things about writing is the extreme susceptibility it shows to the influence of places."

Some of our faculty at the Film School swear they work better in Tallahassee than they do in Los Angeles. The novelist Sheila Ortiz-Taylor works best at writers' retreats. I write best at our farm in rural north Florida, on the porch overlooking the meadow. And Sam Smiley sent me a postcard from Ireland, where he was writing a screenplay. "Somehow creativity really flows when you're away from home."

You may be too young or inexperienced as a writer to know this right now, but again, start paying attention. And, granted, even if you know the place you work best, you might not be able to pick up and go at the moment, but it will help your writing career a great deal if you figure out where that "magic place of all places" is for you and make plans to get there. At least now and then. The sooner you do so, the sooner you'll get where you need to be.

On the micro level, ask yourself what kind of *space* works best for you? As a young writer in Paris, Hemingway loved to work in cafés. Later, in Key West, he worked in a study detached from his house. David Mamet recommends writing in restaurants, and I solved some major structural problems in a book proposal because of the white noise of voices in the food court at our Student Union.

"Again," says Csikszentmihalyi, "it is not what the environment is like that matters, but the extent to which you are in harmony with it."

Once you've found your space, fill it—to the extent that you want it filled—with objects that have significance for you. Anne Lamott keeps a one-inch picture frame on her desk. "It reminds me that all I have to do is write down as much as I can see through a one-inch picture frame. This is all I have to bite off for the time being."

Along with a few of my favorite family pictures, I keep a wind-up butterfly in my study—a gift from my son—to remind me to take off now and then in my writing. Take chances. Lighten up. *Soar.* He also gave me a hilarious toy called a "Critter" that shakes itself silly when I wind it up and reminds me how silly I am (and probably look) when I get so wound up because the writing is not going well. My daughter gave me a cobalt-blue Venetian glass fountain pen that graces my desk and inspires me with its elegant luminous beauty. A good friend, Gene Newcomb, gave me a wooden case where I keep the Mont Blanc pen I bought for myself when I sold two books in one year (the pen leaves my study only for book signings). And my printer is covered with quotations that inspire or move or teach me ("That that is is," one of the most amazing sentences I've ever seen, not surprisingly penned by the greatest of all dramatists, William Shakespeare in *Twelfth Night*) or fortune-cookie fortunes that give me hope or just make me smile ("Depart not from the path which fate has you assigned.") They remind me that my writing doesn't have to be perfect.

Again, this may sound silly. It's not.

> The kind of objects you fill your space with also either help or hinder the allocation of creative energies. Cherished objects remind us of our goals, make us feel more confident, and focus our attention. Trophies, diplomas, favorite books, and family pictures on the office desk are all reminders of who you are, what you have accomplished. . . . Pictures and maps of places you would like to visit and books about things you might like to learn more about are signposts of what you might do in the future.[3]

MADNESS IN YOUR METHOD

How do you work best? In long stretches or short bursts? The screenwriter Mark Spragg prefers total immersion. "I work seven days a week, all day long, 'til I drop, so the subconscious is so saturated, it's what I dream about. When I meditate, it comes up, I've already done so much thinking about it."

Writing tools may seem like a trivial consideration, but you need to know what works best for you: Pencil and paper? Pen? A computer? A typewriter like Barton Fink? (William Faulkner outlined his books on his study *wall*, but I don't recommend this for renters.) I need pen and paper when I start a project—or a piece of one, like this chapter. I need to noodle in longhand before I turn on the computer. I love the scratch of a good fine-point pen across paper; it gets the creative juices going for me while I brainstorm. And noodling (a similar technique is called clustering) is nonlinear, so it keeps me loose, keeps the ideas flowing, keeps the raging perfectionist in me at bay.

Know thyself and thy hang-ups.

I noodled this chapter before I started writing (see page 26):

{Process:}

I'll speak more specifically about actual steps in screenwriting process in later chapters. Here talking about the creative process — writing in general — connecting to your own writing process.

One-inch picture frame / Lamott lowest standards — Janet
Shitty 1st draft : Voices . Do THAT
THE ORDEAL

Tennessee Williams stifled laughter Placenthat...

journal / weekly page Newsweek — medicinal value
Artist's P. 169 way Drought
PLAY! time/space

Do rejection from hell. / Slogged on w/ project I felt no authentic connection
Do THAT.!

No thing time @ Film SCHOOL

Daydream walk
H₂O bathe
my negative ions connect?
lower ions

outline-great — but if the muse starts to talk, you better listen AND TAKE NOTES!!!

Clear a space
no small cheese for film students — deprived into my classes after another all-nighter in the AVID Suite (Try not to take their madness personal)

See Habits p. 76 Artist's way

TAKE THE BREAKS / ELVES OUT ISLANDS

Pay attention
Be a person upon whom nothing is lost / James

Eat well
Get more sleep — Anne's process

prewrite eat sleep write

And remember — you trying to write — meeting obstacles — the dramatic paradigm (WILL HITTING OBSTACLES)

BLOCK / J. MAUNEY / S. TAYLOR — told her to stop & note when she's blocked how she's feeling — ALMOST ALWAYS TIED TO FATIGUE
To sleep — perchance to write . . .

If you pay attention to your own struggle you're a better dramatist

Motion — cradle / swim / dive
H₂O my epiphany! TW

Janet-blocked don't know enough I agree / my experience
Stop, look, listen & Research

Rituals — Hemingway-sharpens pencils + VIVALDI, etc.

Perfectionism —form of Self-hated / Artist's way Just tell the damn story
Be as descriptive —
Vertigo

Figure out your Creative rhythm
am — kids / school

objects / see Creativity p. 356
Frank McCourt "SCRIBBLE"

But discovered — while I've been writing this book — that if I start later I go into a deep creative trance — the afternoon — very productive. Process Does evolve . . . change .

Key is self-knowledge!!

It may look like chaos to you—isn't that where order comes from?—but this noodling helped me see connections, which I noted with arrows. As the chapter began to take shape in my mind, I assembled the various prewritten pieces on the computer, and I was ready to write a rough draft.

When I'm writing a screenplay, I'll noodle a much longer time—*piles* of pages—until the characters and story are clear in my mind; then I work out the structure on my drafting table. I need to know my scenes—at least their dramatic purpose—and the order I'll tell them before I turn on the computer and start drafting the screenplay. Even then, as I reach a new scene, I'll stop and noodle the dialogue and action before I start typing. Some writers work more organically, writing the screenplay to *find out* where the story is going. Barry Levinson dictated the screenplay for *Avalon* into a tape recorder.

Do you work better in silence or with music playing? I never *thought* about writing with music until I began writing scripts with Matt Stevens, and he always did. Vivaldi's *Four Seasons* seems to work best, and it's playing now as I write this chapter.

"Music played an important role in composing the atmosphere of the written page," Lani Sciandra said about writing *Cool Breeze and Buzz*. "I was listening to a lot of electronic music at the time and used a mixed tape of songs I thought captured the feeling of what (I suspected) was going on—sometimes rewinding a track for hours until I got through a scene. St. George Pierre (the composer) was a great influence in shaping the mood from the beginning—I felt his score provided another dynamic to the expectations of a story told against a rural backdrop."

CREATING RITUALS

Ask yourself, too, if there are rituals that help you write better. In an interview for *Fresh Air*, the dancer/choreographer Twyla Tharp said that the rituals we practice before practicing our art help dispel those doubts and fears that plague us. And that isn't all. "Small rituals, self-devised, are good for the soul," Julia Cameron says in *The Artist's Way*:

> Burning incense while reading affirmations or writing them, lighting a candle, dancing to drum music, holding a smooth rock and listening to Gregorian chant—all of these tactile, physical techniques reinforce spiritual growth.[4]

If you're not from California, you might want to try something else.

A Midwesterner, Hemingway began each writing day by sharpening pencils. Southerners, Matt and I make fresh iced tea. When we start writing, one of us paces while the other one types. Hemingway wrote standing up (though not, I suspect, in cafes in Paris); when I write alone, I sit down, usually in the half-lotus position (sitting this way helps my back). Toni Morrison—or is it Maya Angelou?—plays cards until her Muse starts to talk.

In a way, that's what all writers are doing—seducing the Muse, getting her to start talking. So figure out what works for you and your Muse and do more of that. If nothing works—hey, you're creative—create something that does.

TAKING CARE OF YOURSELF

You'll work best when you're taking care of yourself, no small cheese for film students, I know. But remember to eat, and eat well. Get as much sleep as you can; writer's block is often the result of exhaustion. Hit your writing each day, but take breaks, especially when you feel blocked. That way your unconscious as well as your conscious mind can work on it. Ray Bradbury calls the unconscious "the Muse." In *A Writer's Time*, Kenneth Atchity calls it "the out islands." I've nicknamed my unconscious "the elves," and I find my writing goes best when I remember to leave it alone and let the elves work on it for a while.

Go for walks, runs, or long drives. Nothing gets the Muse talking faster than motion. Just be sure, when she does, that you can take notes. Thomas Jackson always carries a small tape recorder in his car. I carry a folded four-by-six card and a pen when I go for long walks. When I drive, I keep a clipboard and a pen on the seat right beside me. I strongly recommend pulling over before you start writing. If you don't, pay attention. For that matter, pay attention *all* of the time. That's the best thing you can do for yourself as a writer. "Be a person upon whom nothing is lost," as Henry James said.

And forgive yourself if your writing's not perfect. Perfectionism is a form of self-hatred, "a circus man strapped to the flaming wheel, turning," to borrow a phrase from the poet Bea Hampton. I know because I'm a recovering perfectionist ("And you want your recovery to be perfect," as one friend drolly said).

"Perfectionism is not a quest for the best. It is a pursuit of the worst in ourselves, the part that tells us that nothing we do will ever be good enough," Julia Cameron reminds us:

> "Perfectionism has nothing to do with getting it right. It has nothing to do with fixing things. It has nothing to do with standards. Perfectionism is a refusal to let yourself move ahead. It is a loop—an obsessive, debilitating closed system that causes you to get stuck in the details of what you are writing or painting or making and to lose sight of the whole. Instead of creating freely and allowing errors to reveal themselves later as insights, we often get mired in getting the details right. We correct our originality into a uniformity that lacks passion and spontaneity. 'Do not fear mistakes,' Miles Davis told us. 'There are none.' "[5]

JUST DO IT

"When all else fails, lower your standards," my father loved to say. Especially on your "shitty first draft," as Anne Lamott calls it, and she's right. As Hemingway said, "The first draft of anything is shit."

Thomas Jackson agrees. "Writing to me is like pulling teeth. I don't know how it works, you just do it every day and eventually something materializes out of all these characters."

So hang in there and keep writing, a little each day. Something will materialize. And you'll have good days and bad. After twenty-five-plus years of writing, I've decided that both are essential: I need two rotten days writing before I can get to a good one.

I hate that.

And keep in mind, too, that trying to write and hitting internal and external obstacles *is* the dramatic paradigm, as you'll see in the next chapter, so pay attention to your own struggle. You'll be a better dramatist for it. Most of all, trust the process. Make some mistakes, take some chances.

Lighten up, take off, *soar*. As I'll say more than once in this book, the last word in screenplay is *play*. In this bottom-line business (grosses and grades), it's much too easy to lose sight of that.

NOTES

1. Mihaly Csikszentmihalyi, *Creativity: Flow and the Psychology of Discovery and Invention*, HarperPerennial, New York, 1996, p. 354.
2. *Ibid.*, pp. 354, 355.
3. *Ibid.*, p. 356.
4. Julia Cameron, *The Artist's Way: A Spiritual Path to Creativity*, G.P. Putnam's Sons, New York, 1992, p. 189.
5. *Ibid.*, pp. 119, 120.

4

CONNECTING TO SCREENPLAYS

A screenplay is a film unfolding on paper. A story told for the screen. A story told to be *seen*. And, like all drama, told *in* scenes.

"The scene is unique to drama—though used sporadically in all story-telling—in being its very bonework," William Gibson says in *Shakespeare's Game*.

A screenplay is a story told in scenes for the screen.

But what is a story?

Definitions abound, but most are similar to the one I just found in the *American Heritage Dictionary* that sits on my desk: *The narrating or relating of an event or series of events, either true or fiction.*

I'm a bit of a word freak, so I took a moment to look up "event": *An occurrence, incident, or experience, especially one of significance.*

Then I looked up "significance": *The state or quality of importance, consequence. From signify, to have meaning or importance.*

A story is the relating of events that have meaning, importance, consequence. That *matter*. That make a *difference*, however subtle, in the character's life. If a screenplay can't answer the question, "How is this day (night, week, month, year) different from any other?" it will raise the dread question "So what?" That age-old challenge, "What difference does it make?" is not idle talk. It's what we want to know when we watch the events of a movie unfold.

Making a difference, in fact, is the first definition of change, at least in my dictionary: *To cause to be different; alter.* And change is the heart of it all. After three decades of writing and a decade and a half of teaching, I've found the most useful, least rule-bound definition of story is *a pattern of human change.*

This change may be subtle, like Aadid's in *My Josephine*, which Barry Jenkins describes as "a pattern of change as glimpsed through a slice-of-life portrait. The film is a slice-of-life in that there's nothing extraordinary occurring within the physical scene: Aadid has done everything we see him do in the film at least five times a week for the last such-and-so weeks of the last such-and-so months, etc. What stands out, however, is the resonance these activities derive from the emotions Aadid assigns them on *this night*."

A screenplay is a pattern of human change told in scenes for the screen.

That pattern of human change has other names—spine, through-line, action—but essentially they mean the same thing. As Sam Smiley says in *Playwriting: The Structure of Action*, "Simply defined, action is human change."

As a writer and a teacher, I prefer thinking of the screenplay as a pattern of human change because it's dynamic. It's a *process* that an audience can see *beginning* (an event occurs that has meaning, importance, consequence), *developing* (the consequences of this event—and others—are played out), and *ending* (the outcome of the events is finally known at the climax). William Gibson says:

> A play is an energy system, and the business of the precip-
> itating event is to introduce a disequilibrium, that is, to
> release energy. Characterization, language, mood and
> tempo, meaning, all the other attributes which will give the
> play its identity, wait upon that release; it animates them,
> they cannot begin to exist without it. And once begun, the
> "play" is that of contradictory energies working to arrive at
> a new equilibrium, if it kills everybody.[1]

Gibson posits that a play—and, I would add, any screenplay—is made up of moves. The precipitating event is the first move, but hardly the last. "It is as in chess, also an energy system, one move provokes another." The example Gibson chooses is *Hamlet*:

> Horatio, once he has seen the ghost, must act; the move is
> his. It requires a decision, and he can decide his eyes are
> failing and go off to the oculist, or the Denmark fog is too
> much and go south for the winter, but these decisions will
> take him and us into a different game, not too inviting. In
> truth, he has no choice, the one decision that moves this
> game forward is
>
> > Let us impart what we have seen tonight
> > Unto young Hamlet; for, upon my life,
> > This spirit, dumb to us, will speak to him.[2]

Jump-started by the precipitating move, the energy system, game, story, pattern of human change is set in motion and will continue until the last move is made, until the energy system comes to an end, until the outcome is known. Until the climax. Until checkmate.

The best screenplays—long or short, serious or comic—create an energy system—a credible, compelling pattern of human change. That's what good screenplays do. That's what we pay our money to see. And we connect because our own lives—good, bad, or ugly—are also patterns of change.

In *The Full Monty*, Gaz—an unemployed steelworker on the brink of losing his son—becomes a one-night-stand stripper to make enough money to regain his son and, in the process, regains self-respect.

In *As Good As It Gets*, Melvin—an obsessive-compulsive writer who doesn't love anything in this world—falls in love with a dog and a waitress.

I could go on all day about features, but the subject here is short screenplays. And when you're writing short screenplays, thinking about story as a pattern of human change is even more useful. Why? Because this definition includes even small, subtle change, *as long as it matters deeply to the character*.

I've had students come into my office and slump in my yellow papasan chair and tell me that so-and-so said their short screenplay isn't a story. Then I ask, "Well, is there a pattern of change and does it make a difference to your character?" If the answer to both questions is yes, I assure students that they have a story. It may need rewriting (all screenplays do); nevertheless, they have a story, and with a lot of work and a little luck, they can figure out how to tell it in a way that connects.

What you're looking for when you write a short screenplay is that small subtle shift, that tiny turn of the screw in a character's inner or outer life. Preferably both. But small is the point. A simple but meaningful pattern of human change. As Patrick Duncan (*Courage Under Fire, Nick of Time*) said in *Creative Screenwriting*, "Let the story be simple and let the characters be complicated." (I'd jot that on a three-by-five card and stick it next to the one that says "Only connect".) And Duncan is referring to *features*. It's far more true for short screenplays.

The worst short scripts I've read suffer from what I call *narrative cram*. Too many big events occurring in too little time. ("Two pounds of shit in a one pound sack," as we say in the South.) A feature plot packed into one or two dozen pages. There's so much going on that nothing seems to matter. Important moments can't *breathe*. The result is suffocating.

In short screenplays, smaller is better.

Small stories that make a big difference.

In *Slow Dancin' Down the Aisles of the Quickcheck*, thanks to external and internal moments of change, Earl is finally able to say—or sing—how he feels to Maybelline.

How do screenwriters make these changes—some might say "miracles"— happen? By creating a pattern of change in their characters' outer life that changes their inner landscape forever. Hamlet was right. Art *does* hold a mirror up to nature, because our lives work the same way—*external events force inner change*.

SURFACE AND DEEP ACTION

When I'm writing a screenplay (or a novel or a play or a memoir, for that matter), I find it useful to break the story I'm telling into the external and internal patterns of change. I call these the story's *surface action* and *deep action*. Just as the best screenplays interweave striving and connecting, they interweave the surface and the deep action. The best drama, in fact, is a dance between the external and the internal: Horatio sees the ghost of Hamlet's father (*external*), struggles to decide the best action to take (*internal*), and tells Hamlet (*external*). And so it goes until death do him depart.

So it's enormously helpful, when you're preparing to write a screenplay, to clarify what these dual actions are. Do so in terms of the main character and an *-ing* verb. This reminds you that both actions are dynamic. And it reminds you that both, though interrelated, are, in fact, different. The surface action is the *external pattern of change*, the events we see happen up on the screen. *Gaz is trying to retain joint custody of his son.* To do this, he has to raise the money he owes his ex-wife. But he refused to work at her factory. So he tries to put together an all-male striptease act.

The deep action—also known as the *character arc*—is the *internal pattern of change* that is occurring in the character in response to external events. *Gaz is regaining his self-respect.*

Boiling your surface and your deep action down to one sentence is harder than it looks—my students are always amazed how tricky this is—so it may take a good deal of thinking and noodling to nail them. Once you do, write them down. You may find that they change as you write (material often has a mind of its own). Fine. Rewrite them. But keep them in plain sight because they're your compass, pointing you in the right direction as you write your screenplay.

MAKING CHANGE

So a screenwriter's job, in a nutshell, is making change. (And, alas, sometimes that's all we make for a while.) Articulating the surface and deep action is just the beginning. Now you have to *make* those patterns of human change happen in a compelling credible way.

But how? How do you build a pattern of change? Think of it as a pathway your character is moving along. What is that path made of?

Stepping stones.

In screenwriting, these stepping stones are specific *moments of change*. Events that make a difference, a.k.a. *dramatic events*. And once you can write a credible, compelling moment of change, you're well on your way to writing good screenplays. So it's of vital importance that you grasp—really grasp— what a moment of change *is*.

As you might expect, I looked up the word "moment," and to my joy and amazement I read: *A brief, indefinite, interval of time . . . A particular period of importance, significance . . . Outstanding significance or value; importance.*

Why did I feel such joy and amazement? Because the word "moment" is screenwriting summed up in one word. It's an interval of time (a scene), but also an interval of time that's important, significant (moment of change), and it comes from the Latin *momentum* which comes from the Latin *movere—to move*. And that's what good screenplays do.

We create stories told in scenes, patterns of human change out of moments of change, moments that matter, moments of moment, if you will, and these moments move our screenplays forward.

Moments of moment create momentum.

Yes, I'd jot that down, too.

But what *kinds* of moments create change in our lives and in the stories we tell? To figure this out for yourself, take a shot at . . .

THE MOOD EXERCISE

So here goes.

On a half-sheet of paper, describe a brief scene (in prose, present tense) in which a character's mood changes. Whatever mood he or she is in when this small scene begins, make sure it has changed by the time the scene's over. (This works best if done in a class or a group, but if you're doing it by yourself, write several brief scenes before you move on in the book. Multiple scenes is what matters.)

If you're not in the mood to make something up, describe a brief scene from your life. Mine might look something like this:

> I'm writing away when the telephone rings. My son, Ross (sixteen at the time) says, "Mom, I'm in trouble." My heart goes *squish squish*. But he's safe. He just ran out of gas, so he pushed the car off the road and walked on to school. "Could you bring me five gallons?" I agree, deciding to be Zen about it. I drive to school humming, then I lurch forward and shriek, "Oh, my *God!*" Up ahead I see his car *nose down in a ditch!* When he pushed it off the road, he pushed it over the edge, a minor detail he failed to mention.

My mood changed a number of times in that scene, but you only have to make your character's mood change once, as students did in these examples submitted anonymously in a screenwriting workshop I taught in Tampa:

> Megan's car turns the corner in front of the school. Mozart is playing on the radio. She smiles, searching for Eddie. She hums the concerto and taps her fingers eagerly awaiting Eddie. Fourteen year old Eddie spots the car, gives his friends a shove, and high-fives a goodbye. He opens the door and gets in.
> "What's new?" Megan says. "How are you, sweetie?"
> "Nothing's new. Don't talk to me."
> Megan shuts off the radio and looks at a pigeon flying by.

Or:

> A young man goes to an electronics store. He purchases a big-screen TV. Young man goes home. In his living room, with a huge ribbon on top, is a big-screen TV.

Or:

> She reaches into her mailbox at the college. Mostly junk. But there were two envelopes. She recognizes the handwriting, the return address. She thought he would send maybe a Christmas card, a note inside. She doesn't dare open it now and get caught reading it. She doesn't trust herself not to cry when she reads his advice about being a scholar. She runs upstairs to her office, tears the letter open, and realizes he's sent the wrong letter. It begins, "Oh, my darling, I love you and I love you and I love you." It was a mistake. And then she sees her name. It was to her.

You get the picture. Short and sweet. A character starts in one kind of mood and ends in another. Don't spend more than five minutes on this. Keep it simple. And don't agonize. It doesn't have to be art ("Let Art do his *own* work," as my friend, Stu Hample, says). So turn off the perfectionist machinery and write a quick scene:

Okay, you've finished your scene. If you haven't, wrap it up. The point isn't perfection. It's making change.

There. Good. Thank you.

If you're in a writing group or a class, collect the scenes and read them aloud. Have each writer identify the *precise* moment of change. What *specific event* happened that altered that character's mood? List these events on the board.

Did the character learn something? Hear some bad news? (I learn that Ross ditched his car.) Good news? (A woman realizes that the love letter she received is really to her.) A surprise? (A young man finds a big-screen TV in his living room.)

When you've finished listing the moments of change and why they changed the characters' moods, look at the verbs that you used—in this case, *learning, finds out, finds, realizes*. Circle them and ask what these words have in common. Is there one word that includes all of them? Take your time. And don't read on until you've taken a stab at this yourself.

Good. Now jot down the word you came up with. I asked my workshop students at the Suncoast Writers Conference in Tampa the same question when we did the Mood Exercise. "Is there one word that includes all of them?"

"They're all discoveries," said one of my students.

"Bingo!" I said. Because a realization or epiphany is a discovery, too.

When I do this exercise with groups of writers or students, it's almost always a discovery that alters the character's mood. Now and then it's a decision (I decided to be Zen about taking Ross five gallons of gas). Both are correct. Because, as Sam Smiley once taught me, discoveries and decisions are the two major categories of change in our lives and the stories we tell. Think about that. How elegant!

Sam also included deed and accident on his list. I tend to think of an accident as a discovery, but deed—or doing—while not a precise *moment* of change—is an essential part of any pattern of change. Remember, "drama" comes from the Greek *dran—to do*. Doing flows out of decisions, and decisions flow out of discoveries.

Again, it's a dance—a complex interconnected dance of discovery, decision, and doing: Horatio sees the ghost of Hamlet's father (*discovery*), struggles to decide the best action to take (*decision*), and tells Hamlet (*doing*, but also a *discovery* for Hamlet). And so the dance (game, energy system, pattern of change) continues to flow until Hamlet can no longer discover, decide, do—or be.

THE PEARL IN THE OYSTER

Each moment of change—discovery or decision—occurs in a scene—the bonework of drama—be it in a play or a screenplay. Which is where we came in.

A screenplay is a story told in scenes for the screen.

I like to think of a scene as an oyster and the moment of change as the pearl—the scene's reason for being. And the pearls—strung together in scenes—are the screenplay's pattern of human change.

It's important to note that some scenes *do not* contain a moment of change. Sometimes a scene is for atmosphere, mood. Or it establishes a situation. Sometimes a character is simply being or doing, absorbing the events that have happened, like Ulee tending his bees in *Ulee's Gold*.

Ulee's writer/director, Victor Nunez, said to me years ago that it's good just to be with your characters for a while in your screenplay. Hang out. It's lovely, important advice. Granted, you don't have much time to do this in short screenplays, but you do need to give your characters and events time to breathe.

But keep in mind that scenes like Ulee tending his bees work because moments of change have already occurred. We sense what he's going through. We're connected to his emotions while he tends his bees. If we weren't—if no moments of change had occurred in the film to stir his emotions (and ours)—then watching him tend his bees—however exquisitely acted, lit, shot—would be far less compelling.

Remember, your purpose is to connect, and you connect through your character's emotions. It's the discoveries and decisions in your story—and the deeper currents of striving and connection—that create emotion in your characters. And this emotion *flows* from scene to scene, from one moment of change to another, holding your story together.

EMOTIONAL FLOW

Just as emotion is the invisible thread that connects an audience to characters up on the screen, *emotional flow* is the invisible thread that connects the individual scenes.

Each scene in a screenplay is separate, distinct. By definition, a new scene occurs when the camera changes time or place (not placement within a scene):

EXT. LIGHTHOUSE—NIGHT

INT. LIGHTHOUSE—NIGHT

EXT. BEACH—DAY

And so forth. The story *leaps* from one scene to another, blessedly leaving the boring stuff out (*Kosher* is a superb example of this art of subtraction, leaping effortlessly from moment to moment, hitting scenes late and getting out early.) We see the pieces of the story that matter, that make a difference, that create—or process—emotion in the characters. And we're able to stay connected to the story—in spite of the leaps—because we follow the emotional flow.

It's analogous to *the persistence of vision:*

> If, while one is looking at an object, it suddenly disappears, the image of it will remain on the retina of the eye for a brief space of time (approximately one tenth of a second) and during that time one will continue to "see" the object although it is no longer before the eye.[3]

I like to call it *the persistence of emotion:*

If, while one is looking at an emotion (the boy reacting to his mother being killed by the bus in *Central Station*, for example) it suddenly disappears because the story leaps to a new scene, the emotion remains on our mind (heart? both?) and we continue to "feel" this emotion during the leap although it is no longer before our eyes.

We—and the character—carry this emotion forward. It *flows* to the next scene when we see him—hunched over, heartbroken. If he were laughing and singing, we'd say, *Huh?* The emotional flow wouldn't work. His happy emotions wouldn't feel *earned* (unless we learned he was in deep denial).

When we watch a film, we're connecting the emotional dots and connecting to the characters as we do. The story—leaps and all—moves forward in what seems to be a seamless emotional flow. And we move forward with it. Even in the wacky mockumentary world of *"Killer Kite,"* which cuts back and forth between the story of the film and the story of the documentary about the making of the film, we are able to follow the emotional flow in each story because the screenwriter provided the dots that we need to connect.

Still, as I said, not all scenes contain a moment of change. The opening scenes of *Slow Dancin'* and *"Killer Kite"* establish mood. The opening scene of *Cool Breeze and Buzz* establishes Paula's character and her world and her relationship to it. But all moments of change *are* contained in scenes. Pearls in oysters. And sometimes the richest, most resonant scenes have more than one pearl. Which brings me to Charlie Chaplin. . . .

EVERYTHING YOU NEED TO KNOW YOU CAN LEARN FROM *CITY LIGHTS*

Okay, that's a bald overstatement. You can't learn *everything* you need to know about writing screenplays from *City Lights*, but you can get pretty close if you pay close attention to one scene in the film.

You've probably seen it—Charlie Chaplin meets the blind flower vendor—but I recommend that you screen it again.[4] Several times, if you can. The scene is only two and a half minutes long. Here's the scene, summarized:

> The Little Tramp (Chaplin) sees a policeman and avoids him by ducking into a parked car and stepping out the other side onto a sidewalk where a young woman (Virginia Cherrill) is selling flowers. She hears the car door slam, assumes he's rich (or affluent enough to own an automobile), and asks him to purchase a flower. It's a silent film and there's no dialogue card for these lines, but you can read her lips, "Flower sir? Buy a flower?" A moustache-twitching moment of deliberating. He's torn. Poor. "Would you buy a flower, sir?" He decides that he will. She holds up two flowers. He points to

the one in her right hand. She offers the other. A little impatient, he touches her right hand. When the flower accidentally falls on the sidewalk, he picks it up. She stoops to get it but when she can't find it, she says in a second dialogue card, "Did you pick it up, sir?" He gives her an "oh, come on" look, holds out the flower, but she doesn't see it. He moves the flower in front of her face and realizes she's blind.

Deeply moved, he tips his hat and gently puts the flower in her hand. She pins it to his lapel and waits for her money. He digs in his pocket for what may be his last coin, looks longingly at it, and puts it into her hand. She curtsies and backs up toward her change box on the cement wall. The Little Tramp takes her hand and helps her sit down. As she starts to make change, the rich man returns to his car, slams the door, and drives away. She calls to him and a second dialogue card appears, "Wait for your change, sir." In a lovely form = content shot, the camera pans back and forth from the car to the flower vendor as the Little Tramp puts it together: She thinks *he's* rich. Deciding he'd like to keep it that way, he tiptoes around the corner out of sight. But offscreen he decides that he wants to see her again, so he sneaks back around the corner and sits by the fountain and watches her adoringly as she walks to the fountain and rinses her water bucket. Unaware that he's there, she chucks the dirty water right in his face. He tiptoes past her out of the frame.

What can you learn from this scene? Five easy lessons:

First, dialogue is *not* essential to creating a pattern of human change in a screenplay. Film is visual. Volumes of speech are conveyed by the actors. As my former colleague, Charlie Boyd, said, "*Thoughts* register on film."

Don't get me wrong, I'm a great fan of talk. If it's highly entertaining and/or illuminates or moves the pattern of human change forward. *Pulp Fiction*—one of the talkiest films in the world—does this better than most. So I don't buy that old saw that talk in screenplays is bad. *Bad* talk is bad. Dialogue that doesn't move the story forward (more on this later), that's too familiar, too cliche-d, or too on-the-nose can be deadly.

Second, this scene from *City Lights* shows us that significant human change can occur in a very short time. In this case, two and a half minutes. As he humors the flower vendor by buying a flower, the Little Tramp is profoundly changed.

So third, this scene is a wonderful illustration of external events forcing internal change. There's a clear surface action—buying a flower—and deep action—falling in love. And, I would argue, gaining compassion. Falling in love/gaining compassion is the Little Tramp's character arc. I find it useful to draw the character arc, and, using my sophisticated screenplay notation, it looks something like this:

In two and a half minutes, because of external events, the Little Tramp's internal landscape is altered forever (or, at least, for the rest of this film).

Amazing.

Fourth, this excerpt shows that a rich and resonant scene often has more than one moment of change. It's an oyster with numerous pearls. Let's look at the scene one more time, this time looking for discoveries and decisions that the Little Tramp makes:

> The Little Tramp (Chaplin) sees a policeman (*discovery*) and avoids him by ducking into a parked car (*decision*) and stepping out the other side onto a sidewalk where a young woman (Virginia Cherrill) is selling flowers. She hears the car door slam, assumes he's rich (or affluent enough to own an automobile—*a false discovery*), and asks him to purchase a flower (a *discovery* for him). It's a silent film and there's no dialogue card for these lines, but you can read her lips, "Flower sir? Buy a flower?" A moustache-twitching moment of deliberating. He's torn. Poor. "Would you buy a flower, sir?"
>
> He decides that he will (*decision*).
>
> She holds up two flowers. He points to the one in her right hand (*decision*). She offers the other. A little impatient, he touches her right hand. When the flower accidentally falls on the sidewalk, he picks it up. She stoops to get it but when she can't find it, she says in a second dialogue card, "Did you pick it up, sir?" He gives her an "oh, come on" look, holds out the flower, but she doesn't see it. He moves the flower in front of her face and realizes she's blind (*discovery*).
>
> Deeply moved, he tips his hat and gently puts the flower in her hand. She pins it to his lapel and waits for her money. He digs in his pocket for what may be his last coin, looks longingly at it, and puts it into her hand (*decision*). She curtsies and backs up toward her change box on the cement wall. The Little Tramp takes her hand and helps her sit down.
>
> As she starts to make change, the rich man returns to his car, slams the door, and drives away. She calls to him and a second dialogue card appears, "Wait for your change, sir." In a lovely form = content shot, the camera pans back and forth from the car to the flower vendor as the Little Tramp

puts it together: She thinks *he's* rich (*discovery*). Deciding he'd like to keep it that way (*decision*), he tiptoes around the corner out of sight.

But, offscreen, he decides (*decision*) that he wants to see her again, so he sneaks back around the corner and sits by the fountain and watches her adoringly as she walks to the fountain and rinses her water bucket. Unaware that he's there, she chucks the dirty water right in his face (a *discovery* for him). He tiptoes past her out of the frame (*decision*).

Thirteen moments of change in two and a half minutes. Six discoveries, seven decisions. You might find more. Each moment of change shifts the direction of the scene's energy and emotional flow. That means the scene has tiny reversals. These give it richness and texture. "Every scene is made up of the texture of the minor reverses a character encounters trying to get his or her way," Brady and Lee write in *The Understructure of Writing for Film and Television*.

If you diagrammed this *City Lights* scene, those reverses would look something like this:

In *Making Shapely Fiction*, Jerry Stern calls this "zigzagging." "Microplotting." "Creating fluctuations of feeling to maintain a high degree of attention." But more important than keeping your audience's attention, Stern says, is psychological truth.

> Zigzagging reflects psychological reality, the way hopes and fears alternate, how in our desperation we leap at solutions that we quickly reject, how human situations can change drastically from one moment to the next. And for readers [or audiences] zigzagging makes each scene electric with suspense.[5]

I like to call zigzagging a scene's EKG. But a scene without change (unless, as previously noted, it provides important mood, atmosphere, or time with the character) looks more like this:

And what have you got? A dead scene.

Fifth, the *City Lights* scene illustrates emotional flow. The Little Tramp comes into the scene concerned about the police who were angry at him in scene one after he was discovered under the tarp at the statue's unveiling (if you haven't seen the whole film, you'll have to take my word for this). So now, when he sees the policeman, he ducks into the car. After meeting the flower vendor and falling in love, he leaves the scene with new emotion, and that will flow to the next scene he's in, the invisible thread connecting the scenes.

Of course there's much more to learn from this scene; I learn something new each time I watch it. Like the brilliant use of surprise: Just as the scene's getting sappy, the Little Tramp gets a bucket of water smack in the face. What a great comic instinct. As Billy Crystal once said, describing what good comedy does, "Take 'em one way, then take 'em another."

And that's the screenwriter's job. Taking the story one way, then taking it another. Making change. Knowing your story's moments of change, why they make a difference to your character, and writing them so well they matter to us. Crafting a credible, compelling pattern of human change out of discoveries and decision and the action and emotions that flow in between. Narrating them in screenplay form. Which brings us to format, something that throws a whole lot of people the first time they see it.

"To this day I remember staring at the page in shock," William Goldman writes in *Adventures in the Screen Trade*. "I didn't know what it was exactly I was looking at, but I knew I could never write in that form, in that language."

What he was looking at wasn't a screenplay, it was a shooting script, full of numbered slug lines and medium shots and close-ups and medium long shots. He didn't know that, so he invented his own screenplay form, an extreme and highly creative reaction, to say the least, but then, this is William Goldman we're talking about.

Screenplay format is really quite simple. It's the *easy* part of screenwriting, once you understand it. And though I don't recommend reinventing the wheel, there's still plenty of room for invention.

DEMYSTIFYING FORMAT

Screenplay format breaks down into five easy pieces:

1. The *scene heading* or *slug line*
2. The narrative description of the *action*
3. The *name of the character speaking*
4. The *parenthetical directions* and *dialogue*
5. *Transitions*

More and more, my students are using screenplay software (me, too). Talk about *easy*. In most people's opinion, it's worth every penny, but it can be pricey (I've listed different software names and phone numbers in the Appendix so you can check on the price and computer compatibility; if you're a student, say so, because they usually offer substantial discounts). It is possible to create a professional-looking screenplay format yourself. To that end, the TAB settings are:

1″	Left margin
2.6″	Dialogue
3.3″	Parenthetical
3.9″	Character name (ALL CAPS)
5.9″	Transitions
7.5″	Right margin (turn off justification)

In either case, use 12-point Courier type, justify your left margin but not your right, leave one-inch margins all around, limit the number of lines per page to 54, number your pages (with a period after the number) in the upper right corner of each page—except for the title page and the first page of dialogue—but don't number individual scenes.

Your title page should be simple—the title in caps, centered, one-third down the page, with "by (your name)" a few spaces beneath it, also centered, or "by" double-spaced and centered beneath it and "your name" double-spaced and centered below that. You can put contact information in the bottom left-hand or right-hand corner.

It's most useful to see how each part appears on the page, so here's the opening scene of *The Making of "Killer Kite"* (the complete script is in Part III of the book):

FADE IN:

EXT. HARLAN LaRUE'S MANSION—NIGHT

The ancient stone building sits dark and lifeless. A single light shines from the room near the roof. Lightning flashes as THUNDER ROARS.

                                                          CUT TO:

INT. LaRUE'S MANSION—NIGHT

The laboratory is cluttered with giant batteries, transformers and dials.

PROFESSOR HARLAN LaRUE, an elderly, disheveled man in a white lab coat, hurriedly makes a last minute inspection of a mélange of coiled wires, flashing lights and bubbling beakers.

His assistant, JONATHAN SCOTT, a young, handsome all-American lad, stands looking out the window.

Lightning flashes.

> JONATHAN
> It's moving in this direction, Professor
> LaRue. In five minutes, we'll be in the
> center of the storm.

The five easy pieces of the format make perfect sense when you remember that *a screenplay is a story told to be seen in scenes for the screen.*

1. The *scene heading* or *slug line*—all CAPS, flush left with the left margin—tells where and when a scene happens:

INT. LaRUE'S MANSION—NIGHT

This is the *master scene* heading, and the action and dialogue can flow uninterrupted. Occasionally you may want to use *mini slugs*—POV, BACK TO SCENE, INSERT, INTERCUT—which appear in CAPS flush left. *Mini slugs*—especially a character's name or an object used as a mini-slug—have spawned a lively new style of screenwriting known as *writing down the page* or *detailing,* which Matt Stevens and I used in our feature, *Behind the Eight Ball:*

EXT. BOOKER JUNIOR HIGH LAWN—DAY

Conrad's car shoots across the lawn.

MRS. MCFADDEN

steps in front of Conrad's approaching car. And puts her hand out like a traffic cop.

CONRAD

tries to slow down.

> CONRAD
> Get outta the way! Get outta the way!

MRS. MCFADDEN

lifts her chin. No way she's getting out of the way!

She leaps up on Conrad's windshield and hangs on like a suction-cup Garfield!

CONRAD'S POV—Mrs. McFadden's face pressed against the glass.

MRS. MCFADDEN
Conrad Howell! I knew you'd get in trouble.

The momentum of his car throws her off the windshield and onto the ground.

She picks herself up and straightens her lapels.

MRS. MCFADDEN
(indignant)
Hmph!

Writing down the page can give a scene great energy, so it's especially useful in action sequences, but it can also eat up a great deal of space, so it's rarely used in short screenplays, particularly if the writer has a page limit.

My students do find it useful at times in short screenplays to use MONTAGE or SERIES OF SHOTS to show the rapid passage of time. A montage is a series of MOS (no dialogue) shots, but more and more, MONTAGE and SERIES OF SHOTS are used interchangeably. Some writers number or letter the scenes; some don't. In our feature *Obscenity*, Matt Stevens and I chose to number our scenes:

A SERIES OF SHOTS:

1. Sara and Joe confer with Bailey about rental figures.

2. Sara and the OWNER of another video store go over adult rental figures. Joe makes notes on his clipboard.

3. ANOTHER OWNER tears off a computer printout and shows it to Sara and Joe.

4. In the conference room, Linda, Joe, and Sara pore over the data. The table is littered with reference books, legal documents, and Chinese food containers. Sara posts figures on a chart on the board.

My colleague, Andy Ruben, producer and co-writer of *Poison Ivy*, letters his scenes and slugs his montages with more information:

INT. LAB—MONTAGE—NIGHT/MORNING

Again, no two screenplays are exactly the same. Just make choices that make your screenplay readable and professional.

2. The *action*—also flush left, single-spaced, with a double space between it and the slug—describes what we see after we fade in on Harlan LaRue's mansion.

The action also describes what is happening *as it happens,* so it's *always* written in present tense. If your description runs longer than four or five lines, break it into smaller sections. Characters' names appears in ALL CAPS the first time we see them.

> PROFESSOR HARLAN LaRUE, an elderly, disheveled man in a white lab coat, hurriedly makes a last minute inspection of a mélange of coiled wires, flashing lights and bubbling beakers.

Too many screenwriting students think describing the action isn't important, but to a master like Hitchcock, it was one form of filling the frame, to him the heart of filmmaking.

> The one thing that the student has got to do is to learn that there is a rectangle up there—a white rectangle in a theatre—and it has to be filled . . . I only consider the screen up there, and the whole film to me should be on paper from beginning to end.[6]

What you're doing in a vivid, economical, *visual* way is filling the screen, describing what's in it (*mise en scène*) and what's going on. Good visual writing is an art and a craft unto itself, creating cinematic tone and mood through language. Bob Gray's opening description of Harlan LaRue's mansion—"the ancient stone building sits dark and lifeless"—is visual and evocative of tone, mood, and genre (and director Matt Stevens underlines and enhances these with the use of a prowling camera—an homage to *Citizen Kane*—in the opening shot).

Thomas Jackson's evokes an entirely different tone and mood in the opening action description of *Slow Dancin'*:

EXT. QUICKCHECK—PREDAWN

> The parking lot is empty and quiet, except for a green 1979 Toyota pickup, a distant train whistle, and the muffled sound of a guitar coming from the inside of the store.

This simple description creates a mood of disconnection and loneliness.

And look at Lani Sciandra's description of the time and place in *Cool Breeze and Buzz:*

> The year is 1967. Dense woods draped in moss align the river's edge. Nearby is a small dilapidated wooden dock garnished with apple snails. A HERON combs the hyacinths on the bank for a meal.

Lani describes the wooden dock as "garnished with apple snails." Garnished. A lovely choice for a screenplay about a young girl who feels a deep love and connection to her world and chooses, in the end, to remain there. An entirely different mood would have been evoked if she had said the dock was "scarred."

Though we tend to think of action description as neutral, the best screenwriters take great care with the words that they choose and create their own writing style. Barry Jenkins uses a spare simple style to create the lovely and deeply-felt emotion in *My Josephine*:

INT. LAUNDRYMAT STOREROOM—NIGHT

Aadid and Adela on opposite sides of the tiny storeroom checking INVENTORY. They both have a CLIPBOARD AND PEN.

Aadid is on one side of the room and Adela another. He counts a stack of cartons and marks his sheet. Adela does the same.

As they both turn to move, they meet under the light. They embrace. They sway. Their lips meet. They kiss.

Mark Spragg described to me how much care he takes with describing the action, consciously filling the frame as he writes. In a scene in his screenplay *Blue Wind*, his main character, Frank, reencounters his step-daughter, Jolee, in a bar. It's been fifteen years since he's seen her.

> I wanted to show big-time contrast, shabby *versus* pearlbutton cowboy sitting next to him. Contrast. She wears short sleeves. Show her strong arms. She owns her own landscaping biz. Minimalism, but within it, I use words like 'cacophony.' I use metaphors. I say a scene has the color spectrum of a Rembrandt. I make it beautiful. And I never pissed off a director by doing this.

When he talks about composing a 16 mm frame, Andy Ruben tells students, "It's a square. Make it *pretty*."

Good screenwriters tell their stories this way. Visually. They fill the frame. They make it beautiful, pretty. They *use* it to help tell their story.

3. The *name of the character speaking* tells who's talking:

BOB (V.O.)

Occasionally, you will need a (V.O.) to the right of the character's name to indicate that the speech is a *voice-over*, i.e., not spoken within the scene. (O.S.)

indicates that the character is speaking *off-screen*, i.e., spoken within the scene but not within the frame.

4. The *parenthetical* indicates tone or inflection, but should be used sparingly. Don't give actors line readings. If the line is well-written, the tone should be clear, but there are exceptions:

BOB
(hostile)
Of course I love you.

And the *dialogue* is the speech that Bob says. Or Jonathan in *"Killer Kite"*:

JONATHAN
It's moving in this direction, Professor
LaRue. In five minutes, we'll be in the
center of the storm.

It's important to note that dialogue forms a *column* that is roughly 3.5 inches wide. It does not go all the way to the right-hand margin of the page.

If you have to break dialogue at the end of a page, always end after the last complete sentence, then center (more) beneath the dialogue block. When resuming the speech at the top of the next page, reslug the character's name and add (CONT'D) beside it. When you're breaking a character's speech to describe action, you don't need (CONT'D). Just reslug the name and continue the speech.

5. *Transitions* appear sparingly in screenplays to help move the story from one scene to the next. FADE IN: and FADE OUT (usually followed by a period at the end of the screenplay) appear flush left on the page. CUT TO: and DISSOLVE TO: appear on the right-hand side of the page (Tab 5.9). You do not need a CUT TO: between every scene; the cut is implied with each new slug line. DISSOLVE TO: means one image is slowly replacing another, usually to show the passage of time. Both are a bit out of fashion, at least for the moment.

Once you understand the basics, the five easy pieces of screenplay format—*the slug line, the action, the name of character speaking, the parenthetical and dialogue, and the transition*—and why they're used in a screenplay, you're ready to use screenplay format.

As you do, remember your goal—*to make the film unfold on paper*.

"The whole film to me should be on paper from beginning to end," Hitchcock said.

So the reader can *see* it unfolding. You want to create a seamless read—"a vivid and continuous dream," as John Gardner once said—for the reader. The *last* thing you want to do is interrupt your own film-on-paper with bad grammar or spelling or boring descriptions or confusing actions. Keep it simple, visual, vivid, and clear. Your goal is to make the film *happen* in your reader's head.

That's connection.

And don't forget how *flexible* screenplay format can be. It's constantly evolving. You have more freedom than you may realize. The more screenplays you read, the more you'll understand what I mean. Read long and short screenplays, preferably in manuscript form, to see how other screenwriters use format. Screenplays in manuscript are available from *script-arama.com* or Script City (1-800-672-2522 or on the Web at *www.scriptcity.net*), among other places, but these, too, can be pricey. Books sometimes are cheaper, but only a few like *Pulp Fiction* are actually printed in manuscript form. *Scenario: The Magazine of Screenwriting Art* (212-463-0600) publishes four issues a year with four (or more) screenplays in each—in the version the screenwriter wishes—and offers deeply discounted student subscriptions. If you're enrolled at a film school, of course, you can check screenplays out of your film library. The point is to read all you can.

Ultimately, the best way to learn to write screenplays is to write them yourself. The conventional wisdom for features says you have to write five before you sell one. I think, with short screenplays, once you've written (and rewritten) the five screenplays here, you'll be well on your way to understanding the craft.

That's what this book is really about.

NOTES

1. William Gibson, *Shakespeare's Game*, New York, Atheneum, 1978, p. 7.
2. *Ibid.*, p. 9.
3. Ernest Lindgren, *The Art of the Film*, New York, Collier Books, 1970, p. 26.
4. *City Lights* is available from *amazon.com* (see availability information in the Films Referenced section at the end of the book).
5. Jerome Stern, *Making Shapely Fiction*, New York, Norton, 1991, p. 255.
6. Eric Sherman, *Directing the Film*, Acrobat Books, Los Angeles, 1976, pp. 331, 332.

CONNECTING TO COLLABORATION

A former screenwriting student, Tom Kurzanski, e-mailed me one day.

> I just wanted to thank you for planting the seeds of writing
> with a partner. The seeds took root and I partnered up with
> a good friend and colleague of mine (Michael Young). Now
> here I am with a T.V. pilot that, I feel, is some of the best
> writing I've ever done.

Tom isn't alone. I've seen the interest in co-writing scripts rapidly rising
among writers and students. And I'm not surprised: Each year the list of
script partners and their successes grows longer (in 2002, *half* of the scripts
nominated for the Best Screenplay Oscar were co-written by ampersands,
the industry designation for writing teams). Why? Because as Tom and Matt
Stevens & I and so many others have discovered, collaborative writing is one
of the most productive and successful ways to write short or long scripts. So
if you're interested in writing with a partner, I strongly suggest that you give
it a try.

Mind you, script partnering isn't easy; in fact, it's one of the most difficult
relationships in the world because it's really *two* relationships—a personal
and a professional one—and both must be nurtured and maintained for the
partnership to work. If the personal relationship goes south, so does the
writing.

"It's hard to fake a working attitude when you're disenchanted," Larry
Gelbart (*Caesar's Hour, Mash, Tootsie*) told Matt and me when we interviewed
him for our book, *Script Partners.*[1]

And writing with a partner is a big time commitment. Nine-to-fivers Scott
Alexander & Larry Karaszewski (*Ed Wood; The People vs. Larry Flynt*) only
half-jokingly compare it to being in prison. Most other script partners
compare it to marriage, but Gelbart disagrees. "It's harder than marriage!"
he told us.

"Why?" we inquired.

He laughed, "Because there's no sex! There's no way to kiss and make up!" (Unless, of course, you and your partner are married or otherwise romantically involved.)

But Matt & I—and the twenty script partners we interviewed—have found that the advantages of writing with a partner far outweigh the disadvantages (the most obvious being sharing the bottom line). There are so many advantages, in fact, that Matt & I compiled a list of the . . .

TOP TEN REASONS TO WRITE WITH A PARTNER

1. Writing is lonely. It doesn't have to be. And it isn't if you co-write your scripts.
2. Writing with a partner doubles your chance for success.
3. Filmmaking is a collaborative art, and co-writing scripts gives you a head start on mastering the collaborative process.
4. It's a dog-eat-dog business—and vice-versa—but when you write with a partner, there's always one person in town looking out for your interests.
5. A writing workout partner helps you stay motivated, focused, and productive in the face of countless rejections (and it's cheaper than anti-depressants).
6. Two imaginations really *are* better than one—better brainstorming and creative breakthroughs.
7. Yin, meet Yang. Complementing (and complimenting) each other can lead to stronger scripts.
8. A partner helps you work through writer's block, if only because it's embarrassing when both of you are staring at a blank page.
9. Collaboration not only improves mental health, it makes you a better writer—and a better person.
10. And, as *Shrek*'s co-writer Ted Elliott (who writes with Terry Rossio) said, "As you struggle as writers to perfect your craft, schlepping from studio to studio trying to make that elusive sale or capture that dream assignment, as you wend your way over the freeways that link Hollywood to Burbank, and Beverly Hills to Century City, there is a final, overwhelming way in which a writing partner can be beneficial. Two words: Carpool lane."[2]

And these are just the top *ten*.

Personally, I never want to write scripts solo again. As Phil Hay said when we asked if he would ever write scripts without his ampersand, Matt Manfredi (*crazy/beautiful*, story for *The Tuxedo*), "It would be very lonely and upsetting."

Andrew Reich & Ted Cohen, head-writers of *Friends*, have continued to co-write their scripts even as they've risen to the rank of Executive Producers. "We both know on some level we could do this by ourselves," Reich said, "but we're better together and we prefer it that way."

Harold Ramis has co-written scripts with different partners, from Douglas Kenney & Chris Miller (*Animal House*) to Peter Tolan (*Analyze This, Analyze That*). "It just adds so much to the work," he said during a break from editing *Analyze That*. "Peter, for instance, will add just tremendously funny things and great scenes, great dialogue. And there's this synergistic benefit—it makes my work better, and together we're better than probably either of us alone. I can enjoy writing alone, but I think I've never been as good as with other people. If I were limited by my own ability, my own imagination, I would be probably less than half as successful as I am," he confessed, laughing.

But for my money, Jim Taylor, who writes with Alexander Payne (*Election; About Schmidt*), said it best when he told us, "Writing with Alexander at my side is much more pleasurable than working on my own." Or as he told *Scenario Magazine*, "Just the writing process itself, of writing on my own, is very unpleasant and unproductive, and it's just no fun."

Fun is the reason Harold Ramis started writing with others.

"Here's the secret," he said. "When I was in college, there were things I was interested in academically, but nothing was as much fun as sitting around a room with really funny guys and laughing all the time. I couldn't think of anything better to do . . . and it occurred to me that people actually make a living doing this. My very good friend in college was a guy named Michael Shamberg, who is Danny DeVito's partner in a company called Jersey Films. And Michael and I literally shook hands and said, 'Let's never take jobs we have to dress up for, and let's only do what we enjoy.' " He laughed. "You know you're gonna struggle anyway, you might as well enjoy it."

FINDING THE RIGHT WRITING PARTNER

But you won't enjoy writing scripts with a partner unless you find the right person.

Okay, you may be thinking, but how do I do that?

It's a question many writers have asked Matt & me since we started our collaboration, and a question we've asked many collaborative writers. And while there's no one-size-fits-all answer, there are some strategies that can help, whether you're looking for a partner to co-write a project or someone to share a writing career.

Collaboration is such an intimate creative relationship, it's best to begin looking for a prospective partner among the people you know. You have a greater chance of working successfully together if you've worked out the bugs of *being* together.

"We knew each other so well, and that's crucial," Reich said of his collaboration with Cohen.

It's no surprise that most of the teams that we talked to evolved out of close personal relationships—friends or family or lovers. Like Reich & Cohen, Alexander & Karaszewski and Manfredi & Hay were best friends before they began writing together. Fay & Michael Kanin (*Teacher's Pet; The Opposite Sex*), Nicholas Kazan & Robin Swicord (*Matilda*), and Lee & Janet

Scott Batchler (*Batman Forever*) chose each other as spouses before they chose each other as writing partners. Olivier Ducastel & Jacques Martineau (*Adventures of Felix; Jeanne and the Perfect Guy*) fell in love before they fell into their collaboration. "It was for us, first and foremost, a relationship as lovers," they explained.

Then there's brotherly/sisterly love. That's not to say other familial combinations aren't possible, but the sibling collaboration is far more prevalent— the Ephron sisters, and the Coen, Wachowski, Farrelly, and Weitz brothers, to name a few of the more famous teams. Consider the amazing success of one of my former students, Matt Chapman and his brother Mike with their charming and wildly popular Web page, *homestarrunner.com*, which features the flash animation short short short films they've created together. Not only do they receive upwards of 300,000 hits every Monday when they add new material (and 5,000 e-mails a day), they are receiving rave reviews all over the country, including *The New York Times* which described *homestarrunner.com* as a "seamless, richly nuanced universe."[3]

But what if you don't have a partner-worthy friend/spouse/lover/ sibling? If you're in film school, look among your creative colleagues: Who has strengths that would complement yours? Who shares your sensibilities about what makes a good story? Your sense of humor? This is *all-important* if you want to co-write comedy. As Gelbart advised, "Say something funny to your prospective partners and if they don't laugh, run don't walk to the next candidate." In fact, the same sense of humor may predict, as nothing else can, a closeness and compatibility in your writing life.

The right partner, however, may not, at first glance, be an obvious choice.

True story: When Matt & I met over a faculty lunch at Florida State's Film School, we *hated* each other. It's too long a story to tell here (we tell all in *Script Partners*), but suffice it to say that by the time lunch was over, I'd decided that Matt was a moral derelict, and he'd decided that I was a self-righteous—well, rhymes with *rich*. After lunch, he actually *crossed the street* so we wouldn't have to share the same sidewalk. Which was just fine with me. But as the year went along and we worked together on student scripts, we discovered that we agreed about what makes a good story, character, scene, saying to each other for the first of countless times, "Get out of my head!" And we cracked each other up. Let's face it—it's impossible to hate someone who laughs at your jokes. Humor studies show that this is one of the most powerful ways to reverse a bad first impression (which is why, as Matt says, he laughs a lot on first dates). Such is the power of humor in creating human connection—and good collaborations.

If you're in college but not in film school, enroll in film or screenwriting classes. Join a drama or comedy group. And if you're not in college, *nil desperandum*. Take classes anyway. Attend writers' conferences. Join writers' organizations. Socialize. If you *still* can't find a collaborator among contacts and colleagues, you can post notices—as many do—in any number of places on the Internet (see Chapter 2 of *Script Partners* for a list). You can also place ads in publications such as *Variety, The Hollywood Reporter*, and *Backstage* (and their online versions as well).

Whatever venue you choose—finding the perfect partner among people you know or among perfect strangers—it's *essential* to find someone with shared sensibilities, complementary strengths, someone who plays well with others (especially you), and above all, someone you respect and who respects you—and your work. Exchange writing samples. If you don't respect their writing (or vice versa), run don't walk to the next candidate. Because Aretha was right—respect matters the most. Hey, we ought to know. We went from zero to sixty on this one.

But in the end, collaboration—like love, friendship, or film—is experiential. No one, not even close friends or spouses or family members, can know if writing together will work until they try it. As Reich described brainstorming the first script with Cohen:

> All of a sudden, Ted said something, and I said, "Then we could do *this*." And he said, "We could do this and *this*." Funny ideas started flowing, and it just felt like *wow*, this is really a good idea! And *boy* is this more fun than I've been having sitting by myself trying to write. With Ted it just clicked.

So choose the most promising partner and see if it clicks when you work together. See if you say, *"Wow."* That's the real acid test. The journey of a collaboration begins with one script.

THE SPACE-TIME CONUNDRUM, THE SEQUEL

Once you've found the right writing partner, you'll have a new problem to solve: Where and when will the two of you work? As I said in Chapter 3, the right place and time are crucial because they influence how well you write. But it's trickier for a team to make these decisions because you have two busy lives to consider, two sets of creative habits, and two circadian rhythms.

Blessed are they who have the same circadian rhythms, but often script partners do not. Matt & I don't. He works best at night and thinks mornings are "heinous." I work best in the morning and I'm a drooling zombie by 10:00 P.M. We respect each other's rhythms—we're talking hard-wiring here—so we compromise and work during the six hours that seem the least heinous to both of us, from 11:00 A.M. until 5:00 P.M. We'll work a little later or earlier if we have a tight deadline, but never too early in the morning or too late at night. And we've discovered that there's an advantage to our circadian incompatibility: I'll go over the script in the morning and have some notes or ideas by the time Matt drags himself out of bed. And he'll do his own version of mop-up after I've crashed at night, often leaving a Post-it™ Note on the screenplay for me to find the next morning: *There's a problem on page 15. Fix it!*

Where you work must work for both of you, too. Like many writers, you might like writing in restaurants. Matt & I enjoy developing our characters and stories over a meal (our collaboration started at a greasy-spoon in Tallahassee) because there's something about the clatter of dishes and conversations swirling around us that fuels the back-and-forth of brainstorming. Not long ago when we started a play/musical and we had nothing but an idea, we were amazed to see the characters and story miraculously materialize over a series of five lunches. But when we get down to the actual writing, we need a more private space, preferably the porch at a friend's beach cottage on St. George Island or the porch overlooking the meadow at Claudia's farm. That's where we do our best work (that's where I'm writing this now). These two places are, for us, "that most magic place of all places where the work goes better than it has gone before," as Tennessee Williams said.

You and your partner, of course, have to solve the space-time conundrum yourselves. You might prefer drafting your scripts in restaurants, or like the nine-to-fivers we interviewed, in a more neutral office space. The key is finding that time and place where you both can relax and write well together.

CO-DRAFTING THE SCRIPT

I said in Chapter 3, too, that no one can tell you your process. This is just as true when you write with a partner. You must work out a way of working that works for you both. As Nick Kazan said, "Deciding your process is part of the process."

This may mean co-writing every word, as Matt & I did when we wrote our first script, but this can take a great deal of time—eighteen months in our case. Depending on your deadline (or age), this may not be practical. Sitcom writers, for example, have a week, sometimes less, to crank out a script. Once "the room" (of writers and producers) has "broken" an episode (into scenes) for *Friends*, Reich & Cohen divide up the scenes and write the first draft solo. They don't *like* writing solo, but it saves time, and they work together to rewrite the script.

Like Alexander & Karazsewski and Manfredi & Hay, Rob Ramsey & Matt Stone (*Life; Big Trouble; Intolerable Cruelty*) co-write every word (they call themselves "the Vulcan Mind Meld"), but many of the teams that we talked to divide up the scenes, each in their idiosyncratic way. Some divide up the acts, and some, like Peter Tolan and Harold Ramis, will split a script right down the middle, as they did with the remake of *Bedazzled*. Tolan wrote the first half, Ramis the second, then Ramis, who directed the film, put them together and polished the script. He and Tolan have also divided the drafts. "That's what Peter and I do—kind of sit in the room and outline and brainstorm, and then I let him do the ice breaking, which is probably the coward's way out." He laughed. "I let him do the heavy lifting. Then I rewrite him." And that's fine with Tolan.

Matt & I found co-writing every word a real pleasure, but when Matt moved to Los Angeles in 1997, we decided to divide up the drafts on our next two scripts, both broad comedies. Matt flew back to Florida, and we worked together for several weeks co-creating the characters, story, and structure, and wrote a detailed scene-by-scene, then Matt flew back to Los Angeles and blasted out the first draft. When he finished, I rewrote it, then we worked together on the third . . . and the fourth . . . and the fifth. If you try this approach, I recommend working closely together co-creating character, story, and structure, to make sure that you're on the same page. And it only works if one of you *wants* to write the first draft, as Matt did with our comedies and I did with most of the chapters of *Script Partners*. The first draft *is* heavy-lifting, and the last thing you want is resentment and possibly ownership issues rearing their ugly heads. Nothing will wreck a partnership faster. You're better off dividing up scenes or acts or co-writing each word. Remember, too, to give the heavy lifter permission to *suck*. This is essential. We tell ourselves it's okay to bang out big, bad, bloated first drafts—"loose and baggy monsters," we affectionately call them—and that freedom allows us to get the words down on paper.

Your process will more than likely evolve over time, maybe even in the course of writing one script, as Tom Kurzanski discovered:

> We tried to work together on the first scenes, agonizing over every line, role-playing to get the dialogue we felt worked the best—and it just took too long. We finally got our sea legs when I suggested we map it out like big studio animators do. We assigned ourselves to certain characters, and would write scenes according to which major characters were featured (e.g., I write the character of Ben, the scene features Ben predominantly over other characters, therefore I write the scene). Once we did that, things worked out great.

For those phases when you do co-write—or rewrite—your script, you'll need to figure out the best way to work together. Who types, who paces? Or sprawls on the couch? With Manfredi & Hay, the one who's most crabby that day gets to lie on the couch while the other one does the typing. Ramsey & Stone sit at two desks facing each other, with Ramsey typing while Matt rules the mouse. Talk about Vulcan Mind Meld! And on some occasions Taylor & Payne *both* do the typing (hi-tech Taylor has figured out a way to rig up two keyboards to the same monitor). When Matt and I are together, he and I sit at a table, and he does the typing, not because he types faster (I do), but because he's trained as an actor and reads our work aloud while I listen (and applaud appropriately). But sometimes we have to co-write long-distance, which involves endless e-mails, phone bills that rival Visa, and compatible software—always, *always* use compatible software. And we've just started using software designed for collaborators (Final Draft 7/CollaboWriter) that allows us to work on a script at the same time when we're in different places.

Again, it's what works best for you both. As we say in *Script Partners*, "How you work is not as important as how well how you work works for you. And how well you work together, even if you're working apart."

DEALING WITH DISAGREEMENTS

At a book signing for *Script Partners* at Drama Books in New York, a young man said to me, "I'd like to write scripts with my wife, but she's reluctant to try because she's afraid we wouldn't be able to handle the disagreements." And Matt & I heard the same fear expressed by others at the Creative Screenwriting Expo in Los Angeles.

It's a common concern, and it should be because disagreements do happen.

"All the *time*," said Alexander & Karaszewski.

Disagreements are an inevitable, integral, and invaluable part of the collaborative process. Even the most compatible, peace-loving script partners disagree occasionally when they co-write a script. Matt & I have a very amicable collaboration, but we've had a few doozies—and they've led to some of our greatest breakthroughs. So don't worry about having disagreements; you and your partner will have them. What matters is how you *deal* with them. If you handle disagreements destructively, this will create a disconnection between you both—the last thing you want or need when you're working together. But if you handle disagreements constructively, however heated they may get, they can make your script—and your partnership—stronger.

Learning to handle disagreements constructively is so important to collaboration that Andrew Reich recommends writing with "someone you've had arguments with or you know you can settle things with without throwing tantrums." I second the motion. But if you and your partner do not yet know how you'll handle disagreements—or even if you do—here are a dozen partnership-saving strategies that can help you keep it constructive:

First and foremost, as I told the young man in New York, and Matt & I told others in Los Angeles, you and your partner need to agree that *your relationship comes first*, especially if you are friends or lovers or spouses. Articulate this to each other. Shake hands on it. You might even put it in writing. Agree that no matter how the writing goes, your relationship is your highest priority. When you agree on this—and act on it—you'll find that it's much easier to navigate the emotional white water of disagreements and write successfully together.

Second, agree that the script comes second, placing it in importance below your relationship but above your individual egos. Resolve to make creative decisions for the good of the script, not yourselves. This means that the ideas you come up with have to stand on their own merit, regardless of who suggests them. Ted Elliott & Terri Rossio call this "egoless arguing."

Tom Kurzanski & Michael Young have taken this advice to heart. "If we ever disagreed or contradicted each other we'd discuss it, presenting our case and decide what was best for the script and the story. The first draft ended up being more than we'd even hoped," Tom said in his e-mail.

Of course, in order to do this, you have to . . .

Three, check your ego at the door. And, hey, this ain't easy. Ego is one of our driving forces as writers. And we're all, in our way, closet control freaks; didn't we become writers, at least in part, so we could create (and rule!) our own universes? As Marshall Brickman (*Annie Hall; Manhattan*) says in his Introduction to *Script Partners*, "It's an enormously powerful feeling, not to be underestimated: the seductive, infantile omnipotence with which someone alone in a room, though he appears to be staring off into the middle distance, is in fact inventing people, starting a war, perhaps, or if it's been an especially rotten day, destroying an entire planet."

But when it comes to collaboration, as Nick Kazan cautions, "Ego is the great destroyer."

If you or your partner can't set yours aside for the sake of the script—and your partnership—you both would be better off as solo writers.

Four, keep it fair, whatever that means to both of you. This is crucial. Why? Consider the case of capuchin monkeys:

> Researchers at Emory University reported in September 2003 that capuchin monkeys have a sense of justice, at least as applied to themselves. They trained monkeys to trade pebbles for food. If a monkey saw a researcher giving her neighbor a grape in return for a pebble, but she herself received only a slice of cucumber, she would signal her displeasure by slamming down the pebble instead of handing it over, or refusing to eat the cucumber.
>
> If a sense of fairness exists in a capuchin monkey, it probably developed early in the primate line, and the genes that promote the behavior are likely to be present in people, too.[4]

In short, we're hard-wired for fairness, so you can't fake this any more than you can fake your circadian rhythms. You must both feel that the division of labor is fair. This doesn't always mean equal. Matt wanted to write the first draft of two of our screenplays, and I wrote the second draft, but I also know that writing the first draft *is* heavy-lifting, so I offered to write the first draft of most of the chapters in *Script Partners*. Even so, we had our sticky moments. When we finished interviewing twenty script partners or teams for the book, we had an Everest of audiotapes to transcribe. Before I left Los Angeles for Florida, I sifted through the tapes and selected the ones I wanted to transcribe.

"Hey," Matt said, "why do you get to choose?"

I started to counter with a quote from Annie Savoy ("Actually, none of us on this planet ever really chooses . . ."), but I knew he was right—we both needed to have a say in the matter. We needed to find a way to divide up the cassettes that would be fair to both of us. And, lo, the answer was right there in our interviews: Reich & Cohen told us they sort the scenes they have to write based on difficulty (hard, medium, easy), then they take turns choosing the scenes they want to write. Inspired by their example, we sorted our tapes by length and difficulty and took turns choosing the ones we'd transcribe. We also agreed if either of us hit total burnout with our transcribing, we could pay a transcriptionist to finish the task. In the end, both of us did.

Five, don't take it personally. This is easier said than done in the heat of an argument, especially considering that "everybody's neurotic and writers are *more* neurotic than most," as Gelbart said. The key is to keep your arguments about the work, not each other, then you'll be less likely to make your criticisms personal or take them personally.

Six, don't keep score. When one of your ideas or jokes or great lines of dialogue gets into the script, resist the urge to remind your partner who came up with that brilliant bit (okay, I'll admit that Matt & I occasionally do this, but it's usually more for laughs than for ego gratification). In the best collaborations, a third voice emerges, and partners are hard-pressed to tell you who came up with what.

Seven, show don't tell. If you're convinced that you know the best way a scene should be written, write it and show it to your partner. We've done this many times. When we're disagreeing about the way a scene should go, one of us will say, "Let me play a minute," and type out the scene. Then the other can see that person's vision—and version—on paper. The proof's on the page. But if you *still* can't agree, you'll have to . . .

Eight, bargain. Cut back room deals. Let your partner have that line you can't stand if you can have that line that you love. Chances are good that neither line will make or break the script.

Nine, defer to passion. This is one of the most common and successful strategies script partners use. In the midst of a creative disagreement, they'll ask, "Who has the most passion?" and defer to that partner. Matt & I have taken this a step further—before we defer to passion we like to explore it. Why does one of us feel so passionately? What's behind it? This has led to cosmic transmissions or at least convinced the less passionate partner that the passionate partner is right.

Ten, defer to the original writer—or to the director. If you've divided up the scenes, acts, or drafts, and you simply cannot agree about some aspect of the script, defer to the writer who first drafted that section. Or, if one partner will be directing the film, defer to that person's vision. "The final say has to be his," Jim Taylor said about Alexander Payne, who has directed their scripts for *Citizen Ruth*, *Election*, and *About Schmidt*. "He will be the one who is on the set trying to make the scene work, so he's the only one who can really say if the scene is working. I'll fight him on certain things up to a point, but then I have to defer to his opinion."

Eleven, create rules to repair the relationship. Unlike love, collaboration means always having to say you're sorry, especially if there's no way to kiss and make up. That is why successful non-conjugal partners like Ramsey & Stone follow rules recommended for conjugal couples:

> We have a couple of little rules that aren't really written
> down. We don't really leave the office mad. (Laughter.) Seri-
> ously, if we've had an argument that day, usually we solve
> the problem anyway by the time we go. But we'll say like,
> "I'm sorry, Matt; I was out of line when I said that," or "I
> didn't mean that,"or whatever. It's not just by rote because
> you want to come in the next day and work, and you know
> you're gonna have these problems.

Twelve, maintain perspective. At the end of the day—or a long argument—it's only a script. Your relationship *is* more important. Which brings
us full circle to number one—the relationship should always come first.
Because, as I said earlier, if the relationship goes south, so will the writing.

When all is said—or shouted—and done, you're not just dealing with
collaborative disagreements constructively, you're constructing a successful
collaboration. You're finding ways "to feed it and keep it running," as Peter
Tolan said, "to evolve with it as opposed to evolving apart."

If you do evolve apart, be honest with each other about it and move on to
different partners or try writing alone. Your time won't have been lost,
because even if the partnership doesn't work out, you will have gained
invaluable insights into collaboration, which is the heart of the art of filmmaking, even for solo writers. As Hanif Kureishe (*My Beautiful Laundrette*),
said so beautifully:

> As a writer, I don't have to work with other people, but I
> do. In a sense, you don't want too much control, you don't
> want to be omnipotent. You can feel yourself going mad if
> you do it entirely on your own terms. The point is to have
> them change you. It's like getting married—you're going to
> find out who you're going to become after a bit.[5]

It's another one of art's rich paradoxes—by working with others, you find
out who you are.

NOTES

1. These quotations and many of the insights in this chapter come from *Script Partners: What Makes Film and TV Writing Teams Work*, written with Matt Stevens;
Michael Wiese Productions, 2003.
2. Elliott, Ted. "Me & My Ampersand." *Wordplayer* 12 October 1999
<*http://www.wordplayer.com/columns/wp18.Me.and.My.Ampersand.html*>
3. Neil Strauss, "Kindred World in Animation," *nytimes.com*, August 28, 2003.
4. Nicholas Wade. "Play Fair: Your Life May Depend On It," *The New York Times*,
Sunday, September 21, 2003.
5. Jed Dannenbaum, Carroll Hodge, and Doe Mayer, *Creative Filmmaking From the
Inside Out*, Simon & Schuster, New York, 2003, p. 98.

PART II

FIVE (NOT SO) EASY SCREENPLAYS

THE DISCOVERY

As you learned in the Mood Exercise, the most frequent moment of change in our lives and our characters' lives is the *discovery*. Learning. Finding out. Realizing.

The best stories are *patterns of discoveries* that make a difference, however subtle, to the characters, like the discovery Hannah makes in *Lena's Spaghetti*:

INT. HANNAH'S BEDROOM—LATER

Hannah jumps on the bed. She flops onto her stomach, picks up the comics, looks them over with a straight face. She turns the page and sees the personal ads. She brightens as she reads.

INSERT—PERSONAL AD

    Like to write? Single male seeks unique female for pen-pal. Please write: Herbert Mack. 8013 Duck Lane. Savannah, Georgia 41256.

MUSIC SWELLS.

Though small and simple, this discovery has great significance for the story, launching Hannah's correspondence with Herbie, a correspondence that alters each of their lives. Likewise the discovery that Paula makes early in *Cool Breeze and Buzz*:

EXT. TRAILER—DAY

ANGLE ON PAULA

skipping along the river's edge reading the comic book. She reaches a clearing and the trailer comes into sight.

HER POV

of the trailer. The red Cadillac is parked in front.

She approaches the Caddy and proceeds to investigate.

CLOSE ON

A) her finger running along the side of the car through a thick layer of dust

B) her hand wiggling the hood ornament

C) the license plate on the front that reads "JACKPOT"

Then suddenly, we hear a MALE VOICE:

> MALE VOICE (O.S.)
> Beauty, ain' she?

HER POV

of a man, BUZZ MCKINNEY, 42, standing in the door at the top of the steps smoking a cigar.

> BUZZ
> (beat)
> Hey, Coolbreeze.

She drops the bag and freezes.

> PAULA
> (staring up at him)
> Hey.

He stands in slacks and a tight short-sleeved v-neck. Upon his belly, a huge brass buckle with a race horse and a large ring on either pinky.

Aunt Barbara appears from behind him.

> AUNT BARB
> Paula, honey, yer daddy's come
> to see you.

And the story is moving. The rest of the story flows from this moment.

Moments of moment create momentum.

In each case, we *witness* a watershed moment in each character's life, a discovery that forces the energy system of their life and emotion to flow a different direction (in *Cool Breeze and Buzz*; in fact, there are double discoveries—the Caddy and Buzz—that make the scene especially rich). The *precise* moment of change is clearly rendered on paper and thus ends up on screen. We *see* the discovery *happen*—that's what we pay our money to see—and we *feel* its emotional impact. We connect.

It's an excellent exercise to have everyone in your writing group (or class) cue up a favorite movie scene where a significant discovery occurs, as my colleague, Dr. Valliere Richard Auzenne, asks her students to do each semester. Screen them. Compare them. Analyze them. Chart their EKG structure. Then, when you're fully acquainted with how discoveries are crafted in the films you admire, you're ready to craft one yourself.

"If you can write a good discovery, you can write a good screenplay," Sam Smiley says. I agree. So learning to craft a convincing, significant discovery is one of the most important aspects of dramatization that you will master.

THE FIRST SCREENPLAY—THE DISCOVERY

To that end, write a three-page screenplay about a character making a discovery that makes a difference to the character. And follow these guidelines:

1. The discovery—the *precise* moment of change— must be clearly rendered on paper and therefore on screen. There's a tendency, especially with beginning screenwriters, to have their discoveries happen off screen. Not in this screenplay. The discovery has to *happen* on screen.

2. The audience must *understand* the difference the discovery makes to your character. They must be able to *see* the shift—however subtle—in your character's life.

3. *Do not go over three pages.* Normal margins and twelve-point Courier type. I know, my students howl, too—*three pages!* But when they're done, they often admit, like Michael Piekutowski (a.k.a. "Pick"), "It makes you focus on what's important. Then you write as much as you can in as few words as possible." Or Kim Baird, "I liked the restrictions. They made you think about what you wanted to say. There was no time for rambling."

"There's no time for lassitude in the screenplay," Mark Spragg told me, and he was talking about *features.*

"What is drama, after all," as Hitchcock once said, "but life with the dull bits cut out?" One of his writers, Jay Presson Allen, described how Hitch did it:

> There was a scene in *Marnie* where a girl is forced into marriage. And I began in the theatre; I only knew to do

absolutely linear things. So I wrote the wedding, and the reception, and leaving the reception, and going to the boat, and the boat leaving. You know, I kept plodding, plodding, plodding. And Hitch—I can't imitate it, I'm sorry I can't because it's so lovely—he said: "Why don't we cut some of that out, Jay. Why don't we shoot the church and hear the bells ring and see them begin to leave the church. Then why don't we cut to a large vase of flowers and there is a note pinned to the flowers that says "Congratulations." And the water in the vase is sloshing, sloshing, sloshing. . . ." You know, I think of that all the time. When I get so wordy and so verbose I suddenly stop and say: think of that vase of water.[1]

In short, cut to the vase. The art of screenwriting is often subtraction. Believe me, I know. After writing features for years, I decided to adapt one of my one-act plays for a short screenplay. The limit was twenty-five pages; my play was thirty, so I thought, *Piece of cake.* Then I started typing the scenes and I realized the screenplay would be sixty pages or more. All that yakketyyak that worked so well on stage had to go. I had to hit my scenes later, cut dialogue that wasn't working hard for the story, boil down my descriptions, select only the most important details, and let the rest go. I cut entire scenes—*everything* that wasn't absolutely essential to telling the story.

Painful? Yes, at first, I admit it, but the finished twenty-five page screenplay was so much better for it, I was delighted. I'm a far better *feature* writer for having done this and a better teacher because I have new sympathy—and *respect*—for my students who have written such rich and resonant short screenplays.

So stick to three pages. Feel free to write a loose and baggy first draft if you want—far be it from me to tell writers their process—but cut it and shape it until it fits in three pages.

4. Remember that you're writing a *screenplay*, not just a scene. Your goal is to write a small story about a discovery and the difference it makes to your character. Like Jay Presson Allen, take advantage of the freedom of the form—the story leap, the power of the image. If your story is built on one conversation, open it up, move it around (this *is* moving pictures we're talking about) the way Nora Ephron does in *When Harry Met Sally*:

EXT. CAR—DAY

The car tooling along a beautiful stretch of highway.

                    SALLY (V.O.)
          You're wrong.

                    HARRY (V.O.)
I'm not wrong.

                    SALLY (V.O.)
You're wrong.

                    HARRY (V.O.)
He wants her to leave. That's why he puts her on
the plane.

                    SALLY (V.O.)
I don't think she wants to stay.

                    HARRY (V.O.)
Of course she wants to stay. Wouldn't you rather
be with Humphrey Bogart than that other guy?

EXT. CAR EXITING (INDUSTRIAL)—MAGIC HOUR

EXT. DINER—NIGHT

Sally's car rounds the corner near some refinery tanks,
heads into a diner parking lot.

                    SALLY (V.O.)
I don't want to spend the rest of my life in
Casablanca married to a man who runs a bar.
That probably sounds very snobbish to you, but I
don't.

The car pulls in front of a diner straight out of the
fifties, Harry driving.

                    HARRY (V.O.)
You'd rather have a passionless marriage—

                    SALLY (V.O.)
—and be First Lady of Czechoslovakia—

                    HARRY (V.O.)
—than live with the man . . .

INT. CAR—NIGHT

> HARRY
> . . . you've had the greatest sex of your life with,
> just because he owns a bar and that's all he does.

> SALLY
> Yes, and so would any woman in her right mind.
> Women are very practical.

She takes out a can of hairspray, sprays her hair.

> SALLY
> Even Ingrid Bergman, which is why she gets on
> that plane at the end of the movie.

EXT. DINER PARKING LOT—NIGHT

> HARRY
> (getting out of car)
> Oh, I understand . . .

. . . he says, realizing she's saying all this because she's never had great sex. A discovery.[2]

One argument, five locations, and two characters making a number of discoveries about each other that seem insignificant, even silly, until Harry comes to his realization that Sally's never had great sex, and she discovers that's what he thinks, and this spawns a new argument that raises the central dramatic question of the screenplay—can a man and woman be good friends? Sally says yes, Harry says no because "the sex thing" is always "out there." They spend the rest of the film working out the answer to this central question.

5. Last, don't let this screenplay's brief length lull you into thinking you're writing a skit. You're writing a significant moment in your character's life. It may be funny or sad or any tone in between, but it isn't a skit. Skits are shallow. Significant discoveries are not.

CHOOSING AN IDEA

The best way to stay out of shallow water with your screenplay is to work with material that you connect to, that has resonance for you as a person. And the best place to find this material is right on your menu. After all, one of the columns is *Discoveries That Made a Difference in My Life*. You might find an idea for a discovery that makes a difference by looking at your own life. If you do, of course, feel free to depart the *donnée* and fictionalize the idea for the screenplay you write.

Look at the other column on your menu—your loves, hates, fears, beliefs. You may have a strong passion or opinion that spawns an idea. This can be a wonderful place to begin. One of my students, Fatima Mojadiddy, believed passionately that the homeless should work, and she wanted to write a short screenplay about this. I agreed, on one condition: She had to talk to homeless people at the shelter in Tallahassee. And there, to her surprise, she discovered that many of the homeless *do* work, an important discovery for Fatima as a human being and screenwriter, and as it turned out, a discovery that makes a difference to the main character in her screenplay. Such is the power of research, which is *essential* when you're creating characters that do not come from your own experience, and they will be more convincing and compelling as a result (for a thorough discussion of the power and importance of researching your characters, see *Script Partners: What Makes Film and TV Writing Teams Work*, pp. 121–125).

You may decide to set your menu aside and create an idea from something entirely different—a bit of dialogue you overheard or an image that struck you just as the image of the river struck Lani Sciandra. Maybe even a sound. Once, walking by a dumpster, I heard a cell phone ringing inside. That scene has stuck with me, and one of these days I'm going to start a screenplay that way—a character hearing a cell phone ring in a dumpster and making a discovery that makes a difference when she answers the phone. Whatever idea you choose, be sure that you feel some connection. And be sure that the idea is small and specific so you can create a pattern of human change that we can see happen on screen in three minutes.

DEVELOPING CHARACTER

Why the discovery makes a difference depends entirely on the character you create. In *Lena's Spaghetti*, Hannah has just moved to a new town. She's lonely, disconnected. When she discovers a personal ad from Herbie, she answers.

And in *Cool Breeze and Buzz*, Paula's discovery that her father is back has tremendous significance for her because she hasn't seen him in years. You have to know—and show—your character so that your audience understands why the discovery matters.

Some writers write a character bio—a brief (or long) description of the character. Television writer Renee Longstreet calls them "character notes," though her notes may run several pages, as they did for her character Andrea Linden in the Lifetime movie, *Mothers and Daughters*. In her notes, Renee describes her character's profession ("Community college art history professor"), appearance ("Attractive naturally—not chic . . . dresses in comfortable clothes. Doesn't pay much attention to appearance. Doesn't exercise much, eats whatever she wants . . . one of those rare birds that other women envy"), situation ("Parenting and working on career—getting degrees, etc. kept her too busy to involve herself with dating, etc. Likes men, has friendships, but not a focus for her"), her time line (College—'73—18 years old—REED College on ROTC scholarship; Pregnant—'75," etc.) and miscellaneous notes ("Jazz buff—has learned to play keyboard as an adult"), including those that offer glimpses into what the character is feeling ("Misses her daughter—harbors some anger at both daughter, mother and sister").

"No one has to see them," Renee told Matt & me, "but I have to write them. So when I do the plot, I already know the person. I really do that. I really have to have my characters."[3]

Then again, her husband and writing partner, Harry, doesn't do character bios, so even within the same writing team, writers have different approaches to creating character.

To be honest, I'm not nuts about bios. All that (albeit important) inert information feels, well, inert. So you may prefer, as I do, to create and explore your characters by answering the following questions:

Character Checklist

1. Name?
2. Physical appearance?
3. Backstory? (the character's story before the screenplay begins)
4. Present circumstances? (occupation, income, geographic location, dwelling, key relationships)
5. Values, beliefs, world view, attitudes, opinions?
6. Loves?
7. Hates?
8. Fears?
9. Wants?
10. Imperfections and contradictions?

You may come up with different questions to ask. Great. Add them to the list. And the more incisive you are with your answers, the better you'll know your character, inside and out.

All this information, of course, cannot end up in your screenplay. Knowing isn't showing. To show, you have to find what Thornton Wilder called "shortcuts to the imagination." Ways of embedding important information—preferably visually—in your screenplay. Ways to give important glimpses into your character and your character's world.

A good place to start is carefully crafting your *Character I.D.*—the brief but *vivid* description of your character when you introduce him for the first time in your script, the way Lani describes Buzz McKinney:

> He stands in slacks and a tight short-sleeved V-neck.
> Upon his belly, a huge brass buckle with a race horse
> and a large ring on either pinky.

The huge brass buckle with a race horse is a glimpse—just a glimpse—into his life as a gambler. A shortcut to our imagination.

When you craft an I.D., you want your character to walk off the page into the head of the reader and stay there the whole screenplay. It drives me crazy when I can't *see* characters the first time I meet them. I know, I know, many screenwriters don't bother, but the very best do. Look how brilliantly William Goldman describes Butch Cassidy the first time we meet him:

> A man, idly walking around the building. He is Butch Cassidy and hard to pin down. Thirty-five and bright, he has brown hair, but most people, if asked to describe him, would remember him blond. He speaks well and quickly, and has been all his life a leader of men, but if you asked him, he would be damned if he could tell you why.[4]

Or how vividly George Lucas, Gloria Katz, and Willard Huyck describe The Toad when he first appears in *American Graffiti*:

> Terry Fields ("The Toad") maneuvers the scooter next to Steve's Chevy but misjudges and ricochets off the trash can before stopping. Terry grins sheepishly. He's seventeen, short but plenty loud, both vocally and sartorially in his pink and black shirt, levis, and white bucks. He looks slightly ridiculous but always thinks he's projecting an air of supercool.[5]

It's one of my great pleasures in screenwriting classes to explicate these two passages, showing how they briefly but brilliantly give us a glimpse of three crucial aspects of character (3-D I.D.s, I like to call them): (1) what the character *looks* like, (2) how the world perceives him, and (3) how he perceives himself.

Talk about exquisitely *crafted*. Perfectly packed little snowballs. Okay, they're a bit on the long side—I'd shoot for two or three sentences, max, especially in short screenplays—but notice that they don't stop the story. Each I.D. is *floated on action*—casing a bank and ricocheting off a trash can—and even as we're introduced to Butch and The Toad, the story keeps flowing.

So take all you know about your character from the Checklist and boil it down into a beautifully crafted 3-D I.D. Avoid like the plague clichés like "avoid like the plague" or sleep-city descriptions like "an attractive female" or "a typical Dad" or the overloaded APB description—six feet tall, brown hair, blue eyes, big feet—actually, big feet has nice possibilities. Select *high* details—specific, illuminating details—that give us a glimpse of the outer and inner person, and write the finished I.D. down on a three-by-five card or a sheet of paper.

DEVELOPING STORY AND STRUCTURE

Now that you know your character, you need to develop your pattern of change. When and where does the story begin? What discovery does your character make? Where? When? And what difference does it make?

When your character makes the discovery—early, middle, or late—in your screenplay is up to you—but the audience *must understand* the difference it makes to your character. *Why* it makes a difference. If the discovery happens early, the rest of your short screenplay might be dramatizing the difference it makes. If the discovery happens late in the screenplay, you'll have to set up your character and situation carefully so we understand the significance of the discovery when it occurs. If you've set your character and situation up well enough, you may not even need dialogue when the discovery happens. In film, such a moment is often more powerful without words.

In *Grosse Pointe Blank*, Martin Blank is speechless when he discovers his home is now an UltiMart. But as he stands there stunned, staring, as this awful information sinks in, we *know* what he's thinking—and feeling. We supply his thoughts and emotions. This is the height of connection between character and audience and the height of success for a screenwriter. The moment is so beautifully crafted, character and viewer become one.

One way to dramatize the difference a discovery makes is to show the shift—however subtle—in your character's life. Martin Blank is heading home, but when he discovers it's an UltiMart, the physical and emotional flow of the story shifts. "You can't go home again," he says to his shrink, "but I guess you can shop there." He calls his secretary, tells her to find his mother, and when he finds her in a mental ward, he finds that she doesn't know who he is. "You're a handsome devil. What's your name?"

The best stories are patterns of discoveries.

Once you've created a pattern of change out of one or more discoveries, decide how your screenplay will end. You don't have to—or want to—tie up all the loose ends. That leads your story into hunky-dory land, and few of us believe it exists. Just find a simple way to bring the magic carpet and your audience back to the ground.

Once you've developed your story, you're ready to create a *Scene-by-Scene*—a list of scenes in the order they occur. I strongly recommend that you work on index cards first—one scene per card—so you can move the scenes around on your desk or table or floor until you find the most effective order and emotional flow. Sticky notes work well, too. The point is to stay flexible, to see all the possibilities your material offers, before you lock yourself and your story into a structure.

If you get inspired about a scene and the index card isn't big enough for the notes or dialogue that you want to write, write them out on a separate sheet of paper (*never* argue with your Muse) and file it, making a note on the index card to look it up later.

Once the order of your scenes is working, type up your Scene-by-Scene. There are no rules about the right way to do this, but I find it useful to give each scene a slug line, double space, then give a brief description of what happens and why, i.e., your dramatic purpose in the scene. An example from *"Killer Kite"* might look like this:

EXT. HARLAN LaRUE'S MANSION—NIGHT (FILM)

The ancient stone building sits dark and lifeless.
THUNDER. Establishes setting and mood.

INT. LaRUE'S MANSION—NIGHT (FILM)

PROFESSOR HARLAN LaRUE and his assistant,
JONATHAN SCOTT, prepare to conduct their experiment
and carry the kite to the roof. Sets up the experiment.

EXT. ROOF—NIGHT (FILM)

A bolt of lightning hits the kite and LaRUE. Jonathan
finds LaRue's empty shoes and realizes he's become one
with the kite. Launches the horror story.

EXT. LABORATORY ROOF—NIGHT (VIDEO)

Liz yells "Cut" and the VIDEO CAMERA zooms out until
we see the CAMERA and the DIRECTOR, COLIN
KISHMAN. Establishes that this is a documentary about
the making of the "cult horror classic," *"Killer Kite."*

You may find it helpful to make a note about the emotion you hope to elicit from the audience in the scene, but don't bog down in too much detail. The simpler your Scene-by-Scene is, the better. That way you—and others— can read your screenplay in a skeletal form, letting the movie run in your— their—head, and confirm that your story and structure are, in fact, working.

DRAFTING THE SCREENPLAY

With your outline as a guide, write with energy and enthusiasm. "Turn the dogs loose and see where they go," as Mark Spragg likes to say. Stir in the I.D. you've already crafted. Make your characters come alive on the page. And make time to work on your screenplay each day, even if you have to get up earlier or stay up later to do it. The cumulative effect of writing each day is amazing.

If your rough draft is too long, grit your teeth and start cutting. A happy problem—subtraction is easier than addition. Try cutting your narrative description (but not necessarily your main character I.D.) in half, making it *more* vivid, visual, and economical. Cut dialogue that isn't essential, that doesn't work hard for you or your story. This is almost *always* a vast improvement as you will see when you read the seven student screenplays in Part III and compare them with their films. Again, a visual reaction from a character is often stronger than words, as Lani Sciandra discovered as she was shooting *Cool Breeze and Buzz*:

> I trusted the notion that less is more—how can we say this without saying it?—redirecting the burden of meaning from writer to viewer—in the script, Paula shouts after the man who dusts her on the dirt road in the red Cadillac—this is an example of me trying too hard to punctuate the point— in the film, it's a silent reaction shot which I felt enhanced the mystery—I realize now how much more I could've let go but I suppose that's how the lesson goes.

When your characters *do* need to speak, let the *text* (what is said) be simple, and let the *subtext* (the river of emotion that flows underneath what is said) be complex.

When your screenplay is finished—at least in this incarnation—give it a title if you haven't done so already. I *never* accept an untitled work, as Barry Jenkins remembers. "When I handed you the script untitled (as it had been for a year), you scratched out *Untitled* and handed it back to me. 'Anything but *Untitled*,' you said, and so I scribbled in *My Josephine*." The title is crucial. It's the first thing your audience sees, your first chance to connect with them and focus their mind on your story.

If you don't have a title, sit down and noodle everything that the story's about. Odd bits and details from the world of your screenplay. Slang for nudity—*The Full Monty*. A wonderful title! I love to do title workshops in class. As I jot miscellaneous words on the board, students start seeing connections. We did this for Chris Tomko's brilliant but untitled short screenplay about two young losers who kidnap a Sharpei dog so they can make enough money to get out of town. And, lo, someone shouted, "Sharpei Diem! Seize the Dog!" It set up the tone and the subject without *telegraphing* (giving the story away). The title stuck—and I love it—bad Latin though it may be.

If you try this alone or in class and you're *still* stuck in what the late great Jerry Stern called "Title Hell"—a place I've been many times—give your screenplay a working title and hand it in. Someone who reads it just might come up with a better one for you.

REWRITING THE SCREENPLAY

Repeat after me: *Screenwriting is rewriting.*

I'm not the first person to say it and I won't be the last. Because truer words that we don't want to hear were never spoken.

"Here is what I always say about screenwriting," Nora Ephron says in the Introduction to *When Harry Met Sally*:

> When you write a script, it's like delivering a great big beautiful plain pizza, the one with only cheese and tomatoes. And then you give it to the director, and the director says, 'I love this pizza. I am willing to commit to this pizza. But I really think this pizza should have mushrooms on it' . . . then someone else comes along and says, 'I love this pizza, too, but it really needs green peppers' . . . then someone else says, 'Anchovies.' There's always a fight over the anchovies. And when you get done, what you have is a pizza with everything. Sometimes it's wonderful. And sometimes you look at it and you think, I knew we shouldn't have put the green peppers onto it. Why didn't I say so at the time? Why didn't I lie down in traffic to prevent anyone's putting green peppers onto the pizza?"[6]

But even *before* a director or producer starts throwing green peppers on your script, you'll be rewriting—to make it better. If you're serious. If you want to be a successful screenwriter. The version published here of *Slow Dancin' Down the Aisles of the Quickcheck* is Thomas Jackson's *fifteenth* draft. "I didn't even have a *story* in my first draft," he told me.

After I read the sixth draft of an M.F.A. Thesis screenplay-in-progress, *The Buse*, I told the co-writer, Rob McCaffrey, what worked for me and what didn't, what was clear and what wasn't, where I thought the emotional flow wasn't working, where a character's emotion wasn't quite earned, what emotional beats he might add to make it work better. A week later, Rob said the screenplay was "beginning to go in the right direction." And it was an excellent script when I read it.

This truth is so important, so fully acknowledged in the profession, that it's spawned a peculiar ritual at the Sundance Screenwriters Lab. "It has become a Lab tradition for the Fellows to burn their scripts to symbolize their acceptance that the writer's work is never done and that the script can always be better," said a 1998 fellow, William Wheeler.

Screenwriting is rewriting. Write it down. Pin it up. Make it your screenwriting mantra. And keep in mind that it isn't bad news.

"Revision," Kurt Vonnegut reminds us, "can make a fool look like a genius."

And as you rewrite, these guidelines might help you along in the process:

1. Be sure you're giving your readers the best script you can, however many drafts this may take. Recently a student gave me a short screenplay with a long note attached telling me she had "literally ripped her hair out" writing and rewriting the script. She wanted to know if there was a way to avoid all that angst and hard labor in the future. Alas, no, I told her, at least none that

I've found. Screenwriting *is* rewriting. Over and over. But I was happy to tell her that her script was terrific. Not perfect, of course, but close. And you should work as hard on your own. As Jerry Stern used to say, "Don't give your writing to a reader until there's nothing more you can do."

2. Get feedback, responses, from the right kind of readers—people who care about you and your work and your future. If the guy who runs your dry cleaners offers to read it, think twice, unless he fits the criteria mentioned above. (I've had my work trashed by one shopkeeper who turned out to be a frustrated writer waiting to take out his frustrations on the first writer stupid enough to offer her work. Now, when I've finished a draft of a screenplay, I only give it to readers I trust). If you're in a workshop or class, you may not be able to choose who sees your work, but there will be those you should listen to more than others. And you will become that same kind of good critic for others.

I try and keep the critiques in my workshops constructive and carefully focused on one common goal—helping the writer strengthen the screenplay. This is an important level of collaboration in the long collaborative effort that is the writing and making of films, and the first level of collaboration if you haven't written your script with a partner.

So I ask my students to tell the writer what is working for them in the script and what isn't. What is clear or unclear; this may be the most helpful feedback of all. What's strong and what could be stronger. How? Is the character's emotional flow working? Why or why not? They must be specific or it just isn't helpful.

You want to know if the precise moment of discovery in your script is clearly rendered. How could it be clearer? Have you clearly shown the difference it makes? Does your audience get it? If not, what could you add or subtract to make sure they do? Are there breaks in the emotional flow? Emotions that seem unmotivated, out of the blue? If a character's emotion doesn't feel earned, we don't buy it. Your job then is to figure out what to add or shade in your script so the emotion *is* earned. And, when you add, of course, you'll have to find something else to subtract.

Take notes as people respond; you'll be amazed how many wonderful suggestions you'll forget. Before the critique is over, your head will feel like an overstocked fishpond.

Most of all, listen closely to everything that is said. More than once I've snickered (to myself) at someone's suggestion only to discover later it's the key to my screenplay. So be open. Check your ego at the door. Constructive criticism is a gift. Your purpose here is creating a screenplay that works. And connects. To do this, you need other people.

3. Look for consensus. If more than one person thinks a moment isn't working, it's probably wise to take a close look. If only one person thinks it doesn't work, and you disagree, diplomatically disregard it. Ultimately

you'll have to run the responses—consensus or not—through your own creative Cuisinart and decide what's best to do.

4. Set the script aside as long as you dare so you can see it fresh when you return to rewrite. "Revise" means *to look or see again*, and you need distance to do this.

5. Make the changes necessary to make your script stronger—from your character I.D. to your curtain line. Sometimes this involves outlining the entire script over again and completely rewriting (*a page one rewrite*); sometimes this involves what Jerry Stern called *embeddings*—small additions you can embed in your existing script that make your story clearer—and stronger.

6. Take heart. Yes, you may have to cut something you love yet doesn't quite work to make room for something that does. But that, as William Wheeler discovered at Sundance, is the nature of the beast. "As I watched my pages curl, smoke and disappear into the flames," Wheeler said, "I realized the feeling of loss and rebirth was one I would always have, one way or another, for the rest of my writing life."

NOTES

1. I am indebted to Stu Hample for sending this quotation from *On Writing*, a collection of interviews held at Writers' Guild of America, East, edited by Arlene Hellerman.
2. Nora Ephron, *When Harry Met Sally*, Knopf, New York, 1992, pp. 7, 8.
3. Claudia Johnson & Matt Stevens, *Script Partners: What Makes Film and TV Writing Teams Work*, Michael Wiese Productions, 2003, pp. 114–115.
4. William Goldman, *Butch Cassidy and the Sundance Kid*, Bantam Books, New York, 1969, p. 1.
5. George Lucas, Gloria Katz, Willard Huyck, *American Graffiti*, Grove Press, New York, 1973, pp. 5, 6.
6. Ephron, pp. xiii, xiv.

7

THE DECISION

Discoveries are often beyond our control, but decisions are not. They come straight from our unique Central Control—experience, values, world view.

"The quickest and best way to know someone is to see that person make a significant decision," Sam Smiley says.

I agree. Our decisions define us. They also define the lives that we lead. It's no wonder, then, that major decisions are powerful moments in screenplays. True watershed moments. In long and short scripts, a character's most important decisions are often the *turning points* of the story—those moments of change that throw the story in a whole new direction.

Rainman is a perfect example: The first turning point at the end of Act I is Charlie Babbitt's decision to kidnap his autistic brother, Raymond, from the institution where he's lived all his life. The climax of the story is the much changed Charlie Babbitt's decision to let Raymond return to the same institution. This second decision is a *measure* of how much Charlie Babbitt has changed in the process. So is Hannah's decision to end the correspondence with Herbie in *Lena's Spaghetti*. And Earl's decision to profess his love in *Slow Dancin' Down the Aisles of the Quickcheck*. And Melissa's decision to let Bear and herself be themselves in *A Work In Progress*. Their growth—character arc—is revealed by the decisions they make.

Decisions are made by characters, and characters are made by decisions.

Who we are dictates the decisions we make and the action we take.

$$Who = Do$$

Again, it's a dance—discovery, deliberation, decision, and doing. So a crucial part of designing that dance is learning to craft a decision.

THE SECOND SCREENPLAY—THE DECISION

Write a three- to five-page screenplay about a character making a decision that makes a difference to the character. The guidelines are similar to those for your last screenplay:

1. The decision—the *precise* moment of change—must be clearly rendered on paper and therefore on screen. You can say "he decides" or be a little more subtle, as long as the decision is *clear*. Look at Andy Dufresne's decision to play Mozart's *Marriage of Figaro* over the prison loudspeaker in *The Shawshank Redemption* after he discovers boxes of records and one phonograph donated by the Library District:

INT. GUARD STATION/OUTER OFFICE—DAY (1955)

Andy shoots a look at the bathroom . . . and smiles. Go for broke. He lunges to his feet and barricades the front door, then the bathroom. He returns to the desk and positions the P.A. microphone. He works up his courage, then flicks all the toggles to "on." A SQUEAL OF FEEDBACK echoes briefly . . .

INT./EXT. VARIOUS P.A. SPEAKERS—DAY (1955)

. . . and the Mozart is suddenly broadcast all over the prison.

After finding the record—*discovery*—he shoots a look at the bathroom (where the guard is)—*deliberation*—and smiles. Go for broke—*decision*. He lunges to his feet and broadcasts the music—the *doing* that follows. The decision is clearly rendered, and the dance of discovery, decision, and doing is beautifully—and *clearly*—choreographed.

2. The audience must understand why your character makes this decision. And you must show—or at least indicate—the difference it makes, the shift, however subtle, in your character's life and emotional flow.

3. *Do not go over five pages.* There's no art without limitation. A real artist welcomes limitations and then finds ways to transcend them.

4. Remember that you're writing a screenplay. Design a small but significant story told in more than one scene about a character who makes a significant decision. You may need a discovery or two to precipitate the decision—that's up to you—but your purpose is making us *see and understand* the decision and the difference it makes.

5. And remember—no skits. Dig deeper.

CHOOSING AN IDEA

As you begin to look for ideas for a significant decision a character might make, it's useful to remember that there are two main kinds of decisions in drama—*expedient* and *ethical*—as Sam Smiley points out:

> Expedient decisions have to do with choice of means, and ethical decisions concern specific ends. Deciding something expediently, such as whether to use a knife or a pistol for a murder, has little relation to good and evil, or rightness and wrongness of conduct. Ethical decision or moral choice, such as deciding whether to murder or not to murder, reveals the quantity of evil in a person and the quality of good in him.[1]

You may want to create a story about a character making an ethical decision or an expedient decision or, if you can manage it in five pages, both, like the women in Aristophanes' great comedy *Lysistrata*.

"The key to the action," Smiley says, "is the ethical decision of the women to join the title character in attempting to end the war; the comedy in the play arises from their decision about how to force men to stop fighting."

This doesn't mean your character has to contemplate murder; taking candy from a baby—or not—is an ethical decision, too. And ethical decisions are the most revealing. As Smiley says, summarizing the thought of philosophers from Aristotle to Sartre, "A man is the summary of his ethical decisions." The same, of course, goes for women.

Look at your menu, at the decisions you've made that made a difference, and see if there's an idea there. Check out your own values and beliefs and think about the decisions they've helped you make—or regret. Consider the people you've known and the difference they've made to you; there might be terrific material there. And feel free to add to any of the columns at any time (some of my students keep the menu on their computer screen and add to it all the time).

If an idea doesn't materialize from your menu, step outside your own life and go sit in a busy mall, a bus stop, airport, and people watch. Make up stories for perfect strangers. What decisions have they made that brought them here now or made them who they are? Or create a surface or a deep action for them: *So and so is coming to decide . . . what?* And what difference does it make? If all else fails, come up with the most outrageous idea you can think of, like Andy Zare when he came up with *tongue*.

Less is usually more in screenwriting, except when you're coming up with ideas. Brainstorm like crazy. Creative composting, I call it. Go wild. Free associate. Noodle. Write it all down. And don't censor yourself. Be *playful* (the last word in screenplay *is* play). When you're done, choose the idea you love the most and save the rest for future screenplays (I keep a file for story ideas, character details, and bits of dialogue that I like). Just make sure you connect to your idea in some significant way. And keep it small and specific.

DEVELOPING CHARACTER

The decisions our characters make—like our own—are hotlines to who they are and what they value and believe.

"People seem not to see that their opinion of the world is also a confession of character," Emerson writes in his essay "Worship," and he said a mouthful, as we say in the South.

So zeroing in on these items on your Character Checklist is an ideal place to start developing your main character. What does she believe? What are her values? World view? Opinions? Once you know, you'll be closer to knowing the decisions she'll make.

It's a terrific exercise to write a monologue for your character. Let her tell you *in her own voice* what she values, believes. Let her rip—emote—about her beliefs. Make them specific. You'll find your character's voice—it's never too soon to do that—and you'll discover who she really is. The speech may or may not end up in your script. That doesn't matter. You're developing character now.

You may discover that you *do* want a piece of it in your script; after all, values and beliefs are a wonderful shortcut to character for your audience, illuminating your character's decisions and actions. Look at the way Crash Davis's beliefs in *Bull Durham* dictate what he does after Annie Savoy says she's choosing him or Ebby to "hook up with" this season:

> CRASH
> Why do you get to choose? Why don't I get to choose?

> ANNIE
> Actually none of us on this planet ever really chooses each other. It's all quantum physics and molecular attraction. There are laws we don't understand that bring us together and break us apart.

> EBBY
> Is somebody gonna go to bed with somebody or what?

> ANNIE
> You're a regular nuclear meltdown honey—slow down.

Crash rises to leave, and heads for the door.

> CRASH
> After 12 years in the minor leagues, I don't tryout. Besides—I don't believe in quantum physics when it comes to matters of the heart . . . or loins.

> ANNIE
> (challenging him)
> What do you believe in?

Crash at the door.

> CRASH
> I believe in the soul, the cock, the pussy, the
> small of a woman's back, the hanging curve ball,
> high fiber, good scotch, long foreplay, show tunes,
> and that the novels of Thomas Pynchon are
> self-indulgent, overrated crap.
> (beat)
> I believe that Lee Harvey Oswald acted alone, I
> believe that there oughtta be a constitutional
> amendment outlawing astro-turf and the
> designated hitter, I believe in the "sweet spot,"
> voting every election, soft core pornography,
> chocolate chip cookies, opening your presents on
> Christmas morning rather than Christmas eve,
> and I believe in long, slow, deep, soft, wet kisses
> that last for 7 days.[2]

You'll notice a number of changes in this speech when Costner says it on screen, but, again, the gist is the same. And these beliefs motivate—and illuminate—his decisions and actions. He doesn't believe in quantum physics when it comes to matters of the heart. And he's an experienced catcher who doesn't try out. So he walks.

In *Sex, Lies and Videotape*, Graham tells Ann his beliefs about keys and responsibility:

> GRAHAM
> Well, see, I have this one key. And this one key is
> all the responsibility I have. Everything I own is
> in my car. If I get an apartment, that's two keys.
> If I get a job, maybe I have to open and close
> once in awhile, that's more keys. Or I buy some
> stuff and I'm worried about getting ripped off, so
> I get some locks. Pretty soon I've got a dozen
> keys, all indicative of responsibility.

> ANN
> You don't like responsibility?

> GRAHAM
> I don't like being responsible for other people.[3]

This wonderfully specific speech helps us understand why Graham can't commit—or connect—to others, especially women, why he makes such peculiar decisions. Incapable of having sexual relationships with women, he videotapes them talking about sex, then finds in these the gratification he needs. In the hands of a lesser screenwriter, this might be cheap and gratuitous, but there's real humanity here because Soderbergh lets Graham let us in on who he is as a person—his beliefs, values, *fears*. And his decisions and actions flow out of that.

DEVELOPING STORY AND STRUCTURE

Spinning story out of character is one excellent strategy for this screenplay (any screenplay). Take your character, his beliefs, values, world view, and place him in a situation where he has to make a decision that will make a difference to him and his story. Crash Davis's decision to refuse Annie's offer alters the flow of the scene—and the story. It takes the rest of the screenplay for events to bring the two of them back together again.

Another strategy is to spin story out of event (though you begin to see that character and event are inseparable. As Henry James said, "What is character but the determination of incident? what is incident but the illustration of character?"). Several years ago, working with script consultant Linda Seger out in Los Angeles, roaring down the Santa Monica freeway in her red sports car, I asked what she considered the greatest weakness in screenwriting.

"Development," she said, without hesitating. "Developing story. American screenwriters don't play the *consequences* of the events that they write. Events occur in a script but they don't make a real difference. Nothing flows out of them. Nothing *develops*."

That phrase "play the consequences" has helped me immensely as a writer and a teacher. It goes right to the *generative* nature of event—*Moments of change generate more moments of change*. When Crash Davis discovers he's a prospect for Annie's sexual spring training, he decides to walk out. In *Kosher*, when Charles discovers he can't marry Rachel because he isn't Jewish, he decides to convert. And these decisions have consequences. So do most decisions. Explore them fully and you'll find your story.

Once you've developed your story, jot the events you plan to include on index cards or sticky notes and arrange and rearrange them until you come up with a structure that works. Your character's decision might occur late in your screenplay, the consequence of a discovery or a series of discoveries she makes (just make sure we understand the difference it makes). Or the decision might occur early (make sure we understand it), and the consequences unfold for the rest of the screenplay. That's up to you. It's your character, story. As long as it works in five pages.

Again, you're designing a dance, a pattern of change, an energy system that your audience can see beginning (the setup), developing (*playing the consequences*), and coming to an end (*climax and resolution*).

Your setup has to be fast. Start your story, your pattern of change, on page one. You can do this with an *inciting event*—the precipitating move or *catalyst* of your story/energy system; dramatists call it the *disturbance*—or you can drop us smack in the middle of things (*in medias res*) the way Tarantino does in *Pulp Fiction*. We fade in—*bang!*—on an argument. The energy system is already flowing.

Don't burn valuable time or pages giving us information about your character's situation. If you want us to know that your character works at a bike shop, don't stop the story to give us that information. *Embed* it. Visually. Let your story flow *through* the bike shop—your character could make a discovery or decision there or process one she's already made—and we'll understand where she works.

Put your scenes in the service of story, not information.

Make sure, in the middle, that we see your story develop. And make sure we see your story come to an end. When you're through designing your screenplay on cards, type up your Scene-by-Scene, take a break or a deep breath, and start writing.

DRAFTING THE SCREENPLAY

This time, raise the stakes on yourself as you draft your screenplay. Work harder for *significant details* in your Character I.D. and narrative description.

"A detail is *concrete* if it appeals to one of the five senses," Janet Burroway writes; "it is *significant* if it also conveys an idea or a judgment or both."

Look at the description of Shawshank Prison in *The Shawshank Redemption*:

> A malignant stone growth on the Maine landscape.
> The moon hangs low and baleful in a dead sky.
> The headlight of a PASSING TRAIN cuts through
> the night.

A little purple, perhaps, but "malignant stone growth" is a fresh, vivid description of a prison that conveys a judgment about how evil it is.

Make your dialogue sound more *natural* this time. When your scenes are written, take a look at your characters' speeches. Are they all the same length? This is deadly. Read your script aloud and you'll see how monotonous it is—downright mind-numbing—to hear this. No sweat. Redo it. Remember that we interrupt one another—and ourselves—when we talk. Long sentences rarely flow like fountains out of our mouths. We talk in fragments. Sometimes. Especially when our emotions are rising. Eisenstein created *montage*—editing—accelerating the pace of the cuts to reflect a scene's rising emotion, a technique Hitchcock perfected in *Psycho*. The same principle applies—within reason—to the way that we talk. When we're upset, our sentences, well, begin to—Break down. Just don't overdo it. Or. It. Could. Look. Pretentious.

Good dialogue is like music—it has rhythm and pace. Crescendos and rests. A pause. Or a silence. Or a *beat*—a snap pause or an indication that a character is changing the subject mid-speech. And, like music, good dialogue has its own notation. When a character is interrupted, it's a *cut line*. You indicate this with two hyphens—at the end of the sentence:

                          BOB
        Look, Sue, I'm—

                          SUE
                     (bitter laugh)
        Sorry?

Or a character might interrupt herself:

                         ANNIE
        I hook up with one guy a season—I mean it takes
        me a couple of weeks to pick the guy—kinda my
        own spring training . . .

Or her voice might trail off, as Annie's just did at the end of the speech. You indicate this with ellipses . . . three dots, no spaces between them in a screenplay.

This lesson in dialogue notation usually precipitates a snowstorm of ellipses in student screenplays . . . Use them sparingly . . . or you'll drive people . . . crazy.

Also don't overdo *punching words* (putting them in italics) for emphasis:

                         CRASH
        Why do *you* get to choose?

Essentially, you're giving actors line readings, so go easy. Let the actors play, too. And note that capitalized words in dialogue indicate shouting. Edward Albee does this AD NAUSEAM! (We forgive him because, well, he's Edward Albee). Do it occasionally—for dramatic effect—or you can simply say in a parenthetical (shouting). Any technique that you overuse calls attention to itself and pops the reader out of the vivid and continuous dream that every screenplay should be. Unless you're trying to make your dialogue sound stylized, work to make it sound natural. Nothing more, nothing less.

REWRITING THE SCREENPLAY

Again, get the best feedback you can and look for consensus. Does your pattern of change begin on page one? Does it develop? Is necessary information embedded in scenes? Is your character's moment of decision clearly rendered? Do we understand it? Can we *see* the difference it makes? Take careful notes when your screenplay's critiqued, then put the notes and your screenplay away for a couple of days if you can. You'll be amazed how much work your unconscious—I call mine "the elves"—will do for you while you're away.

When you return, you'll be ready to reshape your screenplay. Cut what is weak to make room for what isn't. Think of it as pruning a plant; after careful cutting, a plant is healthier, stronger. When you cut away what isn't important, you make room for what is.

NOTES

1. Sam Smiley, *Playwriting: The Structure of Action*, Prentice-Hall, Englewood Cliffs, New Jersey, 1971, p. 88.
2. Ron Shelton, *Bull Durham*, screenplay manuscript dated 5-1-87, pp. 23, 24.
3. Steven Soderberg, *Sex, Lies and Videotape*, screenplay manuscripts dated February 21, 1988, p. 17.

8

THE BOXING MATCH

Since the day you thought about writing screenplays, you've no doubt been told that they must have conflict. As I've said, this is only half true—connection is equally important. And this advice about conflict is not very helpful if you're trying to learn the craft of screenwriting. It gets you obsessing about the wrong thing. You begin to think that conflict is some secret ingredient in a screenwriter's potion—the dramatist's eye of newt—and you wonder where the heck you can find some to throw in your script. But you don't *find* conflict, you *create* it.

Like so many others, Linda Cowgill insists in *Writing Short Films*, "Action in drama and fiction depends upon conflict, which is the starting point of all drama."

With all due respect, this is backwards.

Conflict is not the starting point of drama, drama is the starting point of conflict.

Drama done well is complex, but the root of all drama is simple. Again, the word comes from the Greek *dran—to do*. To perform, execute, bring about, effect, cause, take action. We do because we want something badly. You'll hear different words for it—want, will, desire, intention—but it's all the same thing. Want, if you will, or will, if you want, is the heart of great drama from *Oedipus Rex* to *Pulp Fiction* to *Shakespeare in Love*.

Oedipus wants to end the plague in his country.

Marsellus Wallace wants to get his briefcase back.

Shakespeare wants to finish his play.

Colin, the director in *The Making of "Killer Kite,"* wants to finish his film and he goes to great (and illegal) lengths to do so. Earl wants Maybelline. Aadid wants Adela. Charles wants to marry Rachel. Hannah wants connection. So does Melissa. Buzz wants reconnection. Whatever the story, desire motivates doing.

"An action is an activity designed to bring about an 'end,'" Colin Hardie says, explicating Aristotle's *Poetics*, "We have a desire or wish for a certain state of affairs. From this we argue back by a chain of means, until we arrive at something we see to be in our power here and now."[1]

We desire, deliberate, decide, do. And where conflict's concerned, doing always runs into trouble. Will hits obstacle. That's the dramatic paradigm.

Why is this so satisfying? Why have we gathered for centuries to see it played out over and over? Because it's half of *our* story. Unless we're fully realized *bodhisattvas*, we also want badly. Sometimes we don't get what we want. Sometimes we do, and being human, we want something else. We strive, fail, suffer, strategize, and strive again. So we find it fascinating—and a whole lot more entertaining—to see others do the same thing. It's a major umbilical point between us and the characters we're watching up on the screen. They want. We want. A connection is created between us.

And *conflict* is *created* when will meets obstacle. Again, it's useful to remember the root of the word *confligere*—to clash or strike together. There is no conflict *until* human will clashes with or strikes an obstacle. We want something badly, but life has other ideas. It thwarts us, comes out of left field, hurls obstacles in our path. Or we hurl them in our own path, like Earl's self doubt in *Slow Dancin' Down the Aisles of the Quickcheck*. There are all kinds of obstacles—external and internal—and great drama, like *Hamlet*, like *life*, offers a rich mixture of both.

Say you're late for class (or work). You rush to campus (or your workplace). You try to park. If you're a student, you've no doubt paid a whopping fee for a parking permit which is, you discover, little more than a hunting license. All the parking spaces are taken. First obstacle. Your will is thwarted. Conflict is created. You could park illegally, but you're not that kind of person. Or maybe you are, but you're broke and you already have a half-dozen parking tickets to pay before you can graduate. But you *won't* graduate if you're late for this class. . . .

Suddenly—*aha!*—you see a car pulling out and you race toward it only to realize a van is heading for the same space from the other direction. *Oh, no way!* you think, and you floor it. So does the van. But your car is faster, and you get there first. A little amazed at yourself (or a little ashamed, as I was one day when I did this), you turn off the engine, glance in the rear view mirror, and see the other driver pull up behind you with a look on her face that says, *I want to eat your intestines.* . . .

The conflict increases in energy, intensity—and interest—when another person comes on the scene. Why? There are two wills at war. Two agendas. One person wants. The other opposes. Dramatists call this a *boxing match*—one character wants what another character does not want to give—and the best dramatists use it over and over to create compelling conflict. In *Pulp Fiction*, according to my calculations, Tarantino (with his co-story-writer, Roger Roberts Avery) creates *thirty-eight* boxing matches. The screenplay *opens* in the middle of a boxing match between a young man and young woman. The opening line presents the first obstacle to the young woman's desire to rob liquor stores:

> YOUNG MAN
> No, forget it, it's too risky. I'm through doin' that shit.

But her will is strong; she won't take no for an answer. So the boxing match continues as she tries to persuade him to do it anyway, but he won't.

> YOUNG MAN
> ... It ain't the giggle it usta be. Too many
> foreigners own liquor stores. Vietnamese,
> Koreans, they can't fuckin' speak English. You
> tell 'em: "Empty out the register," and they don't
> know what it fuckin' means.

She wants/he opposes, and we understand why. Conflict is created. So is audience interest, because the outcome of the boxing match is unknown.

It's important to note that boxing matches are *not* arguments. An argument is "a discussion in which disagreement is expressed about some point," but a boxing match is a *pattern of change*. Change does not necessarily happen in arguments; in fact, as Harriet Lerner argues in her book, *Dance of Anger*, we often have the same argument over and over to *avoid* changing. Characters often argue in a boxing match, but change is also occurring. In *Pulp Fiction*, the young woman *discovers* that the young man has another idea—robbing the restaurant they're in—and she *decides* they should do it.

> YOUNG WOMAN
> I'm ready, let's go, right here, right now.[2]

And they do, though Tarantino decides to postpone showing the robbery until the end of the film—thirty-seven boxing matches later—when the robbery has the greatest dramatic and ironic impact.

Whatever the situation or character or will or obstacle, the point is the same: *Conflict isn't the root of drama, it's a by-product of drama.* Once you understand this, you can create all the conflict you want.

THE THIRD SCREENPLAY—THE BOXING MATCH

Write a five-page screenplay about a character (A) who wants something badly that a second character (B) does *not* want to give. And follow these guidelines:

1. Character A's want must be clear.
2. We have to understand *why* your character wants it. This gets at *stake*—what's lost if the character doesn't get what he wants.
3. We must understand why Character B does not want to give it.
4. Let Character A fail at least once, regroup, and try again. This is a screenplay, not just a scene, but even in the best scenes characters try to get what they want with energy and resourcefulness. Let your character try more than one strategy. Let us *see* the dance of deliberation, decision, and doing.
5. The outcome must be clear. Does Character A succeed or fail? There's no right or wrong answer; do what's best for your story, but make sure the outcome is clear.
6. Do not go over five pages.

7. But no skits. Dig deeper and find out what your boxing match is *really* about. One of my students, Ben Edwards, was writing a boxing match about a young soldier in Vietnam trying to get a comic book from another soldier who doesn't want to give it to him. Ben wasn't happy with his rough draft; he said it felt shallow, more like a skit. Then, right in the middle of class, he realized what it was really about. "It isn't about a comic book, it's about how scared this kid is and how he needs diversion, entertainment to keep his mind off his fear." His next draft was terrific.

At Bread Loaf Writers Conference, Terry Tempest Williams told our workshop, "If your writing isn't interesting, you aren't dropping through to what your story is really about." She was talking about nonfiction, but her advice applies with equal force to screenwriting. When Ben realized that his boxing match between two soldiers over a comic book wasn't about the comic book, it was about fear, he found the universal dimension we all can connect to. This deeper level gave the screenplay greater resonance for Ben and—once he rewrote it—for his audience.

CHOOSING AN IDEA

There's a whopping temptation with boxing matches to grab those big TV subjects—rape, murder, drugs. We think, Of *course*! He wants *her* but she doesn't want to give herself to him. Or: She's desperate for a fix, but her best friend won't pony up the horse. Or: He wants to take his enemy's life, but his enemy has other ideas—survival, for instance.

Ideas like this are known as The First Things That Swim By. They swim by first because TV has cut such deep grooves in our consciousness that our imagination shoots down these grooves faster than the dumped water down sluices in *Chinatown*, but as one writer said—I think it was Grace Paley—don't take the first thing that swims by. Keep brainstorming. Piddle around with your passions and perceptions until you come up with a fresher idea, something we haven't already seen in syndication. You may decide to come back to that first idea. That's fine. If you do, there may be a good reason.

When one of my students, David Cypkin, pitched an idea about a boy growing up among drunks and drug dealers at a Miami beachfront hotel, a story that climaxed with a knife fight between a cocaine dealer and a client who still owed him money, my kneejerk reaction was, "Nah, too TV." Then the student explained that he *grew up* at this hotel in Miami, hanging out in the bar with this cocaine dealer who seemed like a nice enough guy until he sliced up a sad, obese client. It was a journey from innocence to experience for him. This deep connection—though no guarantee that the material would make a good screenplay—gave David authentic insight and a shot at making the material more than warmed-over TV.

Having said that, let me quickly add that one of the better boxing matches I've seen is Pick's (Michael Piekutowski) gangster genre piece, *Up To Here*, that opens with two hit men, Marty and Rollins, burying a body they've just murdered. What lifts this story above familiar TV subject matter is the *specificity* of the boxing match that ensues when Marty wants the car keys so he can drive the "aged Cadillac," but Rollins refuses to give them to him. By the time the boxing match ends, *nobody's* driving because Rollins and the Cadillac have sunk in the swamp. The screenplay ends with Marty trudging down the road alone.

There simply aren't any rules. The ideas that produce the best boxing matches do, on some level, have resonance for the writer, but unlike Pick's screenplay, the connection is often *not* autobiographical. Rob Caragiulo's *momma . . . ?* is about Junior, "an eighteen-year-old, mildly inbred son," who wants his exhausted mother to massage his head. He finally gets what he wants, but as the boxing match heats up, his relationship with his mother subtly changes.

In another outstanding boxing match screenplay, *The White Face* by Eric Buscher, Bill Tift, "a lanky man about thirty, wearing messed-up jeans and a long-sleeve shirt untucked with a coffee stain on the pocket," wanders into a bar for a shot of Jack Daniels, unaware that it's a mime bar. Failing to get a real drink, Bill's finally thrown out by the mime bouncer, but he's ever so slightly changed in the process. Neither idea came from these writers' lives, but Rob and Eric did admit to mild obsessions with the mentally impaired and mimes, respectively, and they tapped that obsession to write their screenplays. You might want to add a column to your Menu—What I'm Obsessed About—and look to your own obsessions for good ideas.

Above all, notice that in each of the boxing matches mentioned above, Character A's want is small but significant and *highly* specific. A car key. A head massage. A shot of Jack Daniels. Students sometimes try to write a boxing match about a character wanting someone else's love or respect, but it's tricky to photograph that. That doesn't mean you won't try such a scene in the future; for my money, the greatest boxing match ever written is the final scene between Biff and Willy Loman in *Death of a Salesman*. Biff wants Willy to see—finally *see*—who both of them really are, but Willy refuses. In the hands of Arthur Miller, the scene is breathtaking, heartbreaking, as your scenes and screenplays may be someday, but for the purposes of this screenplay, keep your character's want concrete.

And the best dramatists often do the same thing. Think of Marsellus Wallace's briefcase or Desdemona's handkerchief in *Othello*. As the playwright Jeffrey Sweet says:

> The great plays are filled with brilliant negotiations over objects. You can often dramatize what is going on between your characters through the way they negotiate over an object. This technique is particularly useful because it allows the audience to figure a good deal out for themselves, obvi-

ating the writer from having to go through tedious expla-
nations . . . How much more effective it is to allow the
viewer, by analyzing the negotiation . . . to arrive at his or
her own conclusions as to the nature of the relationship
between the characters.[3]

An object lesson for us all. And one that Arthur Miller follows himself in
the boxing match between Willy and Biff. What Biff wants isn't an object,
but the scene takes off when Biff whips out the piece of rubber tubing Willy
keeps by the gas furnace in the basement because he's contemplating suicide.
And the epiphany that Biff recounts in the scene, the discovery that precip-
itated this great boxing match scene, revolves around an object—the fountain pen that he stole before a job interview:

> I ran down eleven flights with a pen in my hand today. And
> suddenly I stopped, you hear me? And in the middle of that
> office building, do you hear this? I stopped in the middle of
> that building and I saw—the sky. I saw the things that I love
> in this world. The work and the food and the time to sit and
> smoke. And I looked at the pen and said to myself, what the
> hell am I grabbing this for? Why am I trying to become what
> I don't want to be? What am I doing in an office, making a
> contemptuous, begging fool of myself, when all I want is out
> there, waiting for me the minute I say I know who I am![4]

The pen, *per se*, is unimportant, but it precipitates Biff's realization about
what he really wants, and that precipitates the boxing match final scene that
changes his relationship with Willy forever. So, as you choose an idea for
your boxing match, make Character A's want specific, concrete. Then let your
boxing match reveal its significance, meaning.

DEVELOPING CHARACTER

Your character's want is twice blessed: It defines character *and* story. A character's actions flow from the character's want and the character's want flows
from who the character *is*.

Suppose you meet someone for the first time. You've never met him
before, but you *need* to know who he is. Not résumé stuff, who he is *as a
person*. Maybe you need to know badly—he's going to give you a ride or
marry your daughter. If you only had time for one question, what would it
be? It's funny, but that old chestnut that fathers used to ask their daughter's
suitors, "What are your intentions?" isn't far off the mark. If you ask this
person, "What do you want?" and he answers sincerely, you're well on your
way to knowing this person. (And, as the scene with Biff shows, knowing
or discovering what you want is also an avenue to self knowledge.)

In *Zen in the Art of Writing*, Ray Bradbury says:

We know how fresh and original is each man [and each woman], even the slowest and dullest. If we come at him right, talk him along, and give him his head, and at last say, What do you want? (Or if the man is very old, What *did* you want?) every man will speak his dream. And when a man talks from his heart, in his moment of truth, he speaks poetry.[5]

Like Biff when he says what he really wants—"the work and the food and the time to sit and smoke."

Let your character speak her want, in her own voice. Write an "I Want" speech for her. Let him say flat out what he wants, like Charles in the opening of the film *Kosher*:

> CHARLES
>
> I've been meaning to ask you something for a long time. Rachel, we've been boyfriend and girlfriend since Tuesday and you're the coolest girl in school. Will you marry me?

Lest you think characters don't do this in feature-length films, take another look. "I want" speeches are made by characters all the time, like Wayne's in *Wayne's World* when he sees the guitar of his dreams:

> WAYNE
> It will be mine. Oh, yes, it will be mine.

Or Elliot in the opening moments of *Hannah and Her Sisters*, as he watches his sister-in-law:

> ELLIOT (V.O.)
> God, she's beautiful. She's got the prettiest eyes. She looks so sexy in that sweater. I just want to be alone with her and hold her and kiss her and tell her how much I love her. Stop it, you idiot, she's your wife's sister!

Sometimes a character says what he wants and *doesn't* want, like Lloyd Dobler in *Say Anything* when Diane Court's father says, "Yeah, Lloyd, what are your plans for the future?"

> LLOYD
> Spend as much time as possible with Diane before she leaves.

> MR. COURT
> Seriously, Lloyd.

LLOYD

I'm totally and completely serious, sir.

MR. COURT

Oh, really?

LLOYD

You mean like career?
                         (Mr. Court nods)
Um, I don't know. I've—
                         (clears throat)
I thought about this quite a bit, sir. I would have
to say, considering what's waiting out there for
me, I don't want to sell anything, buy anything,
or process anything as a career. I don't want to
sell anything bought or processed or buy anything
sold or processed or process anything sold, bought
or processed, or repair anything sold, bought, or
processed, you know, as a career. I don't want to
do that. So my father's in the army. He wants me
to join, but I can't work for that corporation. Um,
so what I've been doing lately is kick boxing.

He continues to talk about career longevity, the uncertain future of the sport and himself in the sport, then he finishes his monologue by returning to the original want:

LLOYD

I don't know. I can't figure it all out tonight, sir.
I'm just gonna hang out with your daughter.

Again, the speech you write may not end up in your screenplay, but you'll learn a great deal about your character as you write it. If you want to learn more, ask your character *why* she wants what she wants—or doesn't want what she wants—and let her answer (you can develop Character B by asking *him* why he won't give it). Ask Character A what's at stake? What will she lose if she doesn't get what she wants?

We can see stake clearly in "The Bonnie Situation" in *Pulp Fiction*. Jimmie's friend, Jules, has just arrived with a backseat full of brains, and his marriage is at stake if his wife, Bonnie, finds out.

JIMMIE

—I ain't through! Now don't you understand that
if Bonnie comes home and finds a dead body in
her house, I'm gonna get divorced. No marriage
counselor, no trial separation—fuckin' divorced.
And I don't wanna get fuckin' divorced. The last

> time me an' Bonnie talked about this shit was
> gonna be the last time me an' Bonnie talked about
> this shit. Now I wanna help ya out, Julie, I really
> do. But I ain't gonna lose my wife doin' it.[6]

Tarantino is following time-honored dramatic advice—get your character up a tree and throw rocks at him. Jimmie is torn. He wants two things—to stay married and to help his friend, Jules. This creates a *dilemma*.

And we connect because it feels true. We're all torn. We want cheesecake but we want to lose weight. We want to take that job out of town but we don't want to leave our significant other. Our lives are one damn difficult choice after another. And, as Jimmie discovers, deciding is hard. But he makes a decision born of *both* wants. He'll let Jules and Vincent clean up the mess, but they only have ninety minutes before Bonnie comes home. It's one of the oldest dramatic tricks in the book—the time bomb—a sure-fire source of suspense. Will Jules and Vincent get the car cleaned in time? It wouldn't matter to us if we hadn't heard Jimmie's passionate speech, but we did, so it does. What's at stake has clearly been set. We know what Jimmie wants and how badly he wants it because Tarantino has him tell us flat out, hitting it right on the nose in the old "I want" speech.

Like most screenwriters, you may feel reluctant to do this. You've probably heard many times—rightly so—that good screenwriting dialogue is not "on the nose"—but sometimes "on the nose" is where you need to be. My students are always amazed how frequently "I want" speeches appear in good films and how well they work. It may not work for your screenplay, but the option is there if you want to use it.

You might prefer writing a scene that *shows* what Character A wants, like Melissa in the opening scene in *A Work In Progress*:

> She sits in the shade, silhouetted against the bright field.
> A sketchbook rests in her lap as she watches the other
> children playing. She softly smiles at their happiness.
>
> She slowly glances to the empty tire swing next to her.
> The ghosts of herself and others playing on the swing
> slowly appear. Just as Melissa smiles, the apparition
> fades away as slowly as it appeared. Melissa is alone
> again.

Or the scene in *Slow Dancin'* that shows how badly Earl wants Maybelline (he's stolen a Polaroid picture of her and placed it on his bathroom mirror; funnier still, he keeps naming her Employee of the Week so he can have a photo to steal):

> INT. BATHROOM—SAME
>
> Earl stands in front of the mirror in his brown slacks
> and a tank top T-shirt, his middle-age pudge hanging

slightly over his belt. He put the wrapper off a new girdle.

> EARL
> (unsure)
> Maybelline, my heart is a song.

He sucks in his gut, and tightens a girdle around his waist, with all his might, fastening it down. He looks at the picture, and finishes the line, but has trouble due to the tightness of the girdle.

> EARL
> (groaning)
> And you are its melody.

He leans toward the mirror, knocking a can of Ajax off the sink. He starts to pick it up, but the girdle keeps him from bending. He gives up, takes the Polaroid off the mirror and puts it in his pocket.

When we see a character want something this badly, we want him to get it, and that connects us to him and his story.

DEVELOPING STORY AND STRUCTURE

As far as story's concerned, what a character wants is a screenwriter's jackpot. It's the driving force that creates your story, energy system, emotional flow, and pattern of change. Look at *Pulp Fiction*: Marsellus Wallace wants his briefcase. Vincent and Jules want to get it back for him. Bullets barely miss them. Suddenly, Jules wants to retire.

Marsellus wants Vincent to take Mia out on a date. Vincent doesn't want to, given what happened to Tony Rocky Horror, but he wants to do his duty to Marsellus.

Marsellus wants Butch to throw the fight. Butch wants to double-cross him, and he does, but he loses his precious gold watch in the process. He wants it back. Marsellus wants revenge. They collide—literally—on the street. Butch wants to get away. Marsellus wants to kill him. They stumble into a pawn shop, into the owner's wants. They want to get out. Butch does; Marsellus doesn't. Butch wants to save him.

And so the stories spin out. Want after want. Agenda after agenda. *Crossed* agendas. Wanting breeding new wanting.

Develop your story by brainstorming and playing the consequences of your character's want. What does she *do* to get it from Character B? What strategies does she try? What does Character B do to stop her? What does

Character A do when her strategies fail? Or do they? Does she get what she wants? Or not? And what difference does it make to her in the end?

Play the possibilities. Every screenplay has its own rich variations. A character might not get what he wants but he gets what he needs. Look at *Good Will Hunting* and *As Good As It Gets*. Or *African Queen* or *Casablanca* or so many great films, for that matter. Short ones, too. In *tongue*, Joe wants to remain isolated, but life throws him Anna, a young woman with a will of her own, and she wants what Joe does not want to give—connection. A kiss.

"The protagonist has a need or goal, *an object of desire* and knows it," Robert McKee writes in *Story*. "However, the most memorable, fascinating characters tend to have not only a conscious but an unconscious desire. . . . What he believes he wants is the antithesis of what he actually but unwittingly wants."

Which brings us back to character because at the highest level, story *is* character, to paraphrase F. Scott Fitzgerald.

Once you've developed your story, clearly define its surface action/pattern of change/throughline/spine:

Character A is trying to get (object of desire). Nail it in one simple dynamic sentence and write it down on a three-by-five card. Then define your story's deep action/character arc, how Character A's inner landscape is changed by the external events:

Character A is (describe the internal change). Describe the internal change with an *-ing* verb. This keeps it dynamic. Is your character coming to realize something important? Learning something? Reappraising? Overcoming her fears? Nail the pattern of internal change and write it on a three-by-five card, too.

Then brainstorm and decide what moments of change you will need to show to make the surface and deep action *happen*. These are the pearls in the oysters—the scenes—that you'll write (remember, more than one pearl may occur in one scene). Write each scene on a three-by-five card, arranging them until you find the order you want. Dump any scene that doesn't serve your surface or deep action or illuminate it in some way, like the dreams illuminating Joe's fear in *tongue*. Make sure you establish Character A's want nice and early, so your story/energy system/pattern of change *begins* on page one (as you've seen in *Pulp Fiction*, it can begin on *line one*). And make sure it *ends*. Does Character A fail or succeed? Make sure the precise moment when the outcome is known—your screenplay's climax—happens *on screen*. And make sure we understand the significance of this success or failure to Character A.

When you've done all this—and it is a great deal—outline your screenplay in a Scene-by-Scene. Read the outline over and over, letting the short film play in your head, checking your character's emotional flow.

"A strong emotional line is what drives a film or play and engages an audience," Jan Sardi says in the introduction to his screenplay for *Shine*.

We're never more emotional than when we want something badly and our wanting meets obstacles.

DRAFTING THE SCREENPLAY

Put your surface and deep action three-by-five cards where you can see them so you don't lose sight of your screenplay's spine and your character arc as you start to write. If your story starts to drift as you draft, or you otherwise get lost in the fun house, consult these cards to keep your story on track.

Craft your scenes with great care. They're patterns of change in themselves, with a beginning, middle, and end, though you may not want to show all of that. A character's arrival or departure, for example, might not be interesting or contribute to your dramatic purpose. If not, use the magic of the story leap and hit the scene later or get out earlier.

But sometimes you do need to show the beginning, middle, and end, as Robert Benton does in the restaurant boxing match scene in *Kramer vs. Kramer* when Ted and Joanna Kramer meet for the first time since Joanna walked out eighteen months ago. It's a reconnection/disconnection scene between these two characters, so Ted's arrival and departure at Joanna's table are both important.

Cue up this scene on video (it's close to the midpoint) and screen it. It's one of the best examples of a well-written scene, exquisitely crafted with *dialogue beats* (not to be confused with *action beats*—events that move the story forward).

"A beat of dialogue is similar to a paragraph of prose or a verse of poetry," Sam Smiley says.

In the previous chapter I mentioned that the word "beat" in a character's speech indicates a snap pause or a change in subject. You can think of a dialogue beat as a paragraph or short unit of speech about one particular subject.

When you screen the scene in *Kramer vs. Kramer*, outline the beats. Give them brief titles based on each beat's subject. The first beat, for example, might be titled "Hi/hi/chitchat." What are the other beats in the scene?

Why and how do the subjects change or flow to the next beat?

Notice that each *beat* has a beginning, middle, and end. To me, this is one of the most marvelous things about a well-crafted screenplay: The smallest building block—the dialogue beat—is a microcosm for the scene and for the whole screenplay. Each is an energy system that begins, develops, and ends. Somewhere in each beat there's some tiny impulse or change that throws the scene into the next beat (notice the frequent use of questions to trigger new beats). And so the scene and screenplay move forward.

Notice, too, that the beats begin to break down as the scene becomes more emotional. Again, it's Eisenstein's montage applied to dialogue—accelerating the pace of the cuts (in this case, cut lines) to reflect the scene's rising emotion.

I like to think of beats as Legos because they're the smallest building block of drama (I'm not counting words) and they can be moved around, rearranged in a scene or screenplay for the greatest dramatic effect (Sundance tells Butch he can't swim just before they jump off the cliff into the river). And for the most compelling and credible emotional flow.

Take a close look at this excerpt from Robert Benton's screenplay after Ted discovers that Joanna's been watching Billy from the coffee shop across the street from his school:

> TED
>
> You sat in that coffee shop across from school—

> JOANNA
> (completing his sentence)
> Watching my son . . . Ted, I've been living in New York for the past two months.

> TED
> (amazed)
> You've been living here, in the city?

> JOANNA
> (a deep breath)
> Ted . . . The reason I wanted to see you . . . I want Billy back.

> TED
>
> You want what?!

> JOANNA
> (firm)
> I want my son. I'm through sitting in coffee shops looking at him from across the street. I want my son.

> TED
>
> Are you out of your mind?! You're the one that walked out on him, remember?

> JOANNA
> (trying to explain)
> Ted listen to me . . . You and I, we had a really crappy marriage—

> JOANNA (CONT'D)
> (hastily)
> Look, don't get defensive, okay? It was probably as much my fault as it was yours . . . Anyway when I left I was really screwed up—

> TED
> Joanna, I don't give a—
>
> JOANNA
> (she will be heard)
> Ted, all my life I'd either been somebody's
> daughter or somebody's wife, or somebody else's
> mother. Then, all of a sudden, I was a thirty-year-
> old, highly neurotic woman who had just walked
> out on her husband and child. I went to California
> because that was about as far away as I could
> get. Only . . . I guess it wasn't far enough. So I
> started going to a shrink.
> (leaning forward, very sincere)
> Ted, I've had time to think. I've been through
> some changes. I've learned a lot about myself.[7]

Now compare the order of beats to the beats that you outlined when you screened the scene. The lines changed a little, of course—they always do—but sometime, during pre-production or production, the order of the beats was *reversed*. Why? Because emotionally, it just didn't work.

When Joanna tells Ted she wants Billy back, she's dropping a bomb. There's no way in *hell* Ted's going to sit there and listen to her long explanation about going to California and finding herself (a line I never thought anyone could make work, but Meryl Streep did). By reversing the beats—the long explanation *then* the bomb about Billy—the emotional flow is believable. Things are relatively calm when Joanna tells Ted about California—we believe he would listen—but once she says she wants Billy back, he cares about only one thing—keeping her from taking his son. A boxing match.

This switching of beats also makes the scene more dramatic. Now there's a *build* to Joanna's revelation that she wants Billy back (in the screenplay it feels unprepared for, unmotivated, out of the blue). Talk about a moment of change. I mean *kablooey!* The scene explodes, words flying like shrapnel—overlapping, interrupting—the beats breaking down as all hell breaks loose and Ted tells Joanna to go fuck herself. But notice, on screen, he doesn't tell her with words. Benton made a wonderful choice to show it, not tell it, as Ted smashes his glass of white wine—which was a sign of connection—against the brick wall. As Lani Sciandra learned in *Cool Breeze*, the nonverbal reaction is often much stronger.

And so, as you're designing your scenes, noodle your beats. Outline them in the order you think they will happen. But remember they're Legos—moveable pieces—and feel free to move them around until the scene works. Outlining the beats before you draft a scene helps you design scenes that don't spin their wheels—characters talking about the same subject over and over. You may decide to let the wheels spin for dramatic effect. Fine. Just make sure you're not having more fun than your audience. And keep in mind that most scenes work best when the beats change and the story moves forward.

REWRITING THE SCREENPLAY

Beats are also a wonderful tool for revision. Say a scene you wrote isn't working. Outline the beats. You might well discover what's wrong. You might have a beat that doesn't work in the scene, but it's important to the overall story. Try moving it to another scene in your screenplay. I just critiqued a student screenplay where two young women, total strangers, meet on a train. Right off the bat, one starts telling the other her problems. It felt too early for the character. I suggested moving the beat a bit later, and it worked much better. Of course, if the screenwriter had wanted to create a character who goes around accosting strangers with her personal problems, the beat would have been fine where it was.

This is why feedback from others is so very important. They can tell you if your character's emotional flow rings true in your scenes and story. Find out, too, from others if Character A's want is clear. Do they understand why she wants it? Does Character B provide obstacles to this want? Do you play the consequences of Character A discovering these obstacles and/or deciding to do something different? How could Character A's strategies for getting what she wants be improved? Is the outcome of your boxing match clear?

Do we grasp its significance? Does the character's inner change get across? Be open and listen to the answers they give you. Take notes. And as Joanna says to Ted, "Don't get defensive."

Once you've harvested their responses, set your screenplay aside—if you can—before you rewrite. This allows everyone else's opinions to settle until you know in your gut what you need to do. Your considered opinion is usually best.

NOTES

1. Humphry House, *Aristotle's Poetics*, Madeline House, London, 1956, p. 74. (I'm indebted to Janet Burroway for giving me a copy of House's wonderful book).
2. Quentin Tarantino, *Pulp Fiction*, screenplay manuscript, last draft, May 1993, pp. 1–6.
3. Jeffrey Sweet, "An Object Lesson for Playwrights," *The Writer*, December 1989, p. 19.
4. Arthur Miller, *Death of a Salesman*, Viking Press, New York, 1949, p. 132.
5. Ray Bradbury, *Zen in the Art of Writing: Releasing the Creative Genius Within You*, Bantam Books, New York, 1990, p. 36
6. Tarantino, p. 123.
7. Robert Benton, *Kramer Versus Kramer*, screenplay manuscript, revised third draft, July 14, 1978, pp. 75, 76.

9

THE IMPROBABLE CONNECTION

There's no question that conflict is important. And we connect because we also strive, hit obstacles, suffer.

"Life is suffering," Buddha said.

"And such small *portions*," Woody Allen says in *Annie Hall*.

But, as I've said, there is more.

Connection is the other half of the story—of our lives and the stories we tell. Good screenwriters understand this intuitively even though, as I've said, connection is essentially overlooked in screenwriting books. "Nothing moves forward in a story except through conflict," Chris Keane writes in *How to Write a Selling Screenplay*, putting all our screenwriting eggs in one basket.

But, soft! Doesn't *Romeo and Juliet* take a quantum leap forward when Romeo sees Juliet for the first time? He and the story have slowed to a crawl ("What sadness lengthens Romeo's hours?"), but the moment he sees her, the story takes off at emotional warp speed. ("Did my heart love till now? forswear it, sight!/For I ne'er saw true beauty till this night.") Yes, their star-crossed love creates all kinds of conflict that also moves the story along, but so does this initial—and the ongoing, deepening—connection between the two lovers. Again, it's a dance. Conflict and connection. The best stories have both.

Look at the following scene in Ron Nyswaner's screenplay for *Philadelphia* (and then screen the same scene in Jonathan Demme's outstanding film). Andrew Beckett has been fired from his law firm because he has AIDS. No lawyer will take his case, including Joe Miller. Beckett's will is up against an insurmountable obstacle—prejudice—and though this creates conflict, the story is stalled. Beckett is stuck. He decides to handle his case himself and is doing legal research when Joe Miller sees him again:

A CHAIR SQUEAKS and Joe LOOKS UP TO SEE:

Andrew taking a seat across the room (the blotches have been reduced by chemo, but he's struggling with a cold).

Andrew removes notepads and pens from his briefcase.
He takes out a package of tissues, blowing his nose.

> JOE
> (under his breath)
> Shit . . .

Joe slides to the far end of his table, stacking seven or
eight HUGE REFERENCE BOOKS in front of him.

JOE'S POV, PEERING THROUGH THE REFERENCE BOOKS:

Andrew opens a book, taking notes. Rubs his eyes.
Writes something. Sneezes.

A LIBRARIAN delivers a book to Andrew.

> LIBRARIAN
> This is the supplement. You're right, there is a
> section on . . .
> (lowers her voice)
> . . . HIV related discrimination.

> ANDREW
> Thank you.

Andrew takes the book from her—but she remains.

> LIBRARIAN
> We have a private research room available.

> ANDREW
> I'm fine, thanks.

Andrew BLOWS HIS NOSE. Now the other PATRONS are
watching.

> LIBRARIAN
> Wouldn't you be more comfortable in a research
> room?

> ANDREW
> (pleasantly)
> No. But would it make you more comfortable?

> LIBRARIAN
>
> Whatever, sir.
>
> The LIBRARIAN turns away, shrugging to a PATRON, indicating she's done all she can do.[1]

In previous scenes, Joe himself has discriminated against Andrew because he's gay and has AIDS. Earlier, when Andrew came to Joe's office and asked if he'd take the case, Joe refused . . . for personal reasons. And he didn't buy that Andrew had a case. But now, in the library, hiding behind a wall of reference books he's built between himself and Andrew, Joe *witnesses* discrimination in action and its consequence—disconnection—as the librarian tries to segregate Andrew in a research room and other library patrons quickly exit. Witnessing this—and the suffering it causes—stirs a sense of injustice in Joe—and compassion.

"Compassion is the only energy that can help us connect with another person," Thich Nhat Hanh tells us in *The Heart of Buddha's Teachings*.

It is this compassion—mixed with a sense of injustice and, I would wager, a little guilt—that moves Joe to reestablish contact with Andrew:

> Joe approaches, nonchalantly, as if he just *happens* to be sauntering by.
>
> Suddenly he "notices" Andrew.
>
> JOE
>
> Oh, Beckett. How's it goin'?
>
> ANDREW
>
> Fine.

When you screen Demme's film, you'll notice a subtle but important change: Demme has Joe *interrupt* the "Whatever, sir" boxing match beat between Andrew and the librarian. The librarian—a man in the film—looks at Joe, realizes he's outnumbered, and backs down. "Whatever, sir," he tells Andrew and goes. So does a nearby patron. By having Joe come to Andrew's *defense*, Demme creates a richer, more significant moment of connection between these two men.

Connecting is a process, a pattern of change made up of moments of change—*connection beats*. A series of connection beats create and deepen the connection that is occurring in this scene:

> Joe *discovers* Andrew is being mistreated.
>
> He *decides* to come to his rescue.
>
> He *discovers* that no lawyer will represent Andrew, so Andrew is planning to represent himself.
>
> Then, in a lovely, off-the-point beat, Joe *discovers* Andrew's own humanity when he asks about Joe's new baby. Joe, slightly changed, walks away.
>
> Then he *decides* to come back. He asks Andrew how the law firm found out he had AIDS. Andrew tells him. This *discovery* raises other legal

questions and more *discoveries* that play out in a subtle boxing match, Andrew trying to return to his work but Joe keeping him from it, interrupting, wanting answers.

Because of these specific connection beats, Joe is slowly drawn into the case, his connection with Andrew deepening with his understanding of the case law on discrimination and its consequences, stated in bald, unsettling terms in the scene when Andrew reads from a relevant legal precedent:

> ANDREW
> "But because the prejudice surrounding AIDS
> exacts a social death which precedes the actual,
> physical one . . ."

> Joe and Andrew glance at each other, clear their
> throats . . .

In the film, the camera cranes up (a lovely shot called for by the screenwriter) and we look down on Andrew and Joe as they continue to work on the case together, passing notes and books back and forth, their hands almost touching. They have connected as lawyer and client and, more importantly, as human beings. In the following scene—in the screenplay and the film— Joe delivers a summons to Charles Wheeler, the man who fired Andrew. And the story is moving forward again.

It is *connection* that moves it—an *improbable connection* between two men who have been legal rivals, who find each other repulsive (Andrew thinks Joe is an ambulance chaser; Joe thinks Andrew is an infectious pervert). This improbable connection occurs in only four pages—less than seven minutes on screen—but creates breathtaking change in both characters' lives. And it jump-starts the stalled story.

There are moments of change in our lives and stories that are simply not comprehended by conflict.

Moments of change that *create ties between us*, as Stephen Jay Gould so beautifully said. As a screenwriter you can't afford to overlook this crucial fact of narrative life. If you want to write screenplays that connect to others, you need to learn to create and craft a connection.

THE FOURTH SCREENPLAY—THE IMPROBABLE CONNECTION

Write a seven-page screenplay about two characters who initially feel no connection whatsoever—a connection between them is highly *improbable*—but by the end of the screenplay they have come to feel an authentic connection. And follow these guidelines:

1. Establish the improbability of your characters ever connecting.

In *Philadelphia*, the improbability of a connection between Andrew and Joe is carefully set up when Joe refuses to represent Andrew. And it's underlined again in a scene between Joe and his wife—just before the law library scene—when Joe admits that he's prejudiced. He doesn't want to work with a homosexual, much less one with AIDS.

> JOE
> Would you take a client if you were constantly thinking: 'I hope this guy doesn't touch me. I don't even want him to breathe on me?'

This scene clearly establishes the *revulsion* Joe feels toward Andrew Beckett. Yet, in the following law library scene, in four short pages, Nyswaner creates a credible connection between these two men, a short but significant journey for Joe from prejudice to understanding.

2. Create your pattern of change—connecting—with a series of connection beats—discoveries and decisions your characters make that bring them closer together. Connecting is a path; what are the stepping stones—moments of change—in your screenplay?

3. Make sure the connection beats are clearly rendered so we *see* each moment of change *happen* on paper/screen.

4. The process of connecting between your two characters must be believable. You're creating emotional realism, a pattern of human change and emotional flow that we *buy*.

5. If you need a third character to help effect the connection, as Nyswaner does in *Philadelphia*, you may create one, but remember that the focus of this screenplay is the improbable connection between your two *main* characters.

6. This is a screenplay, not a scene, so feel free to open your story up and move it and your characters through various times and locations.

7. Give us a sense of an ending, how the characters are changed by this unexpected connection.

8. Do not go over seven pages.

9. No skits. Connection is one of the deepest, most profound patterns of human change. It's more than *"You* like Chinese food? *I* like Chinese food!"* It may start that way, but you need to dig deeper for a pattern of change that makes a difference to your characters. Your screenplay may be a comedy like *Slow Dancin' Down the Aisles of the Quickcheck*, but the connection must be deeply felt by the characters and the audience alike.

10. Avoid sap. Purple (overly emotional) writing. Sentimentality. Sentiment—authentic feeling and emotion—is important, essential, just don't take it so far over the top that we want to reach for our barf bags.

CHOOSING AN IDEA

As *Philadelphia* so clearly shows, connection is much broader than love or romance. Love isn't off-limits; you just have to work harder to make it fresh, as Thomas Jackson does in *Slow Dancin'*. But be aware as you choose your idea that there are many other kinds of human connection.

Keep in mind, too, that the subject doesn't have to be grim city. Compassion is broader and deeper than feeling sorry for somebody's plight in the world. The word comes from the Late Latin *compassion*, past participle of *compassus*, "to sympathize with." This sympathy might manifest itself in laughter, hilarity, joy. Whatever the nature of the connection you write, you're looking for an improbable but plausible pattern of change—connecting—that leads to your characters' shared understanding, humanity, communion, the two of them *seeing* each other in an authentic way.

When human connection occurs, your characters' feelings drop into a deeper realm. Look at the dialogue from the improbable connection scene in Disney's animated film, *Beauty and the Beast*. Before this scene, Belle ran away, the Beast went to find her and saved her life by fighting off wolves, though he nearly died doing it. As this scene begins, Belle is wringing out a cloth to wash the Beast's wounds:

                    BELLE
    Here now.
                    (he starts to lick his wound)
    Don't do that. Just hold still—

She touches his wound, and he roars.

                    BEAST
    That hurts!

                    BELLE
    If you'd hold still, it wouldn't hurt as much.

                    BEAST
    If you hadn't've run away, this wouldn't have
    happened.

                    BELLE
    If you hadn't frightened me, I wouldn't have run
    away.

The Beast starts to say something, then stops as he thinks about this.

>   BEAST
>   Well, you shouldn't have been in the west wing!

>   BELLE
>   Well, you should learn to control your temper!

He's taken aback, but looks thoughtful.

>   BELLE
>   Now hold still. This might sting a little.
>   (he growls)
>   By the way, thank you for saving my life.

He looks at her, moved.

>   BEAST
>   (gently)
>   You're welcome.

The CAMERA pulls back to reveal a tender tableau—the Beast looking at her as she touches his arm.[2]

The scene ends with a physical and an emotional connection between them.

DEVELOPING CHARACTER

Again, it's tempting to leap for that first thing that swims by: a racist and an African American! An angry teen and an elderly person! A prostitute and a rabbi! Okay, a former student, Aloura Charles, wrote an improbable connection that worked beautifully between a rabbi and a prostitute who meet—and credibly connect—on a subway. But first she had to transcend these character *types* to create specific flesh-and-blood characters who were more than clichés. Clichéd characters are the kiss of death in a screenplay. We roll our eyes, thinking what Chris Keane has stated so bluntly but wisely, "hackneyed" characters are "cheap, lazy, and plagiaristic." You can develop unique characters by going *against* type and cliché. Try gender bending. You might be surprised what you come up with.

Look at your menu for springboard characters. If nothing strikes you, go people watch at your local mall, supermarket, skating rink, street corner, used car lot, gas station. This is a wonderful way to get ideas for characters and situations for an improbable connection.

Dimensionalize your characters by asking *why* the connection between them is improbable. What values, beliefs, or opinions does each character have that make the connection highly unlikely? Why do they have these beliefs and opinions? They may be based on experience or, like Joe Miller, pure prejudice. Explore this backstory in a brief character bio for each character; you'll be amazed what bubbles up as you start to write the backstory down. Then let your characters tell you what they feel and why in their own voice. This monologue and backstory may not get into your screenplay, but it's important to know it.

Then ask yourself what is it about your characters that allows them to overcome these beliefs and opinions? However subtle, the potential for change must be present in your character, or we won't buy the connection. In *Philadelphia*, though the connection between Joe and Andrew is improbable, we believe it in part because we've seen Joe's humanity and capacity for connection in earlier scenes with his wife and baby. So you're developing two different sides of your characters: Who they are when your screenplay begins and who they are when your screenplay ends. But the seeds of change must be there in them from the beginning.

DEVELOPING STORY AND STRUCTURE

A good way to develop your story is to ask yourself what has to happen to bring about this unlikely connection? What discoveries will force your characters to reappraise one another? To see each other in a new light? To realize they're not so damn different? To begin to feel a sense of communion? What decisions do your characters make—and what actions do they take—that deepen the connection between them? As you sift through the possible answers to these questions—again, play the possibilities—you'll find the building blocks—the connection beats—of your story.

Once you know these, put them on cards. Line them up. Rearrange them. The stand-off between Andrew and the librarian is more interesting and intense in the film because Demme rearranged the beats. Joe's decision to come to Andrew's defense occurs in the middle of the boxing match. And Joe becomes a factor in the librarian's decision to back down. This small shift in the order of events makes the emotional flow more powerful and profound, presaging but not predicting the connection that follows.

Once you know your story, create a shapely structure for your screenplay. Define your screenplay's beginning, middle, and end. Does your story have an inciting incident—a moment of change that unleashes your screenplay's energy system and emotional flow? In the law library scene in *Philadelphia*, that incident is Joe's discovery that Andrew is there in the same reading room. He reacts, hiding behind a wall of reference books. But he keeps watching, and what he sees draws him out.

What are your screenplay's *turning points*—the moments of change that turn your story in a new direction? The scene from Philadelphia has two major turning points, giving it a shapely three-part structure. After witnessing the discrimination against Andrew and his suffering, Joe decides to come to his defense. The first turning point. This decision throws the screenplay out of setup into the second part as the story develops. Andrew and Joe are together, but their relationship is still tentative, distanced. They close the distance a little with the discoveries made in the next two beats—Andrew is representing himself; he cares enough about Joe's life to ask about his new baby—but Joe still decides to leave Andrew and his case behind. Then he changes his mind. He decides to come back. The second turning point. This throws the scene into the third section as Joe and Andrew discuss the relevant case law. As they do, their connection deepens with Joe's understanding, a profound change that leads to the scene's climax—Joe's decision to take Andrew's case. It's an offscreen decision, but one that's clearly implied by the end of the scene.

The structure of this pattern of change is carefully crafted. It's shapely, moving the story effortlessly from one moment of change to another until the characters have arrived at an authentic connection. That's what you're working for in your screenplay—a shapely seven-page pattern of change—connecting—that we can see beginning, developing, and coming to an end. Design your structure. Draw it. And then, as you draft, make your scenes so delicious we don't notice your structure.

DRAFTING THE SCREENPLAY

By now you know your own process so well, I need only add that you'll need to give yourself plenty of time to draft this screenplay. As my students discover every semester, creating connection is much harder than creating conflict. It's more subtle. Internal. You're rendering internal change, yet you have to find ways to show it on paper and screen. This is *always* tricky. Your connection beats need to be clear, but you don't want to bludgeon us with them.

It's usually too on-the-nose to let your characters *say* that they feel more connected (though there are always exceptions); let your characters' feelings flow underneath what is said, i.e., push it into the subtext. Joe and Andrew never talk about connecting, but they're connecting as they talk because of the discoveries and decisions they're making. A crucial distinction.

Ideally, you'll find a way to show the moments of change/connection beats through your character's behavior and actions. And you need to describe this moment of change as it happens. My students almost always resist this. "How do I describe a decision? Or realization?" They're afraid if they write "he decides" it will be telling, not showing.

So I ask them, "Can you *see* a person realizing something? Can you photograph that?"

The answer, of course, is yes. So they—and you—have to find fresh ways of describing these internal changes so we can see them. Avoid hackneyed expressions like "her eyes widen" or "he stands there like a deer stunned in headlights." If you need inspiration, as always, read good screenplays. Lots of them. See how other screenwriters render a realization.

In E. Max Frye's screenplay for Demme's film, *Something Wild*, he describes a secondary character's realization this way:

> Donna looks perplexed, then breaks into smiles when she
> realizes she's been the victim of a joke (or was it?).[3]

In *Life Is Beautiful*, when the father, Guido, translates the Nazi's instructions to convince his young son, Joshua, that life in the camp is just a game, screenwriters Vincenzo Cerami and Roberto Benigni spell out Joshua's realization that his father is right:

> Joshua's face has a completely new expression on it. He
> is absolutely convinced that all this is one big game.[4]

If we can see it, you can say it, just be sure you say it so we can see it.

REWRITING THE SCREENPLAY

You'll want to work closely with others on the rewrite of this screenplay. You *need* others to know if the connection really *happens* on paper. Do we see your characters, through a series of connection beats, gradually feel an authentic connection? Are the connection beats clear? Are any missing? Is your structure sound? Do you have a clear inciting incident, a turning point that throws your screenplay out of setup into development and a second turning point that throws the story toward the climax? Is this connection improbable in the beginning of your screenplay but plausible by the end? Remember, you're honoring your characters' emotional flow, and the best way to know if it works is to see if others believe it.

Listen closely, take notes, then put them away with your screenplay. Let the elves work on the script for a while. Then, when you come back to it a few days later, you'll have a clearer sense of what you need to do.

And do it. Reshape your screenplay if necessary. You may have discovered that you need to rearrange your moments of change. If so, outline your connection beats again and redesign your screenplay's structure. Cut and add what you must to make sure the screenplay is working, but make sure that the final draft remains seven pages.

And don't despair if getting it right takes a number of rewrites. Crafting a credible, compelling connection *is* harder than crafting a good boxing match, but both, as you'll see in the next chapter, are essential to writing good screenplays.

NOTES

1. Ron Nyswaner, *Philadelphia*, screenplay manuscript, revised draft, October 15, 1992, pp. 47, 48.
2. Transcribed from the screen, *Beauty and the Beast*, Walt Disney Productions, 1991.
3. E. Max Frye, *Something Wild*, screenplay manuscript, January 26, 1986, p. 46.
4. Vincenzo Cerami and Roberto Benigni, *Life Is Beautiful*, screenplay manuscript, 1998, p. 83.

10

THE LONG SHORT SCREENPLAY

For the past four screenplays, you've focused on essential elements of drama—discovery, decision, conflict, connection—and you've created and crafted these in short screenplays. In the process, ideally, you've learned to write vivid and economical descriptions of setting, character, action, using higher and more significant detail, and you've learned to sharpen your dialogue, letting your characters say far more with less. And along the way, you've probably noticed that these elements of drama—slippery little devils—are tricky to isolate. They tend to hang out together in screenplays— a discovery precipitating a decision, a conflict giving way to connection, and vice versa.

A dance.

So now it's time to clear the creative floor and let these dramatic elements rip in your long short screenplay.

THE FIFTH SCREENPLAY—THE LONG SHORT SCREENPLAY

Write the best ten-page (or shorter) screenplay you can—using the techniques you've learned to tell a good story that makes us connect—a pattern of human change that makes a difference to your main character. And to us.

And follow these guidelines:

1. Choose an idea that has rich resonance for you, that on some (perhaps not obvious) level, is important to you. If you need inspiration, take a look at the seven award-winning screenplays in Part III (and their films) or screen your favorite film of all time, if you have one. Why did you connect? What story could you tell that would connect to others?

2. Make your story simple and your character complex.

112

3. Make sure the story makes a difference to your main character (otherwise you'll face the dreaded *so what?*).

4. Articulate a clear surface action and a deep action (character arc) for your screenplay. Make sure that they are, in some way, interrelated. How do external events in your story create inner change in your character?

5. Make sure your surface and deep action are made of specific moments of change—discoveries and decisions—that we can *see* happen on paper/screen.

6. Explore, develop, and weave together—in whatever proportions are right for your story—conflict and connection. In *Slow Dancin' Down the Aisles of the Quickcheck,* the conflict grows out of a need for connection (wanting Maybelline but not being able to tell her), as it does in *Kosher* and *A Work In Progress.* In *The Making of "Killer Kite"*—a send-up of the horrors of film-making—there's no connection at all. That's one of the hilarious points the story is making. And in *My Josephine* there's only connection, though the film is richly resonant with the underlying conflict and disconnection Muslim-Americans have felt in this culture since September 11, and their attempt to connect by washing American flags for free.

7. Make sure your story checks out with the Screenplay Paradox: Is it unique *and* universal? A story only you can tell us, but one that we want to see?

8. Don't forget, in case you already have (I do all the time) that the last word in screenplay is *play. Enjoy* the freedom of the form: the power of the image (a picture really *does* speak a thousand words, so let your images do most of the talking); the story leap (hit your scenes late, leave them early); and emotional flow (done well, it will connect your scenes and your audience to the story you tell). *Use* the freedom of the form to take your character—and your audience—on a magic carpet ride.

9. Stick to the ten-page limit, unless your instructor and budget allow your script to be longer.

10. Write the film you want to see.

CHOOSING AN IDEA

As you know all too well by now, so much depends upon a good idea. And the best ones—comic or dramatic or a mixture of both—as you also know, come from a deep place inside us:

A passion.
An obsession.
An emotion.
A person.
An experience.
An image.
A perception.
A principle.

You've already tapped some of these in your menu and your four previous screenplays, but now dig even deeper. Explore these deeply felt areas of yourself and your life. What are you yearning to say about life? What stories are you dying to tell? What themes keep recurring? As Wes Ball said about *A Work In Progress*:

> The theme of loneliness has always been a part of my stories. I'm not sure why; I wasn't a lonely kid or anything. Although I wasn't conscious of it at first, I began seeing a pattern in my films. It was a very profound, important realization for me. Once I pinpointed the types of stories that appealed to me, I could quickly dream up concepts for stories that I knew I would be passionate about later, and passion is key to seeing the making of a film through.

"Creating begins typically with a vague, even a confused excitement, some sort of yearning, hunch, or other preverbal intimation of approaching or potential resolution," Brewster Ghiselin says in *The Creative Process*. "[The poet] Stephen Spender's expression is exact: 'a dim cloud of an idea which I feel must be condensed into a shower of words.'"[1]

And, for the screenwriter, pictures—like an American flag tumbling slowly in a washing machine.

Musing about Muses, Rob McCaffrey came up with a funny perception about being alive: If Muses inspire us, is there a comparable spirit that aggravates and undermines us? Rob came up with the Buse, the cosmic creature who makes us spill coffee down our shirt front, lock our keys in the car, have bad-hair days. To share his perception with others, Rob developed a story about a day in the life of a new Buse, a unique story, to say the least, with universal underpinnings because it's a story about finding one's place in the universe, the subject of all great drama, as Arthur Miller once said.

And to write his film *After Life*, writer/director Hirokazu Kore-eda mined his experience and fascination with memory and his unique perception about its role in our lives—and after. "I developed this idea, at a young age, that you forget everything, and then you die." This belief came from his childhood, seeing his grandfather develop dementia and senility. "One day, he no longer recognized our faces. Finally, he could not recognize his own."

So Kore-eda began asking himself the question, "What if you got to hold onto one thing?"[2]

"Dance your own dance," Frank McCourt always tells writers, and he followed his own advice when he wrote his luminous memoir, *Angela's Ashes*.

So create your own version of the previous list. Add and subtract categories. Then dive deep into each one. Explore your own experiences, fascinations, perceptions. And play (that word again!) creative pinball, bouncing from one item on your list to another. The richest ideas often occur when categories cross-fertilize. It's called *homospatial thinking*, bringing two disparate ideas together, like Gutenberg inventing the printing press when he connected the functions of a signet ring and a wine press.

My short play *Propinquity* sprang from such a cross-fertilization. My father's father used to say that people fell in love for only one reason—*propinquity*. Proximity of bodies. There was no sweet mystery to it, no affinity of human nature, just proximity. I disagreed *passionately*. I believed—and still believe—that there are deeper forces at work, or we'd fall in love with every *shlub* we squeeze next to on the subway or bus. And so, when Actors Theatre of Louisville commissioned me to write a ten-minute play, this belief bubbled back up. But it was only half an idea. Luckily, though, the same week a friend and teaching assistant in English said she was sick and damn tired of other teaching assistants complaining about teaching freshmen. She *loved* teaching freshmen because they were young, impressionable, open.

These two passions—hers and mine—intersected, and my play *Propinquity* bloomed whole. I wrote the play in an *hour* ("Good writing doesn't always come hard," Sam Smiley assured me). A simple story: A shy, love-struck freshman, Dale Bender, is trying to tell his T.A. in English, Alexis, that he loves her, while her significant other, Marshall, is trying to leave her. Crossed lines of action. A ten-minute story told in six scenes that I hit late and left early, each with a small but significant moment of change that swept the story onto the next ("A tender and effortless glissando sweeping gracefully from moment to wistful moment," Sylvia Drake wrote—God bless her—in *The Los Angeles Times*).

In one scene, Marshall tells Alexis that the only reason people fall in love is propinquity. Simple proximity. Alexis passionately disagrees. And so does Dale at the end of the play when he delivers his final essay to Alexis:

                    DALE
        Here's my essay. Revised. Very asshole, but it
        has a climax, Miss Saunders. You won't believe
        the climax it has.
                    (beat)
        I didn't write about the House of Usher. I wrote
        an essay on propinquity, what you said the other

> day in your office—that it was the cause of love. I
> hate to tell you this, Miss Saunders, because I like
> and respect you, but that's a crock, a real crock.
> Except possibly for meaning number three—I
> looked it up in the Oxford English Dictionary—
> which defines propinquity as an affinity of
> natures and not simple proximity—

She takes his face in her hands and kisses him.[3]

It is their own affinity of natures that brings them together for this brief moment, and both are changed in the process.

I wrote this short comedy to prove that people fall in love for deeper reasons than proximity, and perhaps I succeeded (the *Irish Times* said "*Propinquity* offers great hope and humanity"), but a play or screenplay cannot succeed on message alone.

"If you want to send a message, call Western Union," Samuel Goldwyn once growled, and I agree, but as Anne Lamott wisely reminds us, "A moral position is not a message." You *can* find wonderful ideas for your screenplay by examining your own beliefs, passion, vision, whatever has the deepest meaning for you, then making a story that shows what you want to say.

"A true plot is an assertion of meaning," asserts Arthur Miller. But it's the *plot* that must assert. Preaching is deadly in drama—I *hate* preaching—and, the truth is, it rarely works anyway.

"You can't tell another," Shelby Foote said, "but with hard work and luck, maybe you can show him."

You must *show* others by creating flesh-and-blood characters going through significant change in specific time-and-place scenes. Screenwriting is an incarnational art. Don't ever lose sight of that.

DEVELOPING CHARACTER

So your not-so-easy task is creating flesh-and-blood characters who will come alive on the page and the screen. You've explored and developed the character checklist, 3-D I.D., the "I want" speech, a passionate speech about the character's values, opinions, beliefs, a brief character bio to create her backstory. All these remain useful tools, but I want to offer a deceptively simple list of questions to answer about your main character in your long short screenplay.

Questions 1–4 define character, Questions 5–9 define story, and Question 10 defines your character arc—how your character is changed by the events of the story. So as you develop your character—*to* develop your character—answer these questions:

1. Who is your character? Answer with a beautifully crafted, significantly specific character I.D.
2. What must your character be connected to in her life or she'll wither up and die (besides the obvious food and shelter)?
3. What does your character want in the story (goal)?
4. Why (motivation)? And why now (how is this day different from any other)?
5. What does your character do to get it (action)?
6. What obstacles—internal and external—does your character meet on the way (conflict)?
7. What's at stake—lost—if your character fails?
8. Does your character succeed or fail?
9. What connections, disconnections, reconnections does your character go through in the story?
10. How is your character changed in the course of the story?

Question 2 always throws my students. What do I mean when I ask what their character must be connected to? Do I mean what the character must be connected to in her life or in the screenplay?

I mean both. If you define what your character must be connected to in her life, you'll bring that *into* your screenplay. Color me stubborn, but I keep this question on the list because I think it offers a less obvious and often richer approach to defining who your character is. Consider yourself and your own life. What must you be connected to or you'll wither and die? This reveals a great deal about your deepest self. For me, it's family, friends, laughter, creativity, beauty, nature, adventure, and chocolate. Okay, maybe I could thrive without chocolate, but not without the other six things.

Knowing what your character *must* be connected to will help you define who she is, where she is, what she does in your screenplay. As we prepared to write our feature, *Winterfort*, Pam Ball and I kicked this question around for our main character, Jack. Two important things surfaced—he must be connected to Claire (the love of his life) and he must be connected to nature (he feels restless, cooped-up, indoors). Jack's non-negotiable need to be connected to Claire gave us the emotional spine of the screenplay, and his need to be connected to nature gave his scenes richness and resonance—and fresher settings. Pam and I shifted scenes once set in kitchens and living rooms (The First Thing That Swam By) to the great lush outdoors of rural north Florida.

The answer to Question 2 may help you find the answer to 3—What does your character want in the screenplay? The answer to Question 4—Why and why now?—further defines your character, her experience, and her situation when your screenplay begins. And Question 5—What does your character do to get what she wants?—brings us to story, though I'm struck again by the interconnectedness of character and action. They're two sides of the same thing—a human being and a human doing.

DEVELOPING STORY AND STRUCTURE

Doing, as you well know by now, is the root meaning of drama. So answering Question 5 is one of the best ways to define and develop your story. Once you've defined what your character wants (goal) and why she wants it (motivation), you can define what she does to get it (action). Though she's talking about features, Linda Seger offers a method for defining and developing a story that's terrific for writing short screenplays. Seger breaks down the story of *Back to the Future* this way, clearly indicating the obstacles Marty meets as he tries to accomplish his goal:

Motivation	Action	Goal
A beefed-up De Lorean forces Marty into the past		
	He overcomes Mother's advances, seeks out the Professor, fights with Biff, dresses as Darth Vader to motivate George to ask Lorraine out. He cajoles, persuades, manipulates, in order to	
		survive and get back to the future.[4]

This exercise—a MAG, I like to call it (motivation, action, goal)—is a dynamic way to develop, define, and clarify your story. You might even create a fourth column—"Or Else"—to clarify stake. (Marty would have never existed, you could say for *Back to the Future*).

It's important to note, however, that wonderful stories have been created where the main character is *not* the *intentional* character—the one with the goal in the story. The main character may be the *focal* character—think Othello—but someone else—Iago—is the intentional one, the character who drives the story. The same is true in *Cool Breeze and Buzz*—Paula is focal, but Buzz drives the story. Again, play the possibilities as you develop your story.

When you've answered Questions 6–8, move on to Question 9—What connections, disconnections, reconnections does your character go through in the story? This can yield rich story possibilities you may not have considered, as well as providing the greatest emotional power to your story and thus the moments of the greatest audience connection. The peak empathic moments in films, long and short, are often the moments of connection, disconnection, and reconnection. Think of *Forrest Gump*. For all its historical conflict and sweep, our greatest points of emotional connection to the story are his moments of connection, disconnection, and reconnection with Jenny, Bubba, and his mother.

Last, as you develop your story, explore Question 10—How is your character changed in the course of your story? This is the character arc, the deep action, the difference that external events made to your character's inner landscape. The change may be small—a tiny turn of the screw—but your character will never be quite the same.

Two other excellent tools for developing and defining your story are the *premise* and the *synopsis,* or *overview.* "Premise" is the word used by Lajos Egri in *The Art of Dramatic Writing* (Woody Allen's favorite book on playwriting) to mean the "theme, thesis, root idea, central idea, goal, aim, driving force, subject, purpose, plan, plot, basic emotion" of a dramatic work. Egri prefers the word premise "because it contains all the elements the other words try to express and because it is less subject to misinterpretation."

"A good premise is a thumbnail synopsis of your play," Egri writes. It implies a character, an action, and an outcome. The premise of *Romeo and Juliet,* he tells us, is *great love defies even death.* The premise of *King Lear* is *blind trust leads to destruction,* and the premise of *Macbeth* is *ruthless ambition leads to its own destruction.*[5]

Egri's speaking of plays, but the same can be said of good screenplays. The premise of *Back to the Future* is *a moment of courage can change the course of a life,* and the premise of *Babe* is *an unprejudiced heart can change the course of life in the valley.* Neither film ever preaches, but the action of each is a wonderful working out of its premise.

A premise is richer and deeper than a *logline,* which summarizes the surface action in one sentence (think *TV Guide*). Premise moves beneath the surface action of a screenplay to its *deep subject*—what it's *really* about. This can help you dig deeper as you develop your story. And ideally, every scene in your screenplay will, on some level, be about this deep subject.

If a premise is a thumbnail synopsis of your screenplay, the next step is writing the paragraph-long synopsis or *overview*—as Brady and Lee call it in *The Understructure of Writing for Film and Television.* This is extremely useful in developing story. A good synopsis—as Rob McCaffrey's for *The Buse* shows—touches on the tone of the screenplay and gives a brief overview of the characters and the story:

> *The Buse* is a modern day fairy tale in which all of the daily, little aggravations which happen to people are personified in the form of spirits called Buses. The story follows a day in the life of a New Buse, whose refusal to torment mortals has gotten him in trouble with the other members of his species. New is desperate to find a line of work which will let him help mankind, but how will he manage it without ticking off his higher-ups? Striking a deal with a Muse which might get him out of his predicament, New agrees to try to inspire a mortal man to win back an old love. The only problem: The lady is getting married to another man the same day!

Rob left us hanging as to the ending (New fails as a Muse but succeeds as a Buse and, realizing how helpful his Buse-ive powers can be, he accepts his rightful role in the great scheme of things), but it's helpful to articulate how your screenplay will end. You might also want to begin your synopsis, as Rob does, by introducing what your screenplay's about ("the daily, little aggravations that happen to people") or as Brady and Lee do in their overview of *Kramer vs. Kramer*: "*Kramer vs. Kramer* is a contemporary marital and family drama about the changing roles of men and women in American society."

You may find it useful, after the synopsis, to develop your story in greater detail in a *treatment*—an expanded prose telling of the story. Bob Gray wrote the screenplay for *The Making of "Killer Kite"* from a one-page story treatment written by Matt Stevens, who directed the film. Or you may want to bypass synopsis and treatment and develop your scenes and story on cards. The important thing is to know your story and the moments of change that move it along from beginning to end. Once you do, you can begin to design your screenplay's structure.

Which brings us to *plot*, too often equated with story. The two, in fact, are not the same, and the distinction is important and useful. *Story is the events or moments of change in the order they happen—A to Z. Plot is the order of events as you choose to tell them,* pure and simple, though there's nothing simple about it.

"Plotting is more than the order of the events," Shelby Foote said.

The events you choose to show and the order in which you choose to show them are major artistic decisions. Why? Because the order of events has a profound effect on how compelling, ironic, or moving your screenplay will be. The whole *is* greater than the sum of the parts.

Your material may work best in a three-act structure—an inciting incident, a turning point at the end of Act One and Act Two, and a climax and resolution at the end of Act Three. But as many fine screenplays—long and short—show, there are other wonderful structural options. Look at *Pulp Fiction*. It's far more compelling and ironic told in a nonlinear structure.

So is *The Making of "Killer Kite."* Told in a nonlinear, mockumentary structure, the film intercuts scenes from the cult horror flick "*Killer Kite*" (shot in film) with scenes of the making of the flick (shot in video), media coverage and reviews of the film, and an after-the-fact interview with the director, Colin Kishman. This structure works extremely well for the subject, increasing the irony and often gut-busting humor (I recently reread the script on the porch at our farm and laughed so loud I startled the ducks from the pond). But it can work well for tragedy, too; *The Sweet Hereafter* intercuts an after-the-fact conversation on an airplane with the story's main action.

We are so tied to seamless realism in this culture, we tend to overlook the fluidity and freedom of film. I recommend Ken Dancyger and Jeff Rush's *Alternative Scriptwriting: Writing Beyond the Rules* if you want to explore alternative structures. Or for sheer inspiration, I strongly recommend screening Michael Verhoeven's German film *Nasty Girl*, a compelling narrative told in a bold mix of past and present, color and black and white, fourth-wall realism and direct address.[6] And closer to home, take a look at Steven Soderbergh's film *Out of Sight*. The screenwriter, Scott Frank, begins the script with an event that actually occurs very late in the story:

FADE IN:

A MIAMI STREET—DAY

The financial district. Lots of people in suits. A shaky, spasmodic ZOOM IN finds . . .

JACK FOLEY—forty, big, focused expression—as he rips a tie from around his neck and throws it down in the gutter. He starts across the street, now peeling off his suitcoat and dropping that, too, right there on the asphalt . . .[7]

We have no idea why Foley rips off his necktie and throws it down in the gutter or peels off his suitcoat, dropping that too (and we don't find out until late in the film), but it's intriguing. We start asking questions. And curiosity is a fabulous hook, a sure-fire way to hold someone's attention. Just ask Pandora.

If you decide to design a nonlinear plot for your story, be sure you don't lose your audience along the way. And there's no shame in choosing a traditional linear three-act structure if that best serves your story and dramatic purpose. As Jerry Stern used to say in his workshops when students complained that they couldn't come up with snazzy, newfangled plots, "When all else fails, chronology works."

Whatever your structure, once it's designed, type up a Scene-By-Scene for your screenplay—the scenes in the order they happen on screen. When you've read it through several times and you're sure your surface and deep action are clear and your character's emotional flow is convincing, it's time to start drafting your scenes.

DRAFTING THE SCREENPLAY

Whether I'm writing a screenplay by myself or with someone else, I find it enormously helpful to noodle the beats in each scene before I draft it—the action beats/moments of change (what has to happen) and the dialogue beats (what has to be said). When you're noodling your dialogue beats, The First Thing That Swims By will often be on the nose. That's okay for now. You're just roughing out the shape of the scene.

Good scenes, like good screenplays, are shapely, like the restaurant scene in *Kramer vs. Kramer* and the library scene in *Philadelphia*. One creates conflict, one creates connection, but both are exquisitely crafted patterns of change. Chart their structure and see for yourself. Then do the same for your scenes.

Once each scene's shape is roughed out, you can focus on the scene's dialogue, searching for the freshest way for your characters to say what needs to be said (it may take a number of drafts before you find it). You're looking for a fresh but in-character way for your characters to say what they're saying. In the screenplay of *Kramer vs. Kramer,* Joanna asks Ted, "How's the job?" and he answers, "Fine."

But on screen, he adds, "Vice president of nothing." It's an embedding that lets us—and Joanna—know that work isn't the most important thing in Ted's life anymore.

With *Winterfort,* once Pam and I had a good Scene-By-Scene, we chose the scenes we wanted to write. I wrote the first draft of a scene where Claire asks her parents for money because she wants to leave her husband, Hutch. Her parents know he's abusive, but he's also the town's football hero, and they just can't let go of that:

> MR. ANDERSON
> Claire, there are four days in my life I'll never forget. One was the day I married your mother. One was the day you were born. One was the day Hutch threw that football thirty-eight yards, and one was the day he married you.

Claire picks up her purse and walks out the door.

But I wasn't satisfied with the scene. I wanted Claire to reply to her father—it's an important moment of disconnection and growth for her in the story—but I couldn't think of what she could say. I didn't want to go on the nose with something obvious like, "Well, I see whose side you're on." So, at a loss for fresh words, I let Claire be at a loss, too, and I let her walk out. But it made the scene a bit flat.

Pam agreed, and she saved it by coming up with a fresh way for Claire to articulate what she is feeling:

> MR. ANDERSON
> Claire, there are four days in my life I'll never forget. One was the day I married your mother. One was the day you were born. One was the day Hutch threw that football thirty-eight yards, and one was the day he married you.

A slight pause.

> CLAIRE
> Well, that's one for me and one for Mama and
> two for Hutch. I guess he wins.

> She picks up her purse and walks out the door.

The subtext of Claire's speech is "I see whose side you're on," but Pam's text is so fresh, deadly, dead on—scorekeeping!—the moment comes alive. So raise the stakes on yourself as you draft and redraft your scenes for your long short screenplay. Make your dialogue work harder for you. Give it greater richness, irony, and levels of meaning. John Hill wrote an excellent article for *Script Magazine*, "Good Dialogue Is To Dye For," comparing great dialogue to dye markers used by the Coast Guard to mark a place on the ocean so divers can find the place where a plane or ship or "whatever is really important" went down:

> It can't be found on the surface; you have to work a little for it. The communication isn't in the 'text,' the words being said, but in the *subtext* ("sub," of course, means below, just under, out of sight but still very accessible—just work a little for it). Really good dialogue "says it without saying it." And when you create that momentary gap in time and space, between hearing the words and realizing the meaning, making the leap to "get it" is something the audience will love you for because it involves them, it brings them into the character's world view and into the story.[8]

In other words, they connect. They enter a screenplay or film, participating, doing some of the work, having some of the fun.

Hill's favorite example—and mine—is Butch Cassidy's line, "I got vision and the rest of the world wears bifocals." I guffawed when I heard it the first time. It still makes me smile. And I still quote it in conversation because it's so damn witty I never forgot it. Imagine writing a line so fresh, so beautifully crafted, that other people remember it. *That's* connection.

You may not have been born with an ear for great dialogue. Few people are. But I'm convinced that you can improve what talent you have by paying attention.

When you're out in the world, *listen* to the way people talk. The other day, on my daily walk through the park in my neighborhood, I noticed a middle-aged city official scooping water out of our creek. "Taking samples?" I asked.

"Yes," he said, nice and cheerful. "Some of our little fishies are dying." *Little fishies.* The combination of baby talk and the news that our creek was polluted was downright chilling (okay, I'd just seen *Civil Action*). And it's dialogue I've filed away to use in a script later on.

When I interviewed TV movie writer/producer Cynthia Cherbak, she told me she did the same thing.

> In the middle of doing a Kirk Douglas movie for HBO, I was robbed in Rural Canyon at gunpoint by carjackers. They told me to get my ring off or they'd cut my fucking finger off, so immediately I lift that out of my true life. I used the exact dialogue the robbers said.

Life's the best teacher, to coin a cliché, but you can also improve your own dialogue by reading plays and screenplays written by great dialoguists—Clifford Odets, Elaine May, Nora Ephron, David Mamet, Quentin Tarantino, Woody Allen, Tom Stoppard. In Stoppard's play *The Real Thing*, the main character, Henry—a writer—grabs a cricket bat to explain to his lover, Annie, why it's so important for writers to agonize until they get the words right:

> Shut up and listen. This thing here, which looks like a wooden club, is actually several pieces of particular wood cunningly put together in a certain way so that the whole thing is sprung, like a dance floor. It's for hitting cricket balls with. If you get it right, the cricket ball will travel two hundred yards in four seconds, and all you've done is give it a knock like knocking the top off a bottle of stout, and it makes a noise like a trout taking a fly . . . (He clucks his tongue to make the noise). What we're trying to do is to write cricket bats, so that when we throw up an idea and give it a little knock, it might . . . *travel.*[9]

Ultimately, that's what all of us are trying to do—write cricket bats so our ideas and stories will travel.

REWRITING THE SCREENPLAY

For the long short screenplay, I strongly recommend that you arrange a *table read*—an informal round-table reading—of a draft of your screenplay. Let one person read the action (they can also read those characters who only have a few lines). Let others read the principal characters. *Do not read yourself.* You need to sit back and listen. This is the best way I know of (short of making a film of your screenplay) to find out which scenes are working and which scenes are not. You'll discover if your dialogue is overwritten, underwritten, if it sounds natural (or stylized, if that's what you want), if your structure is sound, if the story is clear, and if the emotional flow really works. Even a cold reading with inexperienced readers can help you prepare for your rewrite. You might also invite a small audience to the reading and ask for their feedback. Don't object to what they are saying. Listen. Take notes. And look for consensus.

Often, in the early drafts of this screenplay, my students get lost in the fun house. Their story begins to lose focus. And it's hard for them to get fresh perspective because they've been so focused on putting words on the page. Once they put words on the page, the words stick like flies on flypaper. They begin to feel married to them. It's hard for them to pull back and see the big picture (believe me, I know; this happens to me all the time when I'm writing). So in script conferences, I'll turn the "flypaper" screenplay face down on the table and draw three shapes on the back:

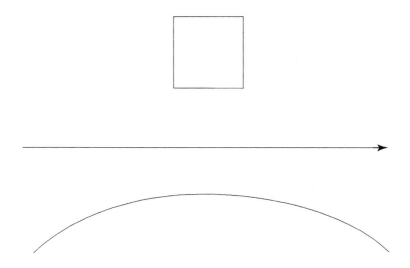

In the square, I ask the student to write what his or her script is about—in one word. There's almost always a long silence. It's a very hard question. At Bread Loaf, when Terry Tempest Williams asked me the same question about a memoir I was writing, I was staggered. "One *word?*" Then the word hit me—*renewal.* On every level, that's what the story was really about. And knowing this helped me immensely as I began designing and drafting the story.

That's what you're looking for—your *deep subject.* Some writers prefer to use the word *theme.* Whatever term you prefer, the point is to find what your screenplay is really truly deeply about. And in the best screenplays, every scene is, on some perhaps subtle level, about this deep subject.

The horizontal arrow is the screenplay's surface action/spine/through-line. Articulate this, if you haven't already, in one sentence with an *-ing* verb. How quickly this gets lost as words fly onto the page! Clarifying your surface action before you rewrite is essential.

The arc is, of course, the character arc, your screenplay's deep action. Articulate this for your long short screenplay, if you haven't, in one sentence with an *-ing* verb. And again, ideally, there's a close connection between the external events in your surface action and the moments of change that move your character along the arc.

When your screenplay's action—surface and deep—is clear in your mind, you're ready to rewrite. And rewrite. And rewrite. And, in most cases, rewriting doesn't stop there.

"Editing is the final rewrite," said Oliver Stone.

And, as you'll see when you read the following seven long short screenplays and screen the seven award-winning films, rewriting doesn't stop until the film's in the can.

NOTES

1. Brewster Ghiselin, *The Creative Process*, Brewster Ghiselin, New American Library, New York, 1952, p. 14.
2. R. Ruby Rich, "Choose One Memory To Take With You, He Says," *The New York Times*, Sunday, May 16, 1999, pp. 11, 19.
3. Claudia Johnson, *Propinquity/Paternity*, two one-acts, Palmetto Play Service, Pendleton, South Carolina, 1997, p. 23.
4. Linda Seger, *Making a Good Script Great*, Samuel French, Hollywood, 1987, p. 120.
5. Lajos Egri, *The Art of Dramatic Writing*, Simon and Schuster, New York, 1960, p. 2.
6. I am grateful to my former colleague, Charlie Boyd, for introducing me to this wonderful film.
7. Scott Frank, *Out of Sight*, *Scenario: The Magazine of Screenwriting Art*, Summer 1998, Volume 4, No. 2, p. 8.
8. John Hill, "Good Dialogue Is To Dye For," *Script*, Volume 4, Number 3, pp. 19, 20, 60, 61.
9. Tom Stoppard, *The Real Thing*, Faber & Faber, Boston, 1984, p. 51.

PART III

SEVEN SCREENPLAYS THAT MAKE IT LOOK EASY

11

KOSHER

By Aimee Barth

INTRODUCTION

Aimee Barth wrote *Kosher* in my Screenwriting II class for the final assignment—a five-page script she would direct for her B.F.A. Filmmaking III project. Like so many terrific short films, *Kosher* was conceived close to home.

> The idea surfaced out of my little brother's desire to be Jewish so that he could have a Bar Mitzvah. When my mother denied his request to convert (we were raised Lutheran), he exclaimed, "You refuse to accept the fact that my soul is entering my body!" Always a precocious kid, (he became a vegetarian at age six citing he would NOT eat the 'flesh of the dead'), he became the model for the main character, Charles, and thus the idea for *Kosher* was born. Of course, like every idea, it changed quite a bit when I put pen to paper and again when we put lens to actor. But, all in all, the final draft of the script and the product on the screen are nearly identical.

Aimee's first draft, however, was a bit loose and baggy (as I encourage first drafts to be), but in the rewrite process, she took to heart the art of subtraction, cutting extraneous scenes, beats, lines, and words.

> I think what made *Kosher* unique was the story's simplicity, and severe editing in the rewrite stage. You and I made sure that no line was wasted, and that translates quite well to the finished product. When you watch the film, it moves quickly, flows easily and doesn't mince words.

I agree. It's a perfect example of how gracefully a screenplay story can be told by hitting scenes late and getting out of them early.

Aimee credits her producer and editor, Emily McMahon, for "helping immensely every step of the way" in the redrafting of *Kosher* during production and post. "Emily's adept grasp of story enabled me to make only the most necessary changes and kept *Kosher* tight and comedic. And we never lost sight of the story we were trying to tell."

Neither did the world. *Kosher* has charmed audiences at film festivals here and abroad, winning numerous awards including Best Short Film Under 10 Minutes from the 2001 Wine Country Film Festival in Glen Ellen, California; Best Student Mini-Film from the 2001 Independents' Film Festival in Tampa, Florida; Best of Category & Show from the 2001 Damah Film Festival in Seattle, Washington; the Joey Award Trophy from the 2001 San Jose Film Commission in California; Best Short Film from the 2002 Flanzer Jewish Community Center 4th Annual Festival of Films in Sarasota, Florida; the Shoestring Award from the 2002 Rochester International Film Festival in New York; Best College Narrative from the 2002 Da Vinci Film & Video Festival in Corvallis, Oregon; Best Arrangement: Cinema in Umbria, Umbertide, Italy, in 2002; and Second Prize for Comedy in 2002 from the Academy of Television Arts & Sciences—a.k.a. the student Emmies.

When I asked Aimee what she's doing now, she said, "I'm in L.A., living the dream. I've been working in craft service while I finish my first screenplay, at the request of a literary agent. I was recently contracted by a production company in the Bay Area, Highway Video, to direct short content films for them. I'm now working as an assistant at a top management agency called 'The Firm.' And I'm being considered as Kate Hudson's body double for her latest film, *Skeleton Key*—keep your fingers crossed!"

KOSHER
By Aimee Barth

EXT. PLAYGROUND—DAY

Autumn leaves fall from a massive oak tree and settle on
the checkered tablecloth of a playground picnic where our
7-year-old hero, CHARLES ROBINSON, and his girlfriend,
RACHEL LEVY, dine during recess. They stare deeply into
each other's eyes. Charles takes her hand in his.

> CHARLES
> I've been meaning to ask you something for a
> long time.

He reaches into his corduroy pants' pocket and pulls out
a little gold box, opening it to reveal a small ring with a
sparkly plastic butterfly.

> CHARLES
> Rachel, we've been boyfriend and girlfriend since
> Tuesday, and you're the coolest girl in school.
> You're always picked first for kickball . . . will you
> marry me?

Rachel is speechless. She eyes the ring.

> RACHEL
> Yes.

Charles slips the ring onto her finger. She admires it,
beaming.

> RACHEL
> Come on! We can get Micah to marry us. He's
> practically a Rabbi.

> CHARLES
> Rabbi?

                                              CUT TO:

EXT. PLAYGROUND BLEACHERS—CONTINUOUS

Charles and Rachel sit before MICAH, an older boy
draped in a talus and wearing a Yarmulke, his hands
folded atop the Torah.

                  MICAH
  I can't. Charles isn't Jewish.

                  RACHEL
  So?

                  CHARLES
  What does that matter?

                  MICAH
  Do you go to Temple, Charles?

Charles shakes his head, not understanding.

                  MICAH
  Do you go to Church?

                  CHARLES
  Sometimes . . .

                  MICAH
  Exactly. He's not a Jew, Rachel. You can't get
  married. It's practically against the law.

Micah yanks his things from the bleachers and stomps
off. Charles and Rachel lower their heads in defeat. An
idea strikes.

                  CHARLES
  I've got it. I'll become Jewish!

                  RACHEL
  You will?

                  CHARLES
  I will. Tell me what to do.

Rachel hesitates.

                  RACHEL
  I think becoming Jewish is a tedious process,
  Charles. It can't be taken lightly.

                  CHARLES
  I love you, Rachel. Tell me what to do.

RACHEL
Well . . . are you circumcised?

CHARLES
Circumcised?

CUT TO:

INT. DINING ROOM—DINNER TIME

Charles and his mother, MRS. ROBINSON, a petite woman with a booming personality, sit before a ham dinner, their hands folded and heads bowed.

MRS. ROBINSON
Come, Lord Jesus, be our guest, and let thy gifts to us be blessed. Amen.

CHARLES
Shabbat Shalom.

Mrs. Robinson's head snaps up.

MRS. ROBINSON
Excuse me?

Charles picks the tines of his fork with his fingers. Mrs. Robinson begins piling Charles' plate with food. He just stares at it.

MRS. ROBINSON
What's wrong, Charles, aren't you hungry?

Charles shrugs.

Beat.

MRS. ROBINSON
Eat your ham, kiddo.

CHARLES
(mumbling)
I can't.

MRS. ROBINSON
Of course you can, it's your favorite.

                           CHARLES
        Yeah, but it's not kosher.

Mrs. Robinson sets her fork down.

                           MRS. ROBINSON
        Kosher?

                           CHARLES
        This food is not clean or fit to eat by the dietary
        laws of Judaism.

                           MRS. ROBINSON
        I know what kosher means.

Charles returns to the task of chasing peas around his
plate. Mrs. Robinson eyes him suspiciously and clears
her throat.

                           CHARLES
        I'm becoming Jewish. I'm marrying Rachel
        tomorrow after school. She's Jewish.

                           MRS. ROBINSON
        Why would you want to do that? You were
        baptized at Holy Cross!

                           CHARLES
        I love her, Mom. I'll do anything to marry her.

                           MRS. ROBINSON
        What do you know about love, Charles?
        You're six years old. Now eat your ham.

                           CHARLES
        I can't!

Mrs. Robinson gathers her strength with a single breath.

                           MRS. ROBINSON
        Charles. You know the rules. You do not
        leave this table until you finish your dinner.

Charles' nostrils flare and he crosses his arms in
defiance. Mrs. Robinson raises an eyebrow. A stand off.

                                            FADE TO:

INT. DINING ROOM—NIGHT

The sun is setting on the dinner table. Charles remains put, glaring at the ham.

FADE TO:

INT. DINING ROOM—NIGHT

Night has fallen. The crickets chirp rhythmically outside. Charles hasn't budged.

FADE TO:

INT. DINING ROOM—DAY

Morning has broken. Mrs. Robinson enters and clears his plate, shaking her head at her stubborn child.
Charles smirks victoriously. He's won.

EXT. PLAYGROUND—DAY

Leaves flutter from the oak tree branches down to where Charles and Rachel stand before Micah, in his robe and talus, clutching the Torah. Rachel is radiant in a white summer dress and flowers in her hair. Charles stands tall in his black tux. A small crowd of little children has gathered for the ceremony.

> MICAH
> Do you, Rachel Levy, take this man, Charles Robinson to be your awfully wedded husband?

> RACHEL
> I do.

> MICAH
> And do you, Charles, take Rachel till death do you part?

> CHARLES
> I do.

Micah turns to the BEST MAN, a tiny little thing with a mop of blonde hair. The Best Man wraps a plastic wine glass in a napkin and hands it to Micah. He gingerly places it on the ground. Charles stomps on the wine glass with fervor.

> MICAH
> You may kiss the bride.

Beat.

> CHARLES
> Kiss her?

Rachel wrinkles her nose.

> CHARLES
> (slamming his palm to his forehead)
> Oy veh!

OVER BLACK:

The Wedding March begins.

MY JOSEPHINE

By Barry Jenkins

INTRODUCTION

It took Barry Jenkins fifteen months to finish the screenplay and film of *My Josephine*. He wrote the first draft in mid-September, 2001, for his B.F.A. Screenwriting II class, and later—much later—directed the film for his Film-making III project.

> It was a very raw film in that first draft. Everything I was feeling about 9/11 was vented right there on the surface of the script. The two characters were broad frames for my sympathy for Arab-Americans in post-9/11 America, and in clinging so much to that aspect of the script I went over-board and presented clichés as commentary on American Society. I was trying to do too much. The frame of the story was always one night in the life of these two characters. In earlier drafts of the script, this frame served only as a vehicle for the extreme act of misplaced vengeance enacted at the script's climax (Aadid is slain by a random, middle-aged American Caucasian male in the first three drafts of the script). It was an extremely sensational and ultimately wrong moment. I tried for months to make this moment work but in the end couldn't get it to translate as anything but sensationalism.

A year after writing the first draft, Barry found himself in my Screenwriting III class with "a mandate" to write another draft of the script.

> I'll admit that by that point I'd given up on the script completely, but I decided to retool it for you. I took all the violence out and made it as simple as I was capable as a writer. There were no flashbacks, gunshots, or American flags; just

a few extremely random scenes between two Arab-American co-workers. I leaned heavily in the direction of the innuendos between Aadid and Adela and strove for a romanticism that wasn't present in earlier drafts. All this I did as a toss off. I wasn't at all serious about making the film but I knew I had to give you something so I just decided to spin something light from the characters. To wit: Napoleon is mentioned in the film because a roommate of mine at the time was a Napoleon buff. While sitting in our kitchen writing the draft to hand to you, I overheard him mention that there were no monuments to Napoleon. I then asked him about Napoleon's love life, and he replied with the story of Mary-Louise and Josephine. I tossed both in and ran with it.

When Barry handed in the script it was titled *Untitled,* something I don't allow. I scratched out *Untitled* and handed it back. "Anything but *Untitled,*" I told him. He scribbled in *My Josephine.*

I expected you to tear it to shreds, but instead got the script back with the succinct coverage—*lovely and subtle.* Your coverage surprised me because I'd never thought of the script playing that way. A few days later a friend mentioned to me a marquee he'd passed at a Laundromat that read AMERICAN FLAGS CLEANED FREE. I took these two elements and ran with them.

The script changed too, in production.

I wrote this script for a particular Laundromat in town that unfortunately (fortunately?) we failed to get. What we were able to acquire was a much smaller Laundromat and this inherently changed some aspects of the script. Things like the water gun fight mentioned in the script did not play well in the smaller setting . . . and areas of the room where I designated certain conversations to take place had to be altered. We basically had, of the sixty shots we planned, twenty-two or so that were absolutely crucial to telling the story and not specific to one Laundromat or the other. It was these scenes that James Laxton (the cinematographer) and I focused on, and the rest became sort of bandry. The other major change during production was the character of Adela and the manner in which she responds to Aadid's affection. I failed to make my actress (a first timer) comfortable in her role, which was a failing on my part as a first-time director. As we got further into shooting (two twelve-hour night shoots), she grew more uncomfortable and as a result became increasingly distant from the other actor. Eventually it got to the point where there were certain scenes we could not pull off, such as them lying together atop one of the laundry tables or reaching for each other's hand in the last shot of the film. We'd talked about them at length but amidst the fatigue and awkward vulnerability that comes with performing in front of strangers, she grew apart from me.

So we adapted. The first and last shots of the film are a perfect example of this. In the script, this last scene called for everything that made the film, except the two characters were also supposed to reach across the doorway to take each other's hand. Somehow, in the hours between the first hour of shooting and this, the last (this was indeed the last shot we did), the moment had grown too saccharin sweet for my actress. She would not do it. At first, I tried to find another way of bringing the two together. I simply had Aadid fold the flag as the script calls for and then stand by her side in hopes of recreating the emotion of what I felt was in the hand reach we'd lost. After two takes of this moment, which had the Laundromat doors closed, I got the feeling something was missing. I looked out at the doorway where the actors stood and, on impulse, ordered the doors opened. We then took the shot again and this time I directed them to stand as far away as possible, on opposite sides of the threshold, with absolutely no interaction whatsoever. When the footage came back the results were amazing, the perfect foot and endnotes. Two very different emotions captured in the same moment.

Other accidents contributed to the film's unique look.

During production, there were a few camera jams where the film got nicked up and shredded as it passed through the projector. These processed nicks and scratches had a surrealistic quality that I really liked, and so I expressed to Meghan Robertson (the editor) that we should get as many of these into the film as possible. Once she understood my affinity for these and the fades to and from white, she became completely absorbed in making the editing reflect Aadid's scattered emotional state running through the film. Fades to black are an accepted filmmaking technique that usually communicate a passage of time. By fading to and from white, we made those fades unique and specific to

Aadid and the sense of this night he's relaying to the audience. Coupled with all the camera scratches and off-focus photography in the film, we strove to create the atmosphere of wandering through Aadid's dreams . . . something akin to that fog of love I mentioned before.

I asked Barry how he felt about the film once it was finished. Was he happy with the result?

I'm pretty satisfied with the way the script translated to film. While there are a few sequences that became very different because of things we did in post, there are also stretches of the script that, when I closed my eyes before production, I saw exactly as they appear on film. The last two minutes of the film play out this way. When I closed my eyes, I saw that cart floating down the aisle—I was in that dryer tumbling, peacefully bouncing around Aadid, listening to his solemn words. I felt the light spilling through the Laundromat doors and I glided along the floor as the film crept onto Aadid and Adela looking out into the city. I was right there. And that, more than the screenings or people's kind words, has been the most satisfying thing . . . the thought that, with the love and help of my friends, I managed to get those things out of my head and onto film so others could see what I saw. Feels damn good.

And no wonder. *My Josephine* has been selected for screenings at home and abroad, winning numerous awards including the Golden Compass Award from the 2003 Baytowne Film Festival in Sandestin, Florida; the Bronze Chris Award from the 2003 Columbus International Film Festival in Columbus, Ohio; and Best Narrative Short from the 2003 Georgetown Independent Film Festival in Georgetown, Virginia.

When I asked Barry what he's doing since he graduated from Florida State's Film School, he said, "I now reside in Los Angeles, CA where I write for the media collective bandry and work as a director's assistant. A self-described 'could-be director who loves thick-rimmed coffee cups,' I recently discovered that wearing a faded work-shirt embroidered with the name Jorge is considerably more attractive to women than reciting the difference between T-stops and F-stops."

MY JOSEPHINE
By Barry Jenkins

First, over BLACK, we hear the faint sounds of a laundromat.

Then:

> AADID (V.O. ARABIC, subtitled)
> A seven minute film about my life.

EXT. LAUNDROMAT—NIGHT

AADID, 22, Middle-Eastern, standing outside a neighborhood laundromat empty save for a few patrons strewn about here and there. Hanging behind him is a NEON SIGN that reads AMERICAN FLAGS CLEANED FREE.

> AADID (V.O. Arabic, subtitled)
> It's funny how . . . there are no streets . . . or buildings . . . or monuments named after Napoleon Bonaparte in Paris . . . or any city.

He pulls a cigarette from his pocket and lights it.

> AADID (V.O. Arabic, subtitled)
> Most people know little about Napoleon. They know he was a conqueror, a tyrant.

As he exhales a long drag, Aadid looks directly at us, oblivious to our watching, inside his own thoughts.

> AADID (V.O. Arabic, subtitled)
> Few people know that Napoleon had two wives. Josephine, his first, he married as general. And Mary-Louise, his second, he married as emperor.

Aadid breaks our gaze and turns his back to us. Through the glass, inside the laundromat, we see . . .

ADELA, 20, also Middle-Eastern, beautiful.

> AADID (V.O. Arabic, subtitled)
> Mary-Louise, for an heir. Josephine . . . for love.

Aadid watches Adela through the glass adoringly.

                    AADID (V.O. Arabic, subtitled)
  Adela. My Josephine.

She's conversing with a MIDDLE-AGED MAN. An
American flag is in a wad under his arm. Adela reaches
out and takes the flag from him. Continuing the
conversation, she unfurls it and begins to fold it neatly.

INT. LAUNDROMAT—CONTINUOUS

                  MIDDLE-AGED MAN
  Is that it?

                  ADELA
  Do you have anything else?

                  MIDDLE-AGED MAN
  No.

                  ADELA
  Your name?

Adela removes pen and paper from her pocket and jots it
down.

                  ADELA
  It'll be ready in the morning.

She tears a piece of the paper and hands it to him.

EXT. LAUNDROMAT—CONTINUOUS

Aadid turning from the scene and leaning against the
glass as the MIDDLE-AGED MAN breezes past. Aadid
takes his last drag and flicks the unfinished cigarette to
the ground.

FADE TO BLACK.

INT. LAUNDROMAT—NIGHT

Adela wandering the laundromat. She stops at a row of
top-loader washers and wiggles her key into one of the
machines, opens the coin box and grabs a handful of
change.

EXT. LAUNDROMAT—CONTINUOUS

From afar, we watch Adela exiting the laundromat, her hands cupped and full of quarters. She crosses the parking lot, cradling the change in her hands, passing from our field of vision just as Aadid steps onto the laundry porch.

Aadid leans against the glass wall, just as he had earlier, looking after Adela.

Resting on a bus bench. THE HOMELESS MAN is semi-conscious, just woken and still lying across two-thirds of the bench.

Adela motions to the bum to cup his hands, and exchanges the coins she has from her hands to the bum's.

The bum counts the change, a coin at a time. Adela watches endearingly, hypnotized.

FADE TO BLACK.

OVER BLACK.

                    AADID (V.O. Arabic, subtitled)
     You learn to like night shifts.

INT. LAUNDROMAT—NIGHT

Aadid and Adela, stone-still statues in front of the laundromat. They're sitting in CHEAP WHITE PATIO CHAIRS playing a game of chess. Behind them, through the glass, we see . . .

LAUNDROMAT PATRONS moving at lightning speed, excited electrons loading machines and folding clothes.

They cycle through washing, drying, and folding frenetically. We observe them until they all disappear.

FADE OUT.

INT. LAUNDROMAT—LATER NIGHT

Adela dumping a bundle of AMERICAN FLAGS on the counter.

> AADID (V.O. Arabic, subtitled)
> We've cleaned flags free for five months. It works.

Adela dumps the flags on the counter and sorts through them.

> AADID (V.O. Arabic, subtitled)
> There's never very many . . . six, seven, eight. We get them every day, clean them every night.

She clamps NUMBERED CLIPS to each one and reloads the cart.

> AADID (V.O. Arabic, subtitled)
> They aren't hard to clean. People run them up in the morning, take them down at night.

Adela pushes the cart of flags through the laundromat, Aadid at her side.

> AADID (V.O. Arabic, subtitled)
> Something that never touches the ground shouldn't be dirty.

INT. EMPTY LAUNDROMAT ROOM—CONTINUOUS

> AADID (V.O. Arabic, subtitled)
> It's a delicate thing.

Aadid and Adela stand beside each other at a large sink. They each have both hands submerged. Soapy foam wraps their wrists.

> AADID (V.O. Arabic, subtitled)
> The colors mustn't bleed. The white stars must be kept from the blue field, the red stripes from the white.

Aadid and Adela's hands wave softly beneath the water. The flags swell and swim around them. There's a play to it all.

> AADID (V.O. Arabic, subtitled)
> You don't scrub them . . . you barely touch them. You're always gentle.

Aadid and Adela continue their work.

INT. LAUNDROMAT—NIGHT

Aadid and Adela atop adjoining washers.

> AADID (Arabic, subtitled)
> What were you talking about?

> ADELA
> Talking about when?

> AADID (Arabic, subtitled)
> With the homeless man?

They pause. Adela focuses her eyes on the counter below.

> ADELA
> About love.

> AADID (Arabic, subtitled)
> In Arabic.

> ADELA (Arabic, subtitled)
> About love.
> (in English)
> What's wrong with English?

> AADID (Arabic, subtitled)
> Nothing.

To this last question Adela does not respond. She simply stares at him, letting the moment linger.

FADE TO BLACK.

OVER BLACK

> AADID (V.O. Arabic, subtitled)
> Adela is a woman who is very good.

INT. LAUNDROMAT—NIGHT

A MONTAGE OF:

Adela standing in the center aisle, staring at us. Slowly, at odd intervals, she takes steps towards us.

Adela, sitting behind a register reading by warm lamplight.

Adela's feet, one before the other, floating down an aisle.

ACCOMPANIED BY:

> AADID (V.O. Arabic, subtitled)
> She's simple. She's not complicated. She's not someone who makes up schemes. She's very gracious. Lovely.

Aadid and Adela together in the laundromat. They're embraced, hip-to-hip, hand in hand, performing a waltz. Neither is very good at it. The smiles on their faces suggest they're aware of this.

INT. LAUNDROMAT—MOMENTS LATER

Adela crouching behind a washer at the end of the center aisle, an extravagant WATERGUN in tow. Across the laundromat, at the opposite end of the aisle, Aadid crouches beside a dryer with a similar WATERGUN.

Adela slides across the aisle, parallel to Aadid, and hides behind another washer. As she settles, Aadid turns towards her and makes his way down the aisle, closing in.

Adela squirms behind the washer. She swivels her body round the corner of the washer and down the next aisle.

Methodically, with poise, Adela eases up from her crouch and peers over the aisle. Aadid does the same. He's dead in her sights, at her mercy and loving it. Aadid lowers his gun and raises his hands. She smiles and a fondness pierces their standoff. Then . . .

Adela triggers her gun. She explodes with laughter as Aadid rounds the corner and chases her down the aisle. They careen past the washers and bend down a row of dryers.

Adela's running while twisting backward to fire at Aadid, joyously screaming. They continue through the laundromat and into the empty parking lot, guns drawn. They circle one another.

INT. LAUNDROMAT STOREROOM—NIGHT

Aadid and Adela on opposite sides of the tiny storeroom checking INVENTORY. They both have a CLIPBOARD AND PEN.

Aadid is on one side of the room and Adela another. He counts a stack of cartons and marks his sheet. Adela does the same.

As they both turn to move, they meet under the light. They embrace. They sway. Their lips meet. They kiss.

FADE TO BLACK

INT. LAUNDROMAT—NIGHT

A LAUNDRY CART floating down the aisle of the Laundromat. We are in this cart, propped atop the folds of DAMP AMERICAN FLAGS.

A wall of dryers approaches us. We observe as a flag is lifted from the cart and hoisted into the dryer.

INT. LAUNDROMAT—MOMENTS LATER

Adela and Aadid facing the dryers, leaning against washers on opposite aisles. They pull change from their pockets.

Working their way down the row, they each load change and start a dryer.

They stand back to watch the American Flags tumble and spin, each one in its own space in this sea of dryers.

DRYER'S POV

Aadid and Adela, staring at us, seemingly unaware of our watching as we twist in the dryer's rotation. The laundromat revolves around them. There's an air to this we've not experienced before. Neither speaks, but we hear:

> AADID (V.O. Arabic, subtitled)
> Every flag, its own dryer. A delicate tumble. Low heat.
> (a pause)
> Sometimes, you can't help but stare at them.
> (another pause)
> It makes you feel . . .

                                            CUT TO:

Aadid and Adela atop a row of washers, together, cradled
beside one another.

                        AADID (V.O. Arabic, subtitled)
    . . . like you should be in love with something.

FADE TO BLACK

INT. LAUNDROMAT—DAWN

The laundromat, dim against the day-lit exterior. Light
creeps along the floor and fades away down the aisles.
It's serene; no patrons, no piles of clothes, only empty
washers and freshly swept floors. In the farthest aisle,
Aadid and Adela.

Silhouetted, they stretch a crisply folded AMERICAN
FLAG between them. Adela releases it to Aadid and drifts
toward the front door. She stands there in its threshold.

Aadid folds the flag into its final shape and lowers it
gingerly to the counter. His face, though somewhat tired,
reflects a calm the freshly folded flags suggest.

Aadid turns from the counter to take in Adela standing
in the morning light. He watches her as though touched
by something ethereal. She's beautiful.

He drifts towards Adela, crossing the threshold to stand
beside her. Their backs to us . . . slowly, nearly
imperceptibly, they each float a hand across the
threshold until . . .

Their hands meet.

FADE OUT.

—————————— *13* ——————————

A WORK IN PROGRESS

By Wes Ball

INTRODUCTION

"The evolution of *A Work in Progress* was a real roller coaster," Wes Ball said about his 2002 B.F.A. Thesis film. "It all began with my previous live-action short, *Jacob: The Movie*, a pretty ambitious student endeavor that ignored everyone's concern about 'scope.' In the end, it had its flaws and I made my mistakes, but I accomplished a lot and gained some confidence in myself. Still, after the scale of *Jacob*, I decided I wanted to go back to basics and tell a very simple story as well as I could. Of course," he added, "because of the way I am, I couldn't just sit on keeping everything simple. I knew the story needed to be simple, but I wantcd to try something new, something challenging, something I or anyone else hadn't done at the school before. This is where *A Work in Progress* was born."

Wes decided to try his hand at full CG animation.

This wasn't an easy sell during my thesis pitch to the faculty. In *Jacob* I had dabbled in CG with a little robot character that shows up, but I had never attempted creating an entire world, its props, and its characters from scratch. But this challenge was really appealing to me, so the faculty let me go figure out a way to pull it off. At this point, the short was going to be entirely animated. I settled on telling the story of a lonely bear (which appeared briefly as a prop in *Jacob*). That was about all I had for a while. After that, the story went through a lot of changes. It went from a bear that was thrown out, to a bear looking for love, and finally to a bear searching for friends. When I incorporated the message of 'be yourself,' the characters suddenly jumped into my imagination all at once.

And something else jumped—or crept—into his imagination as he worked on the animation.

An idea started to creep into my brain: the idea of incorpo-
rating a small live-action sequence about a girl who sketches
these cartoons that would open and close the CG animation.
This was an idea I kept pushing away because at this point
the other thesis films and their shooting schedules had been
worked out by the faculty. I didn't have the guts to ask for
film now that I had convinced them that I could pull off
full CG.

But he couldn't shoo the idea away.

The idea wouldn't leave me alone. So I decided to suck it
up and beg for a roll or two of film and a small equipment
package to go shoot a short live-action scene. Luckily, the
faculty graciously gave me a very small camera package and
400 feet of film to shoot on an off-weekend, but now I had
to convince a few of my exhausted fellow students to help
me out on my shoot. About a week before everything was
lined up and ready to go, another idea suddenly hit me
while driving in my car to my production meeting—
weaving into the animation a live-action story about a
lonely girl also searching for friends. It was a real lightning
flash of inspiration. But I had to scramble to get things
worked out for the new idea. It was both a blessing and a
curse. I had to rewrite, find locations, and cast about a dozen
kids (no small feat in Tallahassee) in about a week. Thank-
fully, the small one-day shoot went off without a hitch. It
was a really great experience—getting back to basics—just
a couple of friends, a camera, and some reflector boards.
After shooting, I edited the scenes together and then set
aside the next two months for animation. Since I was
animating it myself (on my home PC on a program called
Lightwave 3D), I could change things very quickly. Little
ideas and ways to make the scenes more efficient were
always coming while animating. I just let the story grow and
change as I completed it. Aside from the basic story skeleton, the film really was a work in progress.

The screenplay published here is exactly the way Wes sent it to me, in two
parts—a scenario followed by the verses spoken in each of the scenes.

"Writing for animation was a whole new world for me when it came to
screenwriting," he explained. "I never really even wrote a script. I only wrote
a brief description of what happened to the characters during the scene. The
rhyming narration was my dialogue for the story. I knew the time I had for
each scene, what had to happen, and it was just a matter of figuring out the
blocking and details to make it work for the time allotted."

And what did he learn while *A Work In Progress* was a work in progress?

"I found it really is true that you make the movie three times: write it, direct it, edit it. Things always changed and grew, and with this film, being open to that added a ton to its impact."

But he's still amazed by the film's success, a steady stream of national and international screenings and prizes, not least among them the 2003 Bronze Student Academy Award for Animation.

"My little mini-Oscar is sitting in my living room," he said, "collecting dust." He smiled. "I truly had no idea it would be received as well as it has. Working so long and so hard on a project tends to make you lose your objectivity. All together, I couldn't be happier at how the goal of telling a simple story has turned out to be an incredibly rewarding experience. But as usual, I see the little mistakes no one will ever notice, and I'm ready for a new challenge."

He is currently living in Los Angeles where he is "writing and developing several projects in both animation and live-action, one of which is a children's TV series based on *A Work in Progress.*"

A WORK IN PROGRESS
By Wes Ball

Cartoon scenes are not written, only BRIEFLY explained . . . Bear with me . . . no pun intended.:-)

the text for the narration/rhyme follow at the end of the script.

over Black

Sounds of playing and laughter.

FADE IN:

EXT. SHADY TREE CANOPY—DAY

A bright and beautiful sky leads us to an open grassy park filled with playing children. Their laughter carries through the field. We continue through the branches of a towering oak tree, then to an empty tire swing, then to a little girl who sits quietly alone at the trunk of the old tree. Her name is MELISSA.

She sits in the shade, silhouetted against the bright field. A sketchbook rests in her lap as she watches the other children playing. She softly smiles at their happiness.

She slowly glances to the empty tire swing next to her. The ghosts of herself and others playing on the swing slowly appear. Just as Melissa smiles, the apparition fades away as slowly as it appeared.

Melissa is alone again.

She opens her sketchbook to reveal a drawing of a lonely tree with a tire swing hanging from its branches. She looks out to the field one last time, then begins to write. She speaks out loud as she writes.

                    MELISSA
    There once . . . was . . . an old tire that hung from
    a tree.

    Not a soul in sight, no one to see . . .

We slowly push into her pencil drawing. Color slowly begins filling in the pencil lines. Soon the drawing itself slowly takes a three-dimensional shape.

MELISSA
... except for a bear that loved to swing.

By this point, the pencil drawing has completely
transformed into a rich and realistic cartoon world.

EXT. CARTOON GRASSY FIELD—CONTINUOUS

First part of cartoon*

Melissa's rhyme accompanies the introduction.

*An empty tire swing hangs from the branch of a lonely
tree perched atop a grassy hill. The world is empty, not
a soul in sight. A BEAR slowly appears swinging on the
tire swing, then dissolves to the bear swinging himself,
then to the bear gazing out into the empty world. He is
sad and alone.*

MELISSA (V.O.)
When it came to this, he knew everything.

VOICE (O.S.)
(intrigued)
It doesn't just end there does it?

The cartoon quickly transforms into a sketch again.

EXT. SHADY TREE CANOPY

Startled, Melissa looks up from her sketch. She sees a
little girl holding a ball standing in front of her. This is
FAITHE. She seems very comfortable with herself,
definitely not bashful like Melissa.

Melissa
Say what?

FAITHE
Your story. It can't end there.

MELISSA
(looks down to her drawings)
Oh ... well I wasn't done yet.

                              FAITHE
          Oh, okay.
                          (sits down)
          Sorry, go ahead.

Melissa squirms uncomfortably. She isn't used to
company, but she shakes it off and begins to write again.

                              MELISSA
          So the bear found a turtle who was walking under
          the trees.

EXT. CARTOON GRASSY FIELD TRAIL

Second part of cartoon

*Bear finds a grumpy TURTLE trotting down a trail in a
patch of trees. Bear has an idea. Next we see Bear
trying to catch up with a box strapped to his back. He
walks on all fours trying as hard as he can to look like
his new turtle friend. Unfortunately, Turtle doesn't have
the expected reaction. He rolls his eyes and tucks into
this shell. Bear is alone again.*

                          VOICE (O.S.)
                         (disapproving)
          Wait a minute.

The cartoon world stops dead in its tracks.

EXT. SHADY TREE CANOPY

Melissa is surprised to see several children have now
gathered around her. A BOY stands in the middle.

                              BOY
                       (sure of himself)
          He shouldn't give up there.

All the other kids nod their heads approving the idea.

                              BOY
          He should try again.

Melissa, growing more comfortable among the other kids,
nods with a smile and goes back to her writing.

EXT. CARTOON WORLD SKY+

Third part of cartoon

Next we see a FROG squatting on a lily pad in the middle of a pond. We pan to reveal Bear is also squatting on a lily pad trying to be as frog-like as he can. However, a tasty fly buzzes into Frog's sights and he quickly leaps after the fly. Bear drops his head in disappointment.

Just then, the same fly grabs Bear's attention. He watches it fly into the air. Then, Bear sees something that lifts his spirits . . . a bird!

BIRD lazily flaps high up in the sky. Little does he know a Bear with wings made of branches quickly approaches. Bear flaps up next to Bird. Needless to say, Bird is a bit dumbfounded. What Bear doesn't know is that his crude wings are falling apart. Just as Bear notices, he falls from the sky. He tumbles closer and closer to the ground. Just before he hits . . .

> SMALL VOICE (O.S.)
Excuse me.

EXT. SHADY TREE CANOPY

Melissa looks up from her drawing. Even more kids surround her. They are all entranced by her story. A LITTLE GIRL steps forward and builds the nerve to speak.

> LITTLE GIRL
I think he's trying too hard.

The children listen to what she says. Some begin to nod their heads in approval.

> LITTLE GIRL
He should just be himself.

The kids look to each other in agreement.

A smile grows on Melissa's face.

EXT. CARTOON GRASSY WORLD DAY.

Final cartoon story.

Melissa's rhyme sums up her realization of "Just be yourself" as we see Bear at his tire swing again.

This time we see he is pushing the swing. Turtle happily sits in the tire with a huge grin on his face.

We pull out further to reveal Frog and Bird as well. They wait in line for their turn to swing.

Finally, we see a wooden sign slapped together with "Free Swings" painted on it.

EXT. SHADY TREE CANOPY

Melissa slowly looks up to her new audience.

> MELISSA
> Well? What do you think?

No one says anything. The children look to each other with smiles on their faces.

Finally the first audience member, FAITHE, steps forward.

> FAITHE
> Well . . . we were wondering . . . Can you tell us another one?

Melissa grins with excitement and quickly turns to a fresh page in her sketchbook.

> MELISSA
> There once were a bunch of bears, who lived in a forest. . . .

As she tells a new story, her voice slowly grows more distant as we pull out leaving the writer and the audience alone to imagine another story together.

> FADE OUT.

A WORK IN PROGRESS—Narration/Rhyme

OPENING SCENE

There once was an old tire,
That hung from a tree.

Not a soul in sight,
No one to see.

Except for a bear,
That loved to swing.

When it came to this,
He knew everything.

But something was odd . . . on this bright sunny day,
The bear couldn't have fun . . . in his usual way.

You see, the bear was lonely. Friends were far and few . . .
So playing by himself was really all the bear knew.

If only he had a friend, things might be all right.
So he waited for a visit . . . until day turned to night.

TURTLE SCENE

The next day
Bear left the tree in search of a friend.
He just didn't know . . . quite where to begin.

Then he spotted a turtle . . . walking down a trail.
And soon thought of a plan . . . that would not fail.

He strapped a box to his back and called it a shell,
But the grumpy old turtle didn't take it too well.

Bear couldn't understand . . . just where he went wrong.
Bear only knew that he wanted to belong.

FROG SCENE

But, Bear found a frog. And a green one at that!
On top of a lily pad is where the frog sat.

So Bear decided to join him on a pad of his own.
Now he wouldn't have to worry about being alone.

Bear dropped his head, and let out a sigh.
He was alone again, but something caught his eye.

Then, Bear saw a bird way up in the sky.
NOW bear knew what to do! He needed to fly!

BIRD SCENE

The bird looked ahead, as he flew through the air.
He didn't expect to see . . . a flying bear.

He made some wings from a branch off his tree.
Now just like the bird . . . is what the bear could be.

But something was wrong, and the bird knew just why.
Without leaves on his wings, the bear would fall from the sky.

FINAL SCENE

Bear figured it out. He knew what was wrong.
Turns out . . . Bear had the answer . . . all along.

By being himself . . . the bear could clearly see.
He should go back to what he loved . . . his swing and his tree.

And this is where the story ends.
Bear was no longer alone. Bear made new friends.

LENA'S SPAGHETTI

By Rachel A. Witenstein

INTRODUCTION

Rachel Witenstein wrote *Lena's Spaghetti* in my screenwriting class in 1994. The B.F.A. Thesis Script Committee (which chose up to five scripts to produce for thesis films every year) voted unanimously to produce Rachel's screenplay. I asked Rachel to describe the process of writing the script, and she said:

> The "mail relationship" in *Lena's* is an invention that came about through the process of trying to come up with an idea for your screenwriting class at F.S.U. My first idea had something to do with a plant shop run by an eccentric lady, I think, and I just kept flip-flopping characters and situations until it felt like something I wanted to write. If something wasn't inspiring me, I just changed it. I kept adding in bits that I saw in real life, like the character of the father as a breast surgeon. My father isn't a breast surgeon, but I read an article in the *New York Times* about one, and his flamboyance really tickled me, especially in contrast with a girl who is experiencing a certain amount of anxiety about her own development.

But the journey from script to screen was less joyous, more like Nora Ephron's description of The Process, "a polite expression for the period when the writer, generally, gets screwed."

> I had a horrible experience with the production process. But in the end, I learned a lot, and maybe someone reading this will learn from what's happened to me. The screenplay had been chosen for production unanimously by a committee of professors and older students at F.S.U. I received a lot of praise for it. But the director added unnecessary scenes and

took out a lot of the flavor and humor, even to the point of making references to "going to church" when the family was written as Jewish. Ironically, in the editing process, virtually everything that he added was cut, so I felt somewhat vindicated. But there was something irretrievable that definitely did not make it on to the screen and that still makes me sad, even today.

"If you're very lucky as a writer," Ephron says, "you look at the director's movie and feel that it's your movie, too."

In the end, although she admires the film, Rachel cannot honestly say she feels that *Lena's Spaghetti* is her movie, too:

It did win a lot of awards. The production value was good for a student film. Some of the acting was good. The music was ambitious. The credits were ridiculously long, but they showed that a lot of people worked very hard to make *Lena's Spaghetti*—and worked for free. I feel good that I created a story that moved people to work so hard. It must have touched them on some level. But I never felt comfortable using it as a "calling card" to lead to other work after school because the film doesn't represent my style, my range, or my interests as a writer.

But the version of the screenplay published here is hers. It's the final script from my class and the one selected by the B.F.A. Thesis Committee.

Both the script and the film—though quite different—are wonderful works. The film, directed by Joe Greco, won First Place in the student drama category at the Columbus International Film & Video Festival; First Prize in the comedy category at the 26th Annual Canadian International Film/Video Festival; the OSU Photography & Cinema Alumni Society Award, and the Crystal Reel (First Place) for Best Cinematography and Best Actor at the Florida Motion Picture & Television Association. *Lena's Spaghetti* has also been screened at numerous film festivals at home and abroad, including Telluride.

After graduating from F.S.U., Rachel worked in film production in Los Angeles, then went on to study screenwriting at USC, the Charles University in Prague, Conservatoire Audiovisuel (CEEA) in Paris, and earned her MFA in screenwriting from UCLA. Rachel's writing has garnered several international awards, and she is a two-time recipient of the Academy of Motion Pictures Arts and Sciences student screenwriting grant. She sold her screenplay, *Neither Wolf Nor Dog*, and moved to Paris, France, under a writing fellowship from the Franco-American Fund.

Currently, Rachel is working as a writer and producer in Los Angeles. She has created advertising campaigns for films such as *Ocean's 12*, *The Wild*, *Anchorman*, *Eternal Sunshine of the Spotless Mind*, *The Triplets of Belleville*, *City of God*, *Monster*, *Charlie's Angels*, and *Meet the Parents*. She is also the proud godmother of a very special little boy named Will.

LENA'S SPAGHETTI
By Rachel A. Witenstein

FADE IN:

MAIL. Two hands leaf through a stack of mail. They come across a PICTURE POSTCARD. It fills the SCREEN. A MAN kisses an almost transparent angel. The postcard flips over. It is signed in deep red ink: "With oceans of love, and a kiss on every little ripple, Rosalie."

INT. MAILTRUCK—DAY

Settled back into his seat, postman HERBERT MACK, 33, is absorbed in reading the postcard. He waves it in front of his nose and inhales perfume. He sighs, slips the postcard into a bundle of mail and leans out the window to put it all in a mailbox. From the sack beside him, he grabs a new bundle and leafs through it. He finds another postcard to read.

EXT. MAILTRUCK—DAY

Another mailtruck approaches. The driver, ADELE, inches up beside Herbie for the big scare. She HONKS.

                    ADELE
     Caught ya, Herb!

Herb jumps, puts the mail in a mailbox, watches her drive away.

                                        CUT TO:

EXT. QUAINT SUBURBAN NEIGHBORHOOD—DAY

Herbie's truck passes Southern homes. We hold on HANNAH GOLDIN, 13, who sits on a swing hung from a tree, writing in a notebook. A moving truck pulls out of the driveway. CAROLINE AND STANLEY GOLDIN carry bags to their car. THUNDER grumbles.

                    CAROLINE
     Come on, Hannie! It's time to go!

Hannah scowls and scribbles furiously in the notebook.

                                        CUT TO:

CREDITS ROLL:

INT. GOLDIN FAMILY CAR—DAY

The Goldin family car starts and pulls out of the driveway. Rain runs down the back window as Hannah forlornly watches her house disappear.

DISSOLVE TO:

EXT. TO INT. MAILTRUCK—DAY

Through windshield wipers we see Herbie trying to stuff mailboxes without getting wet. He drops a few pieces of mail into the swirling gutter stream. He splashes out into the rain and chases the mail down the street.

DISSOLVE TO:

EXT. HIGHWAY—SUNSET

With the city in the background, the car drives out of town.

DISSOLVE TO:

INT. THE GOLDIN FAMILY CAR—NIGHT

Sunk real low in the back seat, Hannah stares out the window. We hear Caroline SINGING soft harmonies with the RADIO. After giving her mother an annoyed look, Hannah dons headphones, plays a tape.

DISSOLVE TO:

EXT. HERBIE'S APARTMENT—DAY

Wearing his postal uniform, Herbie walks to his mailbox. He opens it, peers inside and closes it, empty-handed.

END CREDITS.

CUT TO:

INT. HERBIE'S APARTMENT—DAY

Canvasses are stacked against the walls. Some are hung. None of the artwork is figurative. It should reflect a mind in isolation. An empty canvas rests on an easel. A table is cluttered with painter's paraphernalia. The shades are drawn. COLA PLUM, Herbie's stylish, fragile mother, opens the shades. Disturbed, she flips through the stacks of artwork. Her concern increases as she inspects a dark, shadowy work. She shakes her head slowly. Herbie enters, already unbuttoning his postal shirt.

> COLA
> (smiling bravely and kissing him)
> Darling. How are you?

She licks her thumb to wipe the lipstick off his cheek.

> HERBIE
> Mom. What a surprise.

> COLA
> I was just passing by . . . I was looking at your paintings, Herbert.

> HERBIE
> Oh. Well?

> COLA
> Very . . . Powerful . . . dark and, well, a little dismal, don't you think, sweetheart?

> HERBIE
> You see what you want to see, Mom. I didn't ask you to look.

> COLA
> Let's just stop this right now. I didn't come here to quarrel.
> (pulls a number out of her purse)
> Herbert, Evelyn's daughter is getting a divorce.

> HERBIE
> Oh, I'm sorry it didn't work out.

Cola stares at Herbie incredulously. Herbie exits to the kitchen. Cola follows, calling after him.

> COLA
> Sorry?

INT. HERBIE'S KITCHEN—SAME

Herbie pulls out a can of spaghetti and opens it with an electric can opener. He starts eating it right out of the can.

> COLA
> She's going to be single! Use a plate.

Herbie dumps the spaghetti on a plate.

> COLA
> Here's her number. You should—

Herbie exits with the plate. Cola follows.

INT. HERBIE'S APARTMENT—DAY

Herbie sits down at the art table and eats amongst the paints and brushes. Cola stands across from him.

> COLA
> Can't you allow me just this small happiness? I'd like to see you paint something . . . beautiful for a change!

> HERBIE
> Mother, I'm sorry. I'm just not interested in that kind of thing.

> COLA
> I see. Should I have gotten her ex-husband's number instead?

> HERBIE
> What?

> COLA
> I've seen your painting, Herbert. Not even one picture of a woman!

Cola exits, leaving Herbie speechless.

CUT TO:

INT. HERBIE'S APARTMENT—NIGHT

ANGLE ON: Herbie's eyes. We pull out to see him
slouched by his easel, tapping his teeth with a dry
paintbrush. The dirty plate is next to him. He stares at
the blank canvas. With one sweep, he knocks it off the
easel, revealing the naked window behind it. He sees his
neighbors through the window of another apartment.
Herbie crosses to the window to get a better look.

EXT. TO INT. DANNY AND JULIE'S APARTMENT—SAME

HERBIE'S POV: DANNY holds the ladder as JULIE climbs
it to unscrew a dead lightbulb. From the ground, he
hands her a fresh one. The window brightens. He climbs
the other side of the ladder to face her. They kiss and
descend the ladder, somehow still joined at the lips. The
lights go off.

INT. HERBIE'S APARTMENT—SAME

Frustrated, Herbie sighs and pulls down the shades.

CUT TO:

EXT. APARTMENT COMPLEX IN HERBIE'S ROUTE—DAY

Herbie stands beside his truck, stuffing the grid of
mailboxes. A young couple, FORD and AMY, approach
him hand-in-hand.

                    AMY
      Got anything for apartment "M"?

Herbie hands them a letter.

                    AMY
      Ford, it's from you?

                    FORD
      Read it, Honey.

Herbie stands next to Amy, waiting for her to move. He
tries to tell her, but can't. Oblivious, she leans back
against the mailboxes to tear open the envelope.

                    HERBIE
Uh, excuse me . . .

                    AMY
              (reading the letter)
Amy Madison. I love you with everything I have.
Will you marry me?
              (looks at Ford)
Really, Sugar?

                    FORD
Yes, Angel. Will you marry me?

                    HERBIE
              (under his breath)
I can't believe this!

                    AMY
              (throws her arms around him)
Of course I will! Yes! I do I do I do!

Herbie tries to sneak behind the smooching couple. Amy
bumps him.

                    AMY
Oh, I'm sorry. I didn't realize . . .

                    HERBIE
It's okay.

Herbie watches as Ford and Amy walk back to their
apartment.

                                        CUT TO:

INT. NEWSPAPER BUILDING—DAY

People swarm around the lobby. Herbie stands in a long
line of CUSTOMERS under a SIGN which reads:
"Classifieds: Employment, Lost & Found, Pets,
Automobiles, Garage Sales, Personals, Obituaries." He
steps forward, accidentally kicking the back of the shoe
of the woman, GINA, in front of him. She gives him a
cold look.

                    HERBIE
So sorry.

The clerk, CLARK, is a bodybuilder, a real "stud." He fills out a form as Gina dictates, but he is actually busy checking her out.

> CLARK

Reward?

> GINA

Of course.

Adele passes though the office, carrying a package. She is in uniform, but her knee socks are bunched around her ankles. She walks with a spring in her step and has sparkling eyes. She spots Herbie.

> ADELE

Hiya, Herb!

> HERBIE

Hi, um . . .

> ADELE

Adele. Read any good postcards lately? Just kiddin', everyone does it. Well, I do anyway. Whatcha doin'?

> CLARK

Can I help you?

> HERBIE

Oh, I uh, lost my cat.

> ADELE

Wow, how sad. What's he look like?

> HERBIE

Well, he's . . . black. And he looks pretty much like a cat.

> CLARK

Reward?

> ADELE

Well, I'll keep my eye out. Bye.

She walks away, balancing the packages precariously on her head.

                    CLARK
     Hey! Reward?

                    HERBIE
     No. No reward. No cat.

                    CLARK
     What?

                    HERBIE
                  (quietly)
     An ad. A personal ad.

Clark snorts a laugh. He pulls out a different form and slaps it down on the counter with a hand.

                                        CUT TO:

EXT. HARVEST STREET FAIR—DAY

A FERRIS WHEEL. A CAROUSEL. And LOTS OF PEOPLE. Three school buses line the street. Bouncing above a CROWD of jostling fairgoers, Hannah Goldin jumps on the trampoline of the HUMAN FLYTRAP. She is dressed in a velcro suit. Small earrings frame her clean face. Each of her fingernails is painted a different color. A DJ broadcasts live over speakers, piping GRUNGE MUSIC through the sunny fair. Hannah smiles at ADAM, a fourteen-year-old teddy bear of a boy. He tosses a baseball and watches with JARRETT, DICKIE, and a group of four BOYS. The radio music tails out.

                    DJ (O.S.)
     We're havin' a blast here at the Harvest Fair! So
     come on down! Bring the kids!

                    DICKIE
                  (elbowing Adam)
     That new girl likes you, Adam!

All except Jarrett laugh. Jarrett scowls.

                              DJ (O.S.)
I think they're ready for a new volunteer at the
dunk tank! Only two tickets gets you the chance
to get this lovely Hooter's girl wet!

Adam and the boys dart through the crowd over to the
dunk tank. Hannah turns as she bounces, helplessly
watching Adam walk away.

                              DJ (O.S.)
We've got lots of rides, lots of games, and of
course, what fair would be complete without the
Human Flytrap!

Frustrated, Hannah flings herself at the velcro wall and
sticks, spread eagle. She laughs, then realizes that she is
unable to move and panics. She yanks furiously with her
arms and legs.

                              DJ (O.S.)
Oh my God! A little boy is stuck to the wall for
our enjoyment! Everybody look!

The crowd looks and LAUGHS. Hannah closes her eyes
and grits her teeth. Her face burns.

                              DJ (O.S.)
Oh, sorry, a little girl! I didn't see the earrings.
Gotta come out folks . . .

                                               CUT TO:

INT. SCHOOL BUS—SAME DAY

Hannah sits alone on the empty school bus, scribbling
furiously in a journal.

                         HANNAH (V.O.)
I hate this school. I hate Adam. I hate our new
house. I hate velcro. I hate my nose—

The greasy BUS DRIVER opens the door. Hannah slams
the notebook shut as kids with carnival prizes pass her
seat. Adam passes without noticing her. Jarrett stops
next to Hannah.

                            JARRETT
                       (yelling to the back)
Dickie Nelson, get the hell out of my seat!

He notices Hannah and snorts a laugh before pushing to the back.

EXT. SCHOOL BUS—SAME DAY

Hannah gets off the bus alone, her backpack over her shoulder. As the bus pulls away, Jarrett and his gang are seen pressed up spread eagle against the back window, imitating Hannah. She runs for home.

                                        CUT TO:

EXT. NEIGHBORHOOD STREET—SAME DAY

Hannah runs down the middle of the road. She stops to catch her breath. A MOVING VAN drives by. She hurls a rock at it as it passes.

                    HANNAH (V.O.)
          Hello, I'm back. Dad says I hate everything
          because I'm thirteen and that I need to put things
          in perspective.

                                        CUT TO:

EXT. RAILROAD TRACK—SAME DAY

Hannah kicks rocks along the tracks, still toting her backpack.

                    HANNAH (V.O.)
          So I've decided to start writing to "Lena," since
          when I'm older, I'll be a famous actress with lots
          of perspective, and "Lena" will be my stage name.

                                        CUT TO:

EXT. HANNAH'S HOUSE—DAY

Hannah trudges through the yard of her new house. She opens the front door and disappears inside, slamming the door behind her.

                    HANNAH (V.O.)
          So, dear Lena, I'm sure you can remember, this
          has been the most humiliating day of my life.

CUT TO:

INT. HANNAH'S ROOM—NIGHT

Hannah sits on her bed under a SMALL READING LAMP,
writing in her journal. She closes it, CLICKS OFF the
lamp and walks to her desk to put her journal away.
Moonlight spills into her room.

EXT. TO INT. HANNAH'S BEDROOM—SAME

Looking very small and young in her nightgown, Hannah
stares out her window.

> HANNAH (V.O.)
> Lena, you are the only friend I have.

FADE OUT:

FADE IN:

INT. HANNAH'S BEDROOM—NEXT MORNING

Hannah lies on the very edge of her bed, awake. The bed
is covered with mounds of meticulously arranged stuffed
animals. The room is filled with unpacked boxes. Caroline
pokes her head in as she buzzes the house. She wears a
smart business suit with no makeup.

> CAROLINE
> Hannah! I'm not going to tell you again.

> HANNAH
> (weakly)
> But Mom, I don't feel good.

Stanley enters the room with a newspaper in one hand,
a thermometer in the other. He places his lips on her
forehead.

> STANLEY
> You don't feel warm. What hurts?

> HANNAH
> My stomach and my head. And I have the chills.

> STANLEY
> Let's take your temp, Babe.

He sticks the thermometer in her mouth.

> CAROLINE (O.S.)
> She's normal, Doctor Goldin.

> STANLEY
> (calling to Caroline)
> With our genes? I doubt it.
> (Hannah rolls her eyes)
> Keep it under your tongue.

Stanley sits at the front of the bed and opens the newspaper. He offers Hannah a section.

> STANLEY
> Got the old paper form back home. Comics?

She puts them aside. Humming an opera, Stanley reads but feels Hannah looking at him. He looks up and speaks after a pause.

> STANLEY
> I know this move was hard on you, Babe.

Hannah's eyes fill with tears but do not spill over.

> STANLEY
> But there's only room for so many breast
> surgeons in one town. Do you understand?

Hannah nods. Stanley looks a little relieved. He tries something.

> STANLEY
> But you know what? I'll tell you a secret if you
> promise not to tell any of my patients. They're all
> beautiful.

Hannah rolls her eyes. Stanley plays now. He acts out the following shapes of breasts to Hannah while he sings this rhyme.

> STANLEY
> There are tubular boobies and conical domes.
> Ptotic droopies and little young ones . . .

Hannah laughs. She spits the thermometer out.

> HANNAH
> Dad!

Stanley picks up the thermometer and reads it.

                    STANLEY
        Well, Mom's right, kiddo. You're normal.
        Congratulations.

                    HANNAH
        Daddy, I feel sick. Can't you take my word for it?

Hannah gives him puppy dog eyes.

                                            CUT TO:

INT. HANNAH'S BEDROOM—LATER

Hannah jumps on the bed. She flops onto her stomach,
picks up the comics, looks them over with a straight
face. She turns the page and sees the personal ads. She
brightens as she reads.

THE PERSONAL AD FILLS THE SCREEN:

"Like to write? Single male seeks unique female for pen-
pal. Please write: Herbert Mack. 8013-B Duck Lane.
Savannah, Georgia, 41256."

MUSIC SWELLS.

                                            CUT TO:

INT. HERBIE'S APARTMENT—NIGHT

Herbie stares at the blank canvas. The phone RINGS.
Suddenly inspired, he feverishly mixes paints. After four
RINGS, his ANSWERING MACHINE can be heard.

                    HERBIE (V.O.)
        Hello, this is Herbert Mack. I'm not home, Mom.
        I'm on a date with Cindy Crawford. And no, I
        haven't gotten a letter yet.

Herbie strokes a deep blue on the canvas. The machine
BEEPS.

                    COLA (V.O.)
        Herbert, change your message!

He stops and looks at what he has done. Dissatisfied, he opens a tube of black and paints over it.

>   COLA (V.O.)
> What if I was a girl calling? It sounds like the only calls you ever get are from your mother. Call me when you get home.

Herbie finishes painting the entire canvas black.

FADE INTO THE BLACK:

IN BLACKNESS:

The sound of RAIN ON ALUMINUM is heard.

INT. HERBIE'S MAILBOX—DAY

Herbie opens the SQUEAKY mailbox door, throwing light into the deep cavern. It is empty. Herbie's disappointed, wet face fills the hole. He slams the mailbox shut.

EXT. MAIL TRUCK OUTSIDE HERBIE'S APARTMENT—DAY

Settled back into her seat, Adele is absorbed in a postcard. She wears her postal uniform but looks more polished than usual. The sound of a DOOR closing startles her. She sees Herbie exiting his apartment. She smoothes her eyebrows. Herbie jogs to the mail truck.

>   HERBIE
> Anything for 8013-B?
>   (recognizes Adele)
> Oh, hello. When did you get this route?

>   ADELE
>   (hands him his mail)
> A while ago. I hope you found your cat, 'cause I saw a black one. On the road.

>   HERBIE
> Uh . . . Oh! No. Nope.
>   (holds up the postcard)
> Did you, uh . . .

>   ADELE
> Yeah. She sounds nice.

CUT TO:

INT. HERBIE'S APARTMENT—DAY

Herbie runs into his apartment, reading the postcard.
After a moment he picks up the phone and dials.

                    COLA (V.O.)
    Hello?

                    HERBIE
    Mom! I got a letter!

                    COLA (V.O.)
    Finally. From a woman?

                    HERBIE
    Yes from a woman!

                    COLA (V.O.)
    Well, read it to me.

                    HERBIE
    Okay. "Dear Herbie. Hi. I am writing because I
    usually write myself, but I thought it would be a
    nice change to actually get a response.
            (he chuckles)
    I'm an actress. I'm from the West and I miss my
    home in the mountains. My favorite food is
    spaghetti. I have two Siberian Huskies with ice
    blue eyes, named Lapis and Lazuli. What about
    you? Lena."

                    COLA (V.O.)
    That's it? What does she look like? Did she send a
    photo?

He waves the postcard in front of his nose and inhales,
grinning.

                    HERBIE
    She's beautiful, Mom.

MUSIC BEGINS: It is a simple, yet lyrical piece.

                                        CUT TO:

EXT. HANNAH'S HOUSE—DAY

Hannah sits on the front steps, writing in her journal. A
mail truck pulls up to the house. She runs to it. The

POSTMAN hands her a bundle of mail. She pulls out a letter on the way back to the house and slips it in her journal.

INT. HANNAH'S HOUSE—SAME

Hannah enters the house. It is a mess with boxes and furniture in the wrong places. There is a grand piano in the foyer. She puts the mail on top and squeezes past it.

> CAROLINE (O.S.)
> (calling from the kitchen)
> Time for lunch, Hannie!

> HANNAH
> Not hungry.

Caroline appears behind the kitchen counter with a phone propped up to her ear by her shoulder. She places a bowl on the counter.

> CAROLINE
> I made Spaghetti O's.

Hannah takes the bowl without her mother noticing.

INT. HANNAH'S BEDROOM—SAME DAY

Hannah closes her bedroom door, flops down on her bed and tears open the letter. She eats as she reads it, delighted.

> HANNAH
> Dear Lena. I can't believe how lucky I am. Your letter was wonderful. You are a charming and witty woman. Life in the theatre sounds so exciting. It's funny, the only thing I cook is spaghetti . . . and not very well. Could you send me your recipe? Herbie.

Wide-eyed, Hannah drops her spoon into the almost empty bowl of Spaghetti O's.

CUT TO:

INT. HERBIE'S KITCHEN—NIGHT

The flame of a gas burner IGNITES. Onions are
simmering, tomatoes are basting, water is boiling. The
counter is a mess with spices and dirty cutlery. Holding
a postcard, Herbie carefully measures ingredients into a
steaming pot of sauce. He opens a can of pineapple
chunks, checks the postcard again and doubtfully stirs
them in the pot. He tastes a spoonful and smiles.

ANGLE ON: The back of the postcard fills the screen. It
reads: LENA'S SPAGHETTI, and is followed by a recipe.

DISSOLVE TO:

INT. SCHOOL BUS—DAY

ANGLE ON: A small painting of a mountain range.
Hannah sits alone among the CHAOS of the school bus,
leaning her head against the window, staring dreamily at
the painting. Jarrett passes by her seat and gives her a
dirty look. She takes out a postcard and begins to write.

> HANNAH (V.O.)
> Dear Herbie. Thank you for the mountains. When I
> look at them, I breath in golden air and exhale
> silver.

DISSOLVE TO:

INT. MAIL TRUCK—DAY

A PILE OF MAIL is stuffed into a mailbox. Herbie stuffs
mailboxes without reading any postcards.

> HANNAH (V.O.)
> I can see through the ceiling to the stars.

EXT. MAIL TRUCK IN A SUBURBAN NEIGHBORHOOD—
DAY

Herbie drives down the beautifully foliated road.

DISSOLVE TO:

INT. HANNAH'S HOUSE—DAY

Hannah helps her father hang a swing in a tree in the
front yard.

> HERBIE (V.O.)
> Dear Lena, Even though it's only once a week, it's
> so good to talk to someone who understands me,
> who thinks the same way I do.

DISSOLVE TO:

INT. HERBIE'S APARTMENT—NIGHT

Herbie sits at his easel, rereading a postcard. He sets it
on top of a stack of postcards and letters, and begins to
paint.

> HERBIE (V.O.)
> I wish I could see your play. I'm sure you'll make
> a great Juliet. I'll be thinking of you. Break a leg,
> Lena.

MUSIC ENDS.

CUT TO:

INT. SCHOOL BUS—DAY

SOUNDS OF CHAOS. Hannah sits in her usual seat, alone,
reading a letter. Across the back seat, Jarrett, Adam,
Dickie and a few other BOYS play a bouncy game of
poker, using a backpack as a table. Several CLASSMATES
watch, hanging over the back seat.

> JARRETT
> (chewing on an unlit cigar)
> Adam, you in? Don't be a wuss.

The bus hits a bump, the cards go flying.

> ADAM
> I'm not playing unless we get a flatter table. This
> sucks.

Jarrett takes the cigar out of his mouth and stands.

> JARRETT
> How about your girlfriend?
> (bellows to Hannah)
> Hey!

Jarrett wads up a piece of paper and tosses it. It lands
on Herbie's letter. Hannah quickly folds it into the
envelope.

JARRETT

Hey! New Girl!

Hannah is caught by the address on the envelope. It reads: "Miss Lena Gold." She takes a deep breath, then stands to face Jarrett.

HANNAH

My name is not "New Girl." It's—

JARRETT

—New Boy? That's right! Adam says we need something flat to play on, New Boy. Any Ideas?

Jarrett's BOYS laugh, give him five, and do the "spread eagle."

BUS DRIVER

No standing on the bus!

HANNAH
(walking towards him)

Yes, Jarrett, I do have an idea. Your flat Neanderthal head!

The entire bus reacts in amazement.

JARRETT
(steps into the aisle)

Eat me!

HANNAH

Barely a mouthful!

STUDENTS

Ooooooooooo!

ANGLE ON MIRROR: The bus driver's eyes dart to the back of the bus.

BUS DRIVER

Sit down, both of you!

They stand eye-to-eye.

BUS DRIVER

Jarrett Buxell! Sit down or I'll write you up.

Defeated, Jarrett sits. His BOYS react, disappointed.

> BUS DRIVER
>
> You too, Girl!

> HANNAH
> (to the driver)
>
> Hannah!

> BUS DRIVER
>
> Sit down or walk!

She doesn't move. The entire bus is quiet. Everyone looks at Hannah with wonder.

> BUS DRIVER
>
> Now!

Hannah sets her jaw.

CUT TO:

EXT. BUS—DAY

The bus WHEEZES as the door opens. Hannah trudges down the stairs and starts walking with her head down. As the bus drives off, we see the faces of her classmates, including a girl, JJ, staring at her out the window.

CUT TO:

EXT. HERBIE'S APARTMENT—DAY

As Adele drives up, she see Herbie leaning up against his mailbox. With paint smudged on his face, he whistles merrily as he waits for the delivery. She checks her hair, leans out the window, hands him his junk mail.

> ADELE
>
> Hiya Herb.

> HERBIE
> (flipping through the mail)
> Hey . . . Isn't it Wednesday?

> ADELE
>
> Can't fool you! Yep, it's Lena Day. And it's a goodie, too.

She holds out the postcard, looking at him oddly. He grabs it but she doesn't let go. She rubs the side of her nose. He doesn't get it. She wipes the paint off of his face.

DISSOLVE TO:

INT. CAROLINE'S BATHROOM—DAY

Hannah sits on the counter and opens a fashion magazine as if it were a Bible. She holds it up to the mirror and mimics the model's expression. She opens a drawer full of Caroline's makeup.

HERBIE (V.O.)
...My mother doesn't believe that you're real. She thinks I'm writing letters to myself. Will you send a picture to prove...

ANGLE ON: HANNAH'S FEATURES

She applies loads of lipstick, eye shadow, blush, etc...

HANNAH (V.O.)
...will not send a photo, because I believe that penpals should remain a bit mysterious. But I will describe myself to you. I have long black hair...

Hannah spies a box of tissues.

ANGLE ON: BOX OF KLEENEX AS HANNAH PULLS OUT TISSUES.

CUT TO:

EXT./INT. CAROLINE'S BATHROOM—LATER

Caroline approaches the bathroom and opens the door, revealing Hannah. She spins around, stuffed to a size "double D." Caroline jumps back, startled.

CAROLINE
Hannah! You scared the crap out of me! Look at you.
(looks her over and smiles)
You want me to teach you how to put it on right?

Hannah nods. Caroline sets down her purse and things and reaches for a washcloth and soap. She wipes the makeup off Hannah's face.

CUT TO:

INT. HANNAH'S BEDROOM—NIGHT

Stanley and Caroline bend over Hannah's bed to kiss her good night. Her room, unpacked now, looks like a little girl's room.

> STANLEY
> (picks up a stuffed dog)
> Don't let ol' Lapis push you out of bed tonight.

He kisses her forehead.

> HANNAH
> He's Lazuli.

> CAROLINE
> Good night, Dolly. I had fun today. Did you?

Hannah shrugs, then grins. Caroline kisses her cheek.

> CAROLINE
> Sweet dreams.

Their arms around each other, Caroline and Stanley turn off the light and exit. Moonlight shines on her bed.

> HERBIE (V.O.)
> Dear Lena. Last night I dreamt that we met. I had cooked for you a nest of spaghetti the size of a bathtub. You insisted on throwing it to the ceiling to see if it was done. It never stuck . . .

CUT TO:

INT. HERBIE'S APARTMENT—NIGHT

Herbie sits at his easel reading a postcard.

> HANNAH (V.O.)
> Dear Herbie. Sometime tonight have you looked up at this beautiful full moon? If you have, then
> (MORE)

> HANNAH (CONT'D)
> we've seen each other, because I've been watching
> it too . . .

He sets the postcard next to the canvas and continues
painting.

CUT TO:

EXT. RAILROAD TRACKS—SUNSET

Hannah lies back on the hill, wearing a flowing skirt and
a bit of makeup. Her hair is longer. She tears open a
letter and begins reading. As she does, her face becomes
worried.

A TRAIN IS OFF IN THE DISTANCE.

> HERBIE (V.O.)
> Lena, have you ever noticed the way stars seem
> to fade if you look straight at them? Well, I need
> to look straight at you, Lena.
>> (she sits straight up)
> All I know is that you are an actress, you have a
> beautiful mind, beautiful handwriting, your
> perfume smells like baby powder and . . . I think
> I'm in love with you.

Hannah stops reading. THE SOUND OF THE TRAIN
APPROACHING. She runs down the hill. The train rushes
past as Hannah runs off.

EXT. STREET—SUNSET

Hannah runs up the street and driveway to her house.

> HERBIE (V.O.)
> What was your childhood like? Do you like red or
> white wine? Angel hair or fettuccini? How old are
> you? When can I meet you?

Hannah runs into her house and SLAMS the door behind
her.

DISSOLVE TO:

EXT. HANNAH'S HOUSE—NIGHT

                                                    CUT TO:

INT. HANNAH'S BEDROOM—NIGHT

Hannah sits on her bed, rereading the letter. There is a
KNOCK at her door. She hides it under her animals.
Stanley enters wearily and kisses her good night.

                        STANLEY
    Sweet dreams, babe. I'm going to bed.

                        HANNAH
    Okay.
               (Stanley walks to the door)
    Dad? Um . . . Nothing.

                        STANLEY
    'Night, kiddo.
               (sighs)
    I guess I shouldn't call you that anymore. You're
    really growing up fast.

                        HANNAH
    I am?

                        STANLEY
    Yeah. And you were such a cute kid. Whatever
    happened?
               (he chuckles)
    Don't let ol' Lazuli push you out of bed tonight.

He exits. Hannah moves to her desk and spreads out the
collection of Herbie's letters. She puts her head in her
hands, then looks at herself in the mirror and steels
herself for the task ahead . . . She picks up a postcard
and her purple pen and writes.

                        HANNAH
    Dear Herbie.

                                                    CUT TO:

EXT. SCHOOL BUS—MORNING

ANGLE ON: Hannah's face in the harsh morning light as
she runs for the bus. We hear the RUMBLE of the school
bus's engine. She pauses at the corner to drop the
postcard into a mailbox, then disappears into the school
bus. The doors close in our face.

CUT TO:

INT. Herbie's APARTMENT—SUNSET

The finished "Lena painting" fills the screen. It is a nude,
reclining female. Her head is tipped back in profile, her
hair cascades abundantly over her body. It tangles with
and becomes a forkful of spaghetti which she holds over
her open mouth as if it were grapes. It looks vaguely
like Adele. Propped up against it is the new postcard
from "Lena." The phone is RINGING. We HEAR Herbie
pick it up.

> HERBIE (O.S.)
> (softly)
> Hello.

> COLA (O.S.)
> (heard faintly on the other end)
> Herbert, Evelyn and her daughter are meeting us
> for lunch on Sunday. Don't say no . . . do it for me
> . . . as a favor . . .

Herbie stands in front of the painting, the phone to his
ear. He reaches for the postcard. Cola's voice FADES as
we HEAR . . .

> HANNAH (V.O.)
> Dear Herbie. Guess what! I got a job with a
> touring company. I won't have an address for a
> while, it could be years if the show goes well. But
> you have been a magnificent friend, Herbie, and
> artist. I'll never ever forget you. Your pen pal,
> Lena.

> HERBIE
> All right, Mom. I'll meet her. I've got to go. Bye.

Herbie hangs up.

CUT TO:

INT. SCHOOL BUS—MORNING

WE MOVE with Hannah down the aisle as she heads for
her usual seat. She stops dead in her tracks. Her seat is
not empty. JJ, a girl with glasses and a soccer ball,
stares out the window. Hannah looks around. There are
no empty seats.

> HANNAH
> (cautiously)
>> You saving this seat?

> JJ
>> No.

CUT TO:

EXT. HERBIE'S APARTMENT—DAY

Herbie walks across the parking lot with groceries under his arm. He sees Adele's truck turning into the parking lot. He ducks behind some bushes, unsure of what to do. Adele gets out of the truck to stuff mailboxes. She has a new hat. It is fairly outrageous, but she wears it with style. She looks radiant. Herbie finally stands up from the bushes.

> HERBIE
>> Hi.

Adele jumps slightly. They are face-to-face, closer than they have ever been.

> ADELE
>> Hi, Herb.

There is an awkward moment.

> ADELE
>> I'm sorry about Lena. She might write soon.

> HERBIE
>> She might.

> ADELE
>> Well, see ya.

> HERBIE
>> I like your hat, by the way. It's a great color.

> ADELE
> (touches the hat)
>> Oh, do you? Wow. Thanks. It's my birthday.

                         HERBIE
It's your birthday?

                         ADELE
Yeah.

                         HERBIE
How old are you?

                         ADELE
Um . . . twenty-nine. Hah! No, actually, I'm thirty-three.

                         HERBIE
No kidding. Me too. Hey, um . . . would you want to grab something to eat? Just as friends, I mean. Or dinner? Do you like Italian?

                         ADELE
Oh wow. Yeah, I do. I'll pick you up at seven?

                         HERBIE
I'll cook.

                                        DISSOLVE TO:

EXT. BUS STOP—DAY

Hannah runs off the bus, followed by JJ. JJ gives the soccer ball a swift kick. The girls chase it down the sun-dappled road together.

                                        FADE TO BLACK:

THE END.

15

COOL BREEZE
AND BUZZ

By Lani Sciandra

INTRODUCTION

Lani Sciandra wrote *Cool Breeze and Buzz* in my screenwriting class in 1994 and directed it for a B.F.A. Thesis Film in 1995. When I asked her how the screenplay changed during production, she said:

> We really didn't have a solid ending for the story throughout production—I had to communicate with and discover it through the actors—within the guidelines of the written scenes we re-invented as we went along—we all had to believe it was happening—I was never really convinced of my own dialogue and drew upon the silence more than the words for meaning—in fact, it was Sally (Aunt Barbara) who came up with the non-dialogue exchange between her and Buzz in the last scene that represents the crystalline moment of under-standing for all of them, and solidifies the ending for me.

And the script continued to change in editing:

> There are certainly moments left in the film that don't quite land—tiny moments of trying to push meaning—since Jen-nifer (the editor) and I were still learning how to juxtapose images, the tendency was to relate the elements linearly—as we arrived at a fine cut, I became unsettled about what we had achieved—it felt stilted and forced, as if the motion were dragging itself—I thought it could propel itself more by cutting back the bulk—dismantle the safety net and trust the danger—we brought in our editing teacher Charlie Boyd to help deconstruct the narrative to a more visceral level—approaching it like a piece of music—despite great opposi-tion, we cut into it with effective results—it turned out to be a monumental lesson in identifying with and nurturing (my) instinct.

In 1995, *Cool Breeze and Buzz* won the Gold Award in the Student Category at Worldfest Charleston and the Gold Award at Worldfest Houston. In 1996, it was the winner of the Independent Film Channel Student Film Showcase; the CINE Eagle Award (Preprofessional/Amateur); the OSU Photography and Cinema Alumni Society Award from the Columbus International Film & Video Festival; and the Student Award at the Florida Film Festival. Also in 1996, *Cool Breeze and Buzz* was named Best Narrative at the Big Muddy Film Festival; Best Narrative Film at the Utah Film and Video Festival; the Trophy Winner for Movies On A Shoestring at the Rochester International Independent Film Festival, and best film in the dramatic category at the Tacoma Tortured Artists Festival. In 1997, it won the Juror's Choice Award at the Victoria Independent Short Film & Video Festival in Canada. In addition, *Cool Breeze and Buzz* has been screened at film festivals worldwide, including the AFI Los Angeles International Film Festival in 1996 and the Women in the Director's Chair 16th Annual International Film & Video Festival in 1997.

Lani is currently living in New York City. When I asked what she's been doing since *Cool Breeze and Buzz*, she said, "Macrame."

COOL BREEZE AND BUZZ
By Lani Sciandra

FADE IN:

BLACK SCREEN

We HEAR four long, deep BREATHS (CREDITS BEGIN)

CUT TO:

EXT. ST. MARK'S RIVER—DAY

CLOSE ON PAULA MCKINNEY

13, up to her shoulders in the water. She takes four
more slow BREATHS then quickly ducks under water.

INDIAN SITAR MUSIC FADES IN AS CAMERA HOLDS ON
WATER

until Paula emerges from under the surface, out of breath,
having uncovered a broken arrowhead. The year is 1967.
Dense woods draped in moss align the river's edge. Nearby
is a small dilapidated wooden dock garnished with apple
snails. A HERON combs the hyacinths on the bank for a
meal. Paula is petite with a gritty edge about her as she
sits on the bank, her hair bleached from the sun, cleaning
her findings from the river. She's got on a bathing suit, a
pair of low-top Chuck's and scrapes on either knee. She
holds up a dark specimen.

ANGLE ON SPECIMEN

It is a piece of a large jawbone, blackened from years
under water. The teeth are still intact. She then places it
in an old cigar box.

ANGLE ON CIGAR BOX

There is a fading b/w photograph of a young couple on
the beach amongst various small artifacts.

THE MUSIC FADES (CREDITS END)

We hear LOCUSTS in the canopy of trees above. In the
background is a silver Airstream trailer with a large
canopy laced with small party lanterns and windchimes.

AUNT BARBARA (O.S.)
(from the trailer)
Pau-la.

Her voice is DEEP AND RASPY. Paula doesn't answer and
continues.

AUNT BARBARA (O.S.)
(louder)
Paula!

Paula gathers her things and puts the findings in a
bucket and walks to the trailer. She sets the bucket down
before entering.

INT. TRAILER—DAY

It is a rather large-sized interior, adorned with a collage
of unmatching, outdated furniture and knick-knacks. A
large velvet painting of JFK centers over the TV. Paula
enters and the screen door SLAMS behind her. "The Ed
Sullivan Show" BLARES from the set as AUNT
BARBARA, 46, watches from the couch in a robe and
curlers wrapped in a pink scarf. She lights a cigarette.
Paula enters the kitchen and fixes a Kool-Aid.

AUNT BARBARA
(pointing toward kitchen)
Paula honey, grab me my purse. I need for ya t'
run up to the store fer me.

Paula grabs the purse off the counter and hands it to her.

PAULA
What'cha need?

Barb digs through her purse.

AUNT BARBARA
I need ya t' git me some Epsom salts.

She looks down to her foot.

AUNT BARBARA
My bunyons r'on fire.

Paula holds her hand out as Barbara counts change from
the bottom of her purse, extinguishing her cigarette in
the process.

> AUNT BARBARA
> An' I got a splittin' headache . . . Please pay
> attention when I call you, girl.
> (beat)
> Whew! This heat is unbearable.
> (handing her change)
> Jus' git the smallest one they got.

Paula guzzles down her drink, wipes her mouth with the
length of her arm then sets the glass in the sink. The
drink has left her with a Kool-Aid moustache. Barbara
reaches for her leather cigarette case and discovers it's
empty.

> AUNT BARBARA
> Ya' got any smokes?

> PAULA
> No, I've been bummin off'a you, 'member?

Barbara takes a quick check in the purse. No more
change.

> AUNT BARBARA
> (sighing)
> Well, the salts'll do.

Paula throws on a pullover raincoat and cut-offs over her
suit and exits. Barbara cringes as the screen door
SLAMS.

EXT. CANOPY DIRT ROAD—DAY

Paula is walking down the barren dirt road, her coat tied
at the waist. Suddenly, a large red CADILLAC
CONVERTIBLE zooms by from behind, blowing a dense
cloud of dust up.

> PAULA
> (shouting to car)
> Slow down before you kill somebody!

She begins coughing hysterically, brushing off the dust.

HER POV

of the Cadillac as it drives over a bridge and disappears
in the trail of dust.

INT. FLOYD'S KIT N' KABOODLE—DAY

Paula opens the door and the bell RINGS. It's a typical small town general store with short aisles and shelves of medication behind the counter. A large FAN with streamers attached blows in a corner. Paula thumbs through a comic book at the magazine rack.

> FLOYD
> (to someone O.S.)
> Kin I help ya' find sumpthin'?

Paula peers over the comic book down the aisle.

HER POV

She sees a BLACK MAN in a business suit perusing the snack aisle.

She looks back to Floyd, who's becoming increasingly uneasy. Paula quickly shoves the comic book into the front pocket of her coat, unnoticed, then quietly meanders about the store as the Black Man approaches the front counter to pay. Floyd hands him his change.

> BLACK MAN
> No, keep it.

The Black Man leaves, and Floyd shrugs off the courtesy and puts it back in the register. Paula suddenly appears at the register.

> FLOYD
> (startled)
> You nearly scared the wits outta me, little missy.

He leans in, his eyes following the Black Man out the door.

> FLOYD
> You kin never turn yer back on 'em. Rob ya blind ev'rtime.
> (turning to her; beat)
> Now, what kin I do fer ya'?

Paula displays a mischievous grin.

> PAULA
> (looking to shelves behind him)
> Um, yeah. I need a box'a Epsom salts, please.

                    FLOYD
     O-kay.

Just as he turns his back to scan the shelf, she reaches
for a pack of generic cigarettes on the counter.

                    FLOYD
                 (slowly)
     Epsom salts . . .
                 (grabbing box)
     Here ya'r—

                    PAULA
                 (overlapping)
     No! The uh, smaller one.

She quickly shoves the pack in her coat and pulls her
hand back just in time and smiles as if nothing
happened.

                    PAULA
                 (quickly)
     It's for my aunt.

                    FLOYD
     That'll be sixty-five cents.

She unloads the contents of her pocket onto the counter
and weeds through the change.

ANGLE ON CONTENTS

comprised of a bubble gum comic strip, a polished tiger-
eye stone, a Zippo lighter and strands of twine and lint.
Curiously, Floyd picks up the stone, but Paula quickly
rips it from his hand.

                    PAULA
     I'll take that.
                 (admiring it)
     It's my good luck rock. I found it. Cool, huh?

Floyd nods and counts the change.

                    FLOYD
     Fifty-nine, sixty . . . Sixty-five. It's all here.
                 (handing her the bag)
     Thank you.

                            PAULA
                      (taking bag)
              No, thank you.

She smiles and parades toward the door.

                            FLOYD
              A bit hot fer a coat don't 'cha think?

She stops in her tracks then turns.

                            PAULA
                      (beat)
              Nope.

She turns and exits.

EXT. TRAILER—DAY

ANGLE ON PAULA

skipping along the river's edge reading the comic book.
She reaches a clearing and the trailer comes into sight.

HER POV

of the trailer. The red Cadillac is parked in front.
She approaches the Caddy and proceeds to investigate.

CLOSE ON

A) her finger running along the side of the car through a
   thick layer of dust.
B) her hand wiggling the hood ornament.
C) the license plate on the front that reads "JACKPOT."

Then suddenly, we hear a MALE VOICE.

                      MALE VOICE (O.S.)
              Beauty, ain' she?

HER POV

of a man, BUZZ MCKINNEY, 42, standing in the door at
the top of the steps smoking a cigar.

                            BUZZ
                      (beat)
              Hey, Coolbreeze.

She drops the bag and freezes.

                    PAULA
              (staring up at him)
     Hey.

He stands in slacks and a tight short-sleeved v-neck.
Upon his belly, a huge brass buckle with a race horse
and a large ring on either pinky. Aunt Barbara appears
from behind him.

                 AUNT BARBARA
     Paula honey, yer daddy's come to see you.

There's an awkward pause.

                 AUNT BARBARA
     Buzz, you gotta be hungry from all that drivin'.
     What do ya say I fix us a nice lunch. How's that
     sound?

There is a pause, then Barb enters the trailer.

                    PAULA
              (nodding to the car)
     Nice wheels.

He walks down the steps toward the car.

                    BUZZ
                 (proudly)
     Won her in Atlantic City last Christmas.
                  (beat)
     Me an' a couple of poker buddies were runnin' the
     tables that night.

He smiles as he recalls the events. Paula listens.

                    BUZZ
     Little did we know, was some House big shot
     waitin' in the wings all night for his shot. By
     dawn, he finally
              (reenacting the man's movement)
     swaggered down a thick wad of 100s and
     challenges us a round, double or nothin'. So the
     boys elected me. An' I ain't never been one to
     turn down—

Aunt Barbara appears at the screen door.

                    AUNT BARBARA
                (overlapping)
        Ya'll gonna stand out there all day? Le's eat.

                      PAULA
                 (guessing)
        So, you bought the car with the money?

                      BUZZ
                 (grinning)
        Even better.

He straightens out the hood ornament and takes out a
handkerchief from his back pocket.

                      BUZZ
           (polishing the ornament)
        Beat him so bad he had to insist on another
        round. She's been mine ever since.

                      PAULA
                (enchanted)
        Cool.

He looks at her for a moment and smiles.

                      BUZZ
        Come on.

They head for the trailer.

INT. TRAILER—DAY

CLOSE ON PLATE

as Barbara places it on the table, covered with Spam
finger sandwiches and pigs-in-blankets. Toothpicks in
their centers. On the table, a jar of pickles, boiled
peanuts and ginger snaps.

                      BUZZ
                (poking fun)
        Barb, I see you haven't lost your touch.

                    AUNT BARBARA
        Oh, now you jus' back off. If I'da known I'd be
        entertainin'—

                    BUZZ
                 (overlapping)
        You'd still serve up the same slop.

They all dig in at the same time, each one scarfing as
much as possible off the plate. Conversation has come to
a standstill. We listen to them CHEWING their food.

                    AUNT BARBARA
        So where'd ya' say you were headed?

                    BUZZ
        Well, a colleague of mine in Miami gave me a tip
        that could very well make your little brother a
        very rich man.

ANGLE ON AUNT BARBARA

rolling her eyes.

ANGLE ON PAULA

listening.

                    AUNT BARBARA
                 (skeptical)
        An' what's this tip?

                    BUZZ
                 (beat)
        Vegas.

                    AUNT BARBARA
                 (flabbergasted)
        Las Vegas? Whatcha wanna move to the middle of
        the desert for?

                    BUZZ
                 (wiping his brow)
        So what! A little sun never killed no one. Can't be
        much worse than the swamp you're livin' in.

                    PAULA
                 (interrupting)
        I hear Vegas is wild!

                    AUNT BARBARA
        But it's the desert, fer Chrissake!

                                BUZZ
What's the difference? You're gonna sweat your
balls off either way.

Barb gives him a look for the comment.

                                BUZZ
                    (to Paula)
Sorry, honey.
                    (to Barb)
Look, Barb, I got a plan and it's fool-proof. It can't
fail.

                          AUNT BARBARA
A plan.

                                BUZZ
What can I say? Business has been good. And
right now, in the trunk of that car, I got enough
money for a down payment on a club of my own.

                          AUNT BARBARA
A what? A club? You know what kinda risk that
is? The things involved in something like that?
                    (beat)
And what if it don't work out. Where you gonna
go then?

                                BUZZ
Look, I'm tellin' ya', it's gonna work. It's got to
work. I can feel it, B.

He notices Paula is just playing with her food.

                                BUZZ
Hey, Coolbreeze.

Paula looks.

                                BUZZ
What do you say we go out tonight. The three of us.

                          AUNT BARBARA
Can't. Tonight's single's bingo at St. John's an' I
ain't never missed a night. But you two go, don't
worry about me.
                    (looking at watch)
Oh, heavens! It's nearly three-thirty!
                    (getting up)
I gotta get ready, do my hair . . .

Barb unties her scarf and scurries to the bathroom.

                    BUZZ
                 (to Paula)
     When's bingo?

                    PAULA
     Six.

They snicker.

                    BUZZ
     Wait here, I'll be right back.

He heads out the screen door to his car. Barbara pokes
her head out the bathroom door.

                    AUNT BARBARA
                 (indiscreetly)
     Paula, I think the two of you goin' out's a good
     idea. Give you some time alone to catch up.

She goes back in the bathroom. Buzz returns with a
large dress box and hands it to Paula.

                    PAULA
     For me?

She appears pleasantly surprised. She opens the box and
pulls out a frilly pink dress that looks suited for a six-
year-old. She holds it up with the tips of her fingers as if
afraid to touch it.

                    BUZZ
     Whatcha think?

                    PAULA
                 (hesitating)
     Wow. It's pink.

                    BUZZ
     You can wear it tonight!

                    PAULA
     But . . . I don't wear dresses.

                    BUZZ
                 (enthusiastically)
     It'll look great on you!

(pause)
Tell you what. I'll make a deal with you. You wear
the dress and we'll do anything you wanna do.

                    PAULA
              (surrendering)
Well . . .

                    BUZZ
Okay, great!
              (beat)
So, what's to do around here?

Paula looks at the hideous dress then looks to him
mischievously.

                                        CUT TO:

EXT. WOODS—DUSK

Paula is in the dress and her Chuck's seated on a log.
Buzz is knelt on the ground trying to light a fire with
matches that keep blowing out. The Caddy parked in the
background.

                    PAULA
              (handing her Zippo)
    Try this.

Buzz makes another unsuccessful attempt with the
lighter. Paula kneels down and gathers some dry grass
then takes the lighter, flips the lid and lights it in one
motion. The fire starts.

DISSOLVE TO:

EXT. WOODS—NIGHT

Paula and Buzz are roasting marshmallows over a bright
fire. Buzz SMACKS a bug on the back of his neck.

                    BUZZ
    Ya'ouch!

                    PAULA
    You get used to it.

There is a pause.

                    BUZZ
    So, uh . . . your Aunt Barb's been taking good care
    of ya'?

                    PAULA
Oh, yeah. She can have her moments, but I guess
I do, too. I take care of her, and she takes care of
me and all that junk. Yeah, she's cool.

                    BUZZ
Good, good . . . Glad to hear it.

                    PAULA
So you're really just passin' through then, on
your way to Las Vegas . . . Wow, how cool.

                    BUZZ
Y'well, I'm not just passin' through. I came to see
you. Is that cool?

                    PAULA
Oh, yeah. I just meant most people are just
passin' through anyway.
               (beat)
Woodville ain't nowhere anyone really wants to
be, they just gotta pass through us to get to
wherever it is they're goin'.

                    BUZZ
               (pause)
Y'know, I was a little afraid you weren't gonna
remember me.

                    PAULA
Really? I remember lots of things.

                    BUZZ
               (pleased)
Really? Like what?

                    PAULA
Like . . . I remember you used to have that real
long shaggy beard that used to itch so bad when
you picked me up.

                    BUZZ
               (amused)
Mmhmm.

He SMACKS another bug.

                    BUZZ
Dammit!

                    PAULA
Funny though, I remember you being a lot taller.

He laughs then looks at her profile illuminated by the fire light.

> BUZZ
>
> You know, you look so much like your mother. Do you remember her?

> PAULA
>
> Not really. I guess I was too young or something ... But I remember everyone being really sad and crying and I didn't really understand all of it. Except when you took my hand and told me not to let go. And I didn't, 'cause I remember I got the worst cramp from squeezing so hard.

> BUZZ
>
> You didn't let go, did you?
>> (pause)
> I really loved your mom ... But when you can finally let go, it's tough turning back.
>> (beat)
> I couldn't turn back.

The firewood POPS and the CRICKETS GROW LOUDER. They both stare off into the fire. Paula yawns.

> BUZZ
>
> Whelp. We'd better hit the hay. I'd like to get an early start.

They get up and lay out their sleeping bags.

> FADE TO BLACK:

The sound of CRICKETS and FROGS intensifies. We then hear a soft RUSTLING in the woods.

> CUT TO:

CLOSE ON BUZZ

as his eyes pop open from the SOUND in the woods. He springs up in his sleeping bag, waking Paula.

> PAULA
>
> What is it?

> BUZZ
>
> Shh. Listen ... There's something out there.

He stands and is apparently uneasy.

                                 BUZZ
You, you hold tight.
                (grabbing a stick)
I'll uh, take care of it.

They sit still and listen. Buzz peers into the blackness
and throws the stick. We hear SMALL FOOTSTEPS scurry
away.

                                 BUZZ
There it is, you hear it!

                               PAULA
Relax, it was just some harmless critter making
his rounds.

                                 BUZZ
Oh. Yeah. Well, still, you can never know. Can't be
too careful.

He grabs a bigger stick and lays back down and tries
zipping the sleeping bag as far as it can go. She scoots in
closer.

                               PAULA
Don't worry Dad, I'll protect ya'.

She smiles.

FADE TO BLACK:

                                            CUT TO:

EXT. WOODS—DAY

Paula slowly wakes from her slumber. There is no sign
of Buzz. His sleeping bag is empty. She stands up and
scans the area noticing that their cooler has been tipped
over and its contents are spread everywhere.

                            BUZZ (O.S.)
                      (shouting)
Shit! Ouch! Ooo—

Buzz suddenly appears from behind a tree trying to zip
up his pants.

                        BUZZ
    Ants! Ah! Y'ouch!

Paula giggles as Buzz hits the floor swatting his bare
feet.

                        BUZZ
    What's so funny?! And did you see what your
    little critter friend did! That was my breakfast.
    Our breakfast!

He gets up and marches to the campsite still trying to
swat the ants. Paula is amused by the whole scene.

                        BUZZ
                (under his breath)
    Harmless . . . I'll show you harmless . . . Great
    outdoors my . . .

He wraps everything off the ground in one of the
sleeping bags and dumps it into the backseat of the
Caddy. Paula, trying not to laugh, follows his lead and
boards the car.

EXT. MOVING CAR—DAY

A funky 60s soul SONG plays as Buzz performs a
cigarette trick for Paula as they drive a long stretch of
countryside.

                                        CUT TO:

EXT. TRAILER—DAY

Paula removes her findings from the bucket on the porch
and lays them out to dry. Buzz exits the trailer in clean
clothes carrying a small suitcase to the car, then joins
Paula under the canopy.

                        BUZZ
                (referring to outside decor)
    I like what you did to the place. What'cha got
    there?

                        PAULA
    Just some stuff I found in the river.

He looks at the small collection and picks up the piece of jawbone.

                    PAULA
    Mastadon teeeth.

                    BUZZ
    Masta—what?

                    PAULA
    Mastadon. Sorta like a woolly mammoth but
    without the wool. They're like ten or twenty
    thousand years old.

                    BUZZ
    Impressive.

He sets the piece down.

                    PAULA
    So, you got everything?

                    BUZZ
    I'd like to think so.

He sits on the step and watches her sort her findings.

                    BUZZ
               (beat)
    Maybe you can come stay with me.

She looks to him.

                    PAULA
               (puzzled)
    You mean, like visit?

                    BUZZ
    No, I mean for real.
               (beat)
    What do ya' say?

                    PAULA
    Wow, you mean like all the way to Las Vegas?
    With you?

                    BUZZ
    All the way. With me.

She is stifled by the offer and doesn't say anything.

> BUZZ
> Well look, I'll have to go out there first to set up
> camp, but you think about it and as soon as I get
> everything in order, I'll come back for you.

> PAULA
> You know for sure if it'll really work?

> BUZZ
> (rubbing her head)
> Now that's not for you to worry your pretty little
> head over.

He looks to his watch.

> BUZZ
> I should really hit the road.

She says nothing. He stands and hugs her.

> BUZZ
> You just sit tight and I'll come back.

He boards the Caddy, and she watches him back the car
to the road. Suddenly, she dashes out to the road.

> PAULA
> Take this.

She hands him the polished rock.

> PAULA
> It's for luck.

> BUZZ
> (driving away)
> Just hold tight.

She stands in the road and waves.

HER POV

as the car heads down the dirt road.

CUT TO:

LONG SHOT

from the river of Paula watching the Cadillac drive off.
Dust trails the road as the car disappears behind the
trees. She goes to the top of the steps and pauses and
looks up to the trees overhead and then to the river.

INDIAN SITAR MUSIC FADES IN

She disappears into the trailer.

FADE OUT.

16

THE MAKING OF "KILLER KITE"

Story by Matt Stevens
Screenplay by Robert S. Gray

INTRODUCTION

The Making of "Killer Kite," written and shot in 1991 as an M.F.A. Thesis Film, is a reincarnation of a spoof that Matt Stevens wrote, directed, and shot on Super 8 mm in high school:

> Like every other young male filmmaker—I'm talking about when I was in high school—I made the obligatory inanimate-object-attacking-people film. *Killer Kite 2*, a supposed trailer for a sequel that, of course, didn't exist. I decided to do the attacking kite in the context of a spoof since I was relentlessly bombarded by ads for *Jaws 2* during my latchkey kid phase of watching hours and hours of television after school. So it was a spoof of the trailer for *Jaws 2*. Maybe it was my war on over-hyped cheesy horror films!

Years later, as a graduate student at the F.S.U. Film School, Matt turned "*Killer Kite*" into a one-page story treatment for a mockumentary about the making of a low-budget horror film, "*Killer Kite*":

> The plan was to follow an inept crew during the difficult production of a beleaguered project. In an ironic twist, the film (within my film) would turn out to be so bad that it would be good—becoming an instant cult classic, a la *Rocky Horror Picture Show*. *The Making of "Killer Kite"* would include interviews with cast and crew (who would take themselves *way* too seriously), as well as clips from the supposed film. I think I was partly making fun of filmmakers who took themselves too seriously—and filmmakers who hadn't evolved beyond that phase of producing films about inanimate objects attacking people. Of course, I was also

209

making fun of the filmmaking process itself, which is so inherently on the edge of farce anyway! And, hey, I was just trying to make people laugh.

After the faculty selected Matt's story for an M.F.A. Thesis Film, they selected Bob Gray to write the screenplay:

> I was given the assignment of writing the screenplay and, it became apparent that, in order to tell the story of the making of the fictitious film, "*Killer Kite*," I would first have to write, at least, a detailed treatment of the "film" itself. I decided to use the classic structure and characters from any of a dozen horror films from the 50s and 60s (i.e., the Mad Scientist and Young Assistant who unwittingly unleash the terror, the Niece of the Mad Scientist who becomes the love interest and partner of the Young Assistant in destroying the beast, and, of course, the final scene that leaves open the possibility of a sequel). Once the story of "*Killer Kite*" was set in my mind, it became possible to write about the making of the "film."

Matt credits Bob with most of the ideas about the plot of the film-within-the-film, but also with most of the verbal wit in the script ("What is she trying to achieve?" "An orgasm."/"Get the ugly kid out of here or I'll cut your stinking heart out . . . P.R., that's all I do."). Matt stuck to shtick:

> I remember that I had always proposed a number of gags, including: A conflict between the filmmakers—one who wanted raw sex and violence on the screen, and another who thought he was making an artistic masterpiece; terrible actors auditioning for the film; on-set disasters that would lead to continuity errors which would be revealed in the clips; a dolly that wouldn't work or had to be returned, so that the crew had to resort to ridiculous things like using a kid's red wagon to get that money shot; a stunt kite that wouldn't work, so the actress would have to wrestle with the kite to make it look like a fight; a ridiculously overdone scene where a girl with a lollipop would be chased by a kite, and it would cut to a stand-in finishing the scene for her because of shooting difficulties. And I believe that I had large brushstroke ideas for certain set-pieces—the creation of the Kite; a chase scene involving a child actress who is tortured by the crew and a stage mother; a sex/nude scene that turns disastrous; a final climactic battle with the Kite; and rabid fans of the film outside a showing.

As for the mockumentary part of the screenplay, Bob took a different approach:

> I decided to pattern *The Making of "Killer Kite"* after *Spinal Tap*, which is to say I would try to make the "documentary" as real and believable as possible to help sell the wacky, over-the-top subject it purported to document. I consider it the greatest compliment when someone finds the "documentary" so convincing that they want to know where they can rent a copy of the "film" "*Killer Kite*."

A feeling I had myself when I saw the mockumentary the first time. But pulling the two stories together on paper and screen was tricky, Bob said:

> The greatest challenge lay in telling both stories simultaneously. I tried to weave the stories, dropping hints and skipping around, referring back in a scene to something that was set up several scenes earlier. I think it works and, in the end, the viewer has a good grasp of both stories.

Getting there, though, wasn't easy:

> Creating the script and the eventual film became an exercise in schizophrenia. All of the "documentary" portions would be shot on video and should have the sound, look and feel of hand-held, impromptu footage, while all of the "film" portions would be shot on film and have the sound, look and feel of a scripted and rehearsed—albeit schlocky— motion picture. Hence the VIDEO or FILM at the head of each scene in the script. This schizophrenia carried through the production for me as well since I was also the Director of Photography/Camera Operator. I would spend a morning shooting run-and-gun video and the afternoon shooting traditional, motion-picture-style tripod/dolly cinematography.

In production, a number of changes occurred. As director, Matt threw in some "visual things" during production, just as Bob did as D.P. on the project.

And the actors, Matt said, made valuable changes in the screenplay and film:

> I depended a lot on the contributions from the actors— improvisations, etc.—while rehearsing and shooting. Especially since much of it was supposed to have a documentary feel, I wanted to give them that freedom to play. And there are several funny ad-libbed moments that made it into the film.

Matt also did some restructuring during post. He and Bob both said they were happy with the final product. As Bob summed it up:

> In the end, I think *The Making of "Killer Kite"* is a good script that became a very good film through the efforts of the multi-talented Matt Stevens and the incredible cast who were, to a person, able to take the "documentary" and make it seem off-the-cuff and personal and then turn around and play the intentionally-bad "film" script right to the top without going over. The film was as much fun to make as it is to watch, and the many accolades it's received have been very gratifying indeed.

In 1991, *The Making of "Killer Kite"* won the top student Emmy—First Prize for Comedy from the Academy of Television Arts & Sciences College Television Awards. It also won First Place in narrative from the Ft. Lauderdale International Film Festival and Best Student Entry from the Canadian International Film Festival in Ontario. It was a Top Five Finalist in the Lucille Ball Festival of New Comedy in 1992 and it has been screened in venues across the United States, including the Director's Guild of America.

Since *The Making of "Killer Kite,"* Bob Gray has been "working steadily but wearing a lot of different hats to work steadily," he told me. He shot an independent feature, *Samantha,* and wrote a Movie-of-the-Week, *Invisible Angels,* based on the book *Born to be Hurt* by Ida Muorie. He has also developed and produced a cable series about boating, *Sail Away,* with former CNN anchor Patrick Emory, and is currently producing a national TV series called, *Inside Tennis With The Koz,* which airs on The Tennis Channel. "It's a monthly, thirty-minute, magazine-style show," Bob told me. "We've covered events from San Diego to the Cayman Islands to New York to Moscow. In addition, I'm producing a variety of educational and documentary programs for The Education Channel as well as some commercials." He lives in Sarasota, Florida, with his wife and two children.

Matt Stevens is now a Los Angeles-based writer/producer who has sold both fiction and documentary projects, produced biography shows for E! Entertainment Television, and worked as a script analyst for Creative Artists Agency and other companies. His short films have been screened at national and international festivals, winning many awards, and two of his feature-length screenplays, *Obscenity* and *Psycho Bitch* (both co-written with me), were 2002 finalists for the Sundance Screenwriters Lab. He's the co-author (also *avec moi*) of *Script Partners: What Makes Film and TV Writing Teams Work.* Before relocating to Los Angeles, Matt taught screenwriting and directing at the Florida State Film School, where he and I first met and took an instant dislike to each other (we tell the story of the unlikely evolution of our writing partnership—an improbable connection if ever there was one—in *Script Partners*). "I've also been working a lot in new media," Matt told me, "writing about film for E! Online and contributing to numerous other Web sites. I even try to find time to squeeze in some acting, singing, and voice-over work."

THE MAKING OF "KILLER KITE"
Story by Matt Stevens
Screenplay by Robert S. Gray

FADE IN:

EXT. HARLAN LaRUE'S MANSION—NIGHT (FILM)

The ancient stone building sits dark and lifeless. A single
light shines from a room near the roof. Lightning flashes
as THUNDER ROARS.

CUT TO:

INT. LaRUE'S MANSION—NIGHT (FILM)

The laboratory is cluttered with giant batteries,
transformers and dials. PROFESSOR HARLAN LaRUE, an
elderly, disheveled man in a white lab coat, hurriedly
makes a last minute inspection of a melange of coiled
wires, flashing lights and bubbling beakers. His assistant,
JONATHAN SCOTT, a young, handsome all-American lad,
stands looking out the window.

Lightning flashes.

> JONATHAN
> (checking his watch)
> It's moving in this direction, Professor LaRue. In
> five minutes, we'll be in the center of the storm.

> PROFESSOR
> All right Jonathan. No time to waste. Ten years of
> research and it all comes down to this moment.
> Prepare the kite.

Jonathan throws a large switch and a glass case begins
to pulse with green light, growing brighter until a black,
bat-shaped kite becomes visible inside. The two stand
staring into the case, their faces an eerie green.

> PROFESSOR
> Think of it, my boy. In the future when they
> power an entire city with the power from one
> storm, men will speak of this night. The

                              PROFESSOR (CONT'D)
              night Harlan LaRue changed the course of history.

Jonathan opens the glass case and connects two wires to
either "wing" of the bat kite. He carefully removes the
kite from the case.

                              JONATHAN
              The kite is ready, Professor.

                              PROFESSOR
              Onward, into the future.

The two go up the stairs to the roof.

                                              CUT TO:

EXT. ROOF—NIGHT (FILM)

The Professor and Jonathan, with kite in hand, come out
onto the roof. They set the kite to sail almost effortlessly.
The Professor grabs the kite string and holds on tightly,
wind gusting, lightning flashing and THUNDER
CRACKING.

                              PROFESSOR
                              (yelling)
              Check the connections.

Jonathan runs back down into the laboratory as the
Professor looks mechanically into the sky. Suddenly, a
bolt of lightning hits the kite and the Professor. Jonathan
returns to the roof.

                              JONATHAN
              It worked. The batteries are charged. Professor?

He sees the Professor's empty shoes sitting on the roof,
smoking.

                              JONATHAN
              Professor LaRue?

He looks up to see the kite as it flies off. Now, there is
the hint of an evil smile on its face.

CUT TO:

EXT. LABORATORY ROOF—NIGHT (VIDEO)

From a different angle, we see Jonathan standing on the
roof, watching the kite.

                    LIZ (O.S.)
    Cut.

The VIDEO CAMERA zooms out until we see a film
camera on a dolly sitting only a few feet in front of
Jonathan. Behind the camera is COLIN KISHMAN. As the
shot continues to widen, we see the roof is actually a set
on a soundstage. CREW MEMBERS wander about.

                    COLIN
    Perfect everybody. Really. Good job. Let's just do it
    one more time.

GROANS are heard from the Crew.

CUT TO:

INT. COLIN'S OFFICE—DAY (VIDEO)

Colin Kishman is in his late 20s and very hip; in a black
shirt, buttoned to the throat, wire rim glasses and hair
that is lacquered straight back. Awards, film posters and
books decorate his tastefully conservative office. He sips
a mineral water as he sits back casually in his over-
stuffed chair.

                    COLIN
    "Kite" had been a dream of mine since I was in
    film school in Iowa but it was too far ahead of its
    time for school and none of the studios were
    interested so we did it as an independent.

JUMP CUT:

                    COLIN
    It's set in the horror film genre but it's actually a
    neoexpressionistic vision of the classic struggle
    between man and his inner demons.

                                                    CUT TO:

INT. BARREN ROOM—DAY (VIDEO)

CARL KISHMAN, mid-thirties and looking older, is
dressed in a plain blue work shirt as he sits at a metal
table. Behind him is a cold concrete wall. He smokes
constantly as he runs his fingers through his hair. There
is a nervous tic in the corner of his eye.

                        CARL
        Well, yeah, that's the great thing, you know, it's got
        something for everybody. I mean, it scares your
        pants off to begin with plus, it's got a little . . .

He uses his hands to indicate breasts.

                        CARL
        You know? I mean, you've got to show a little
        skin if you're going to sell the thing.

                                                    CUT TO:

INT. COLIN'S OFFICE—DAY (VIDEO)

                        COLIN
        I just didn't want to do that same old, tired,
        bedroom love scene that's been done to death.
        Setting it in the laboratory, I thought, was not
        only thematically correct but very sensual.

                                                    CUT TO:

INT. CARL'S ROOM—DAY (VIDEO)

                        CARL
        And, where the guy ends up buffing the broad
        right on the giant battery . . . I mean, is that great,
        or what?

                                                    CUT TO:

INT. COLIN'S OFFICE—DAY (VIDEO)

                        COLIN
        Casting? Don't remind me. No, honestly, ours was
        tough but worth it. We ended up getting the best
        talent in Hollywood.

CUT TO:

EXT. KISHMAN PRODUCTION TRAILER—DAY (VIDEO)

An old trailer sits on a vacant lot. Concrete blocks serve
as stairs. Next to the door is a sign that reads,
"Kishman Brothers Productions—Hollywood, Florida."
There are about a DOZEN ACTORS lined up in front. LIZ
BOWDEN exits the trailer and addresses the actors.

                    LIZ
     All right, who hasn't filled out a form?

A few actors raise their hands. She goes to the FIRST
ACTOR and offers them a form.

                    LIZ
          (coldly)
     Any union affiliations?

                    FIRST ACTOR
     No, ma'am.

                    LIZ
     Good.

A COWBOY exits the trailer, slamming the door.

                    COWBOY
     Don't waste your time, boys. These idiots don't
     know talent when they see it.

                    LIZ
     Well, I do. And, believe me, I didn't.

CUT TO:

EXT. TRAILER—DAY (VIDEO)

An OLDER ACTOR is practicing his lines in a baroque
and theatrical voice.

                    OLDER ACTOR
     The night Harlan LaRue changed the course of
     history.
          (beat)
     The night Harlan LaRue changed the course of
     history.

CUT TO:

EXT. TRAILER—DAY (VIDEO)

A definite CHARACTER ACTOR.

> CHARACTER ACTOR
> I'm going to read for the lead. I've paid my dues doing characters and I think I'm at that leading-man stage in my career, now.

CUT TO:

EXT. TRAILER—DAY (VIDEO)

A precocious YOUNG GIRL stands reading her lines while her doting STAGE MOTHER kneels beside her, brushing her hair.

> YOUNG GIRL
> Mother, do you mind? I'm trying to learn this.

> STAGE MOTHER
> Sorry, honey. Go ahead.

The Young Girl goes back to the script, pauses and then lets out a blood-curdling SCREAM.

CUT TO:

INT. KISHMAN PRODUCTION TRAILER—DAY (VIDEO)

The two Kishman brothers sit at a table stacked with resúmés and photos. Carl is now wearing a shirt and tie that is loosened at the neck. He does not run his fingers through his hair or have a nervous tic. Colin has much longer hair than before and wears a T-shirt that says, "Film Iowa." Film and Iowa share the letter "I". The two appear very fatigued.

> COLIN
> (unenthusiastically)
> Very good. Really.

He looks to Carl for confirmation but gets only a glaze of disinterest.

> COLIN
> Really, very nice.

We see that it is the Character Actor.

COLIN
It's not exactly what we had in mind for the lead
but, if we decide to go that way, we'll be in touch.

We jump through a series of lines being read by different
actors. Each one is worse than the last:

FIRST ACTOR
It's moving in this direction, Professor LaRue.

SECOND ACTOR
I can't stop seeing that poor child's face and that
. . . thing.

OLDER ACTOR
The night Harlan LaRue changed the course of
history.

THIRD ACTOR
Tammy, it's too dangerous. We should . . . wait, can
I start over?

FOURTH ACTOR
We should leave it to the authorities. That fiend
has already killed five red-haired children.

FIFTH ACTOR
(snickering)
Make love to me, Jonathan.

SIXTH ACTOR
(seductively)
Make love to me, Jonathan.

SEVENTH ACTOR
(sternly)
Make love to me, Jonathan.

The Brothers are rocked awake by the Young Girl's
SCREAM.

YOUNG GIRL
Shall we proceed with the audition, gentlemen?

CUT TO:

INT. LABORATORY—DAY (VIDEO)

ASHLEY DAVENPORT is sitting on the laboratory set for
her interview.

>   ASHLEY
>   Tammy is the pivotal character here. It's really
>   her story and I want to give her a very positive,
>   can-do, sort of 90s-woman quality.

JUMP TO:

>   ASHLEY
>   (proudly)
>   Yes, I was the "Love-My-Floor-Wax" lady. It ran
>   for six months in the Jacksonville area.

JUMP TO:

>   ASHLEY
>   I'd rather continue doing dinner theatre here than
>   move to California. It's just that whole L.A., show-
>   biz, starlet thing is definitely not me.

CUT TO:

BILL PRINZ is sitting on the same set.

>   BILL
>   This is Jonathan's story. He is the central
>   character around which all the supporting
>   characters revolve. I mean, he helps build the
>   beast, he destroys the beast and he gets the girl.
>   Gets her right here, in fact. That should prove
>   interesting.

JUMP TO:

>   BILL
>   My looks are holding me back as an actor, I
>   think. I mean, all I'm offered are the leading-man
>   roles and, just once, I'd kill for one of those juicy,
>   character parts. Oh, well.

CUT TO:

INT. COLIN'S OFFICE—DAY (VIDEO)

Colin holds up a large poster for "Killer Kite." Near
the bottom of the poster, we see a child sitting on the
sand, a small shovel in hand and a pail at her feet. Near
the top of the poster is a large, menacing bat-shaped
kite.

> COLIN
> This was the original poster idea but I felt it was
> too derivative of JAWS, so . . .

He holds up a second poster. Instead of the child at the
bottom, we now see a couple, running in terror from the
kite.

> COLIN
> We came up with this which I thought was better
> but still didn't grab me so . . .

He holds up the final poster. It is a close shot of Ashley
and Jonathan, partially undressed and in passionate
embrace. On the wall, in the background, is a small
shadow of a kite.

> COLIN
> I designed this one myself. I just felt the story
> was not about some kite, really. It's about people.

CUT TO:

INT. BARREN ROOM—DAY (VIDEO)

CARL is once again in the stark concrete room where we
first saw him.

> CARL
> My advice to young filmmakers?
> (beat)
> Hire Lizzy Bowden as your A.D.

CUT TO:

EXT. IRICK PARK—DAY (VIDEO)

Film equipment and CREW are everywhere. Colin sits
behind the camera atop the dolly crane while Carl paces

nervously, checking his watch. Liz holds a red wig and addresses the Young Girl in a whisper as her Mother looks on from the background.

> LIZ
> Yes, your mother did a wonderful job but the kite only attacks red-headed children. So, you can either put on the wig or I'll shave your head with a rusty razor. Got it?

CUT TO:

EXT. IRICK PARK—SHORTLY LATER (VIDEO)

The child is now wearing the red wig. Just behind her the kite is being suspended in the air by ASPEN GREENWALD, the stunt coordinator.

> LIZ
> Ready on set?

Aspen looks high in the tree to his assistant SHORTY LOGAN, who holds the other kite line.

> ASPEN
> Ready, Shorty?

> SHORTY
> Ready.

> LIZ
> Okay, quiet everybody. This is a take. Roll sound.

> SOUND MAN
> Speed.

> LIZ
> Roll camera.

> COLIN
> Speed.

> LIZ
> (slating)
> Killer Kite. Scene 43, take 1.

                              COLIN
    And . . . action.

The Girl runs from the kite which is closing in on her.
She looks back, SCREAMS and falls.

                               LIZ
    Cut. Good for everybody?

                          SOUND MAN
    Sound good.

                              COLIN
    Sorry, I lost her when she fell. Let's just do one
    more.

                                                    CUT TO:

EXT. IRICK PARK—LATER (VIDEO)

Liz, agitated, holds the slate in front of the camera.

                               LIZ
    Scene 43, take 15.

She marks and drops the slate to reveal the Young Girl
spattered with dirt and wig askew.

                              COLIN
    Action.

The Young Girl starts running and turns to scream. This
time, it is a raspy and pale imitation of its former self.

                               LIZ
    Cut.

                                                    CUT TO:

EXT. IRICK PARK—LATER (VIDEO)

Carl paces as he talks to Colin.

                              CARL
    You just don't get it, do you? We've got the dolly
    for two more hours. That's it. Then, no more dolly.

                    COLIN
We only need it for three more shots.

                    CARL
You've already spent four hours on this one.

                    COLIN
We're fine.

Carl's cell phone RINGS. He turns it on and puts it to his
ear.

                    CARL
Your brains are in your ass.
          (becoming nervous)
Oh, no. Not you, Mr. Van Arsdale. Ha, ha. No, it
was just . . . one of the actors.
          (to no one in particular)
You'll never work in this town again.

                                        CUT TO:

EXT. IRICK PARK—LATER (VIDEO)

The Stage Mother sits comfortably as the Young Girl
limps over, tired, defeated and on the verge of tears.

                 YOUNG GIRL
          (hoarsely)
I can't do't again.

The Mother sprays antiseptic in the Young Girl's throat.

                STAGE MOTHER
Like hell. You'll do it all day if they tell you to.
          (softly)
Okay, honey?

The Young Girl turns and lets out a piercing SCREAM,
right into the microphone. The Sound Man rips off his
headphones and begins chasing the Young Girl, murder in
his eyes. Liz jumps up and brings him down with a
flying tackle. She looks up with a face full of dirt.

                    LIZ
Okay people, that's lunch.

CUT TO:

EXT. IRICK PARK—LATER (VIDEO)

Everyone is again in position to re-take scene 43.

>LIZ

Scene 43, take 22.

>COLIN

Action.

The Young Girl takes off running and screaming. She falls, looks up and, instead of screaming, begins choking.

>LIZ

Cut. What the hell's the matter now? Aspen?

>ASPEN

The line's wrapped around her throat. Give me some slack.

>CARL

Careful. Easy, you're tearing the kite.

The Stage Mother runs over to assist the Young Girl.

>STAGE MOTHER

My baby.
>(to Carl)
You'll be hearing from my lawyer.

Liz yanks the line and, unnoticed by anyone, Shorty is pulled from the tree, landing with a THUD. The Young Girl and Stage Mother head for their car.

>LIZ

Where are you going?

>STAGE MOTHER

I'm taking my daughter to the hospital, if that's all right with you, bitch.

Liz yanks the wig off the Young Girl's head.

>LIZ

Christ, never work with kids.
>(to Colin)
Okay, we've wasted five hours, we still don't have this shot and we've lost our actress. So, who are we supposed to get to finish this scene?

Colin turns slowly to look at Liz, the only woman on the set. The implication of his look sinks in.

> LIZ
> Oh, no. No, no. No way.

CUT TO:

EXT. IRICK PARK—LATER (VIDEO)

Liz is now in the red wig as an ASSISTANT is strapping her breasts with an Ace bandage.

> COLIN
> Believe me, it will cut. No one will ever notice.

He gives her a quick kiss on the cheek and leaves.

> LIZ
> (to the assistant)
> I can't believe this. I've worked with Bob Altman, Mike Nichols . . .

The Assistant is unimpressed.

> LIZ
> Anson Williams.

The Assistant looks up, awestruck.

> ASSISTANT
> Really?

CUT TO:

INT. BARREN ROOM—DAY (VIDEO)

Carl continues his interview.

> CARL
> Of course, the ironic thing is that the special effects are what made the film, in some ways, but also what . . . broke it, actually, with the lawsuit and all but, God, don't remind me of that.

He takes a long drag off his cigarette and blows smoke into the air, staring blankly as his eye twitches quickly.

EXT. LABORATORY ROOF—DAY (VIDEO)

Aspen stands next to Shorty, who's dressed in a full-body, bat kite costume. A patch covers one eye; a scar on the cheek below.

> ASPEN
> (to camera)
> This next stunt is really revolutionary. It's never been tried before. This kite costume, that my test pilot Shorty here is wearing, is like a small hang glider so, when he jumps off here, they'll be able to get these great shots of the kite circling and circling. Really menacing looking stuff, man. But the really wild thing is, there's a camera stuck inside Shorty's costume here so, at the same time, he'll be getting these great aerial shots. I told him, "Hey, make 'em pay you D.P. rates."

He slaps Shorty on the back, playfully. Shorty looks over the rail, panic stricken. It is a long way down.

> ASPEN
> (to camera)
> No, we haven't had time to test it yet but, if anybody can do it, Shorty can.
> (to Shorty)
> Right, buddy?
> (to camera)
> There's nothin' he won't do.

> CUT TO:

INT. COLIN'S OFFICE—DAY (VIDEO)

Colin's interview continues.

> COLIN
> Probably the most rewarding thing about "Kite" was the relationships that developed on the set, especially between the actors and myself. There was a real simpatico there.

CUT TO:

INT. LABORATORY—DAY (VIDEO)

The set is lit, the equipment in place and the actors in costume. Colin, fatigued and nervous, addresses Bill and Ashley.

> COLIN
> (to Ashley)
> No, I don't think they would go to his room. This is something they do in the heat of passion. Okay? This isn't a romantic weekend in the Keys. This is raw animal lust. Get it . . . got it . . . good.

> ASHLEY
> But, I don't understand Tammy's motivation here. It seems so submissive. What is she trying to achieve with this?

Carl, with a three-day growth of beard and clothes straight from the floor, passes through.

> CARL
> An orgasm.

LAUGHTER is heard around the set.

> COLIN
> All right, people. Let's have quiet. This is a very difficult scene for everybody so, let's just cooperate.
> (to Ashley)
> Tammy realizes she is becoming the same isolated, lonely, embittered person that her uncle Harlan had become and the only way she can avoid that is to dare to love another and her disrobing is merely symbolic of her losing the veils of secrecy that have enshrouded her soul.

Ashley is moved by his words.

> COLIN
> Okay, let's try one.

JUMP TO:

> ASHLEY
> Jonathan, we may not live to see another day and I don't want to die a woman who never knew love. Make love to me, Jonathan.

They embrace and kiss passionately. Ashley begins snickering.

                    LIZ
  Cut.

                                        JUMP TO:

                  ASHLEY
    Make love to me, Jonathan.

They kiss, her face to the camera side of his.

                    BILL
    Sorry, but shouldn't my face be on the other side?

                    LIZ
  Cut.

                  COLIN
    No, Bill, we'll want to see Tammy's face here.

                                        JUMP TO:

                  ASHLEY
    Make love to me, Jonathan.

They embrace and kiss. She rips the buttons from his shirt. He unbuttons her blouse and, as he finishes, she self-consciously begins to re-button it.

                    LIZ
  Cut. Damn it, what are you doing?

                  ASHLEY
    Sorry, I'm . . . I just . . . Can we do it again? Sorry.

                    LIZ
  Okay, let's get Jonathan another shirt.

                                        JUMP TO:

They are set to retake the scene. Bill's shirt is a different color, now.

                  ASHLEY
    Make love to me, Jonathan.

Again, they embrace, kiss and begin to disrobe each other. This time, as he finishes unbuttoning her shirt, she manages to turn her back to the camera. He wrestles to turn her back around, kissing all the while.

> LIZ
> Cut. Where does it say, "Tammy and Jonathan wrestle"?

> ASHLEY
> I'm sorry. This isn't easy, you know?

> LIZ
> I don't care. Act if you must.

> ASHLEY
> Fine. You think it's so easy, then you get naked in front of them.

She points to the crew, who look around embarrassed and guilty. Ashley leaves the set in tears.

> CUT TO:

INT. SOUNDSTAGE—SHORTLY LATER

Carl and Liz are off to one side of the set, talking quietly.

> CARL
> We've got to have this scene. I mean, we've got to have it. No "R" rating, no sale. It's that simple. We've got to have it.

Colin joins them.

> COLIN
> It's no use. She says it's purely exploitive and she won't do gratuitous nudity.

> CARL
> We'll pay her.

> COLIN
> I offered. She said, "I'm an actress, not a stripper."

                    CARL
That's it. We're screwed.

                    LIZ
That's your answer.

The brothers only look confused.

                    LIZ
Pay someone to body double the rest of the scene.

Colin and Carl come alive at the simplistic genius of her
suggestion. Together, they turn to look at Liz.

                    LIZ
Oh, no. Absolutely not. N-O, no. Forget it. Hire a
body double.

                                              CUT TO:

INT. COLIN'S OFFICE—DAY (VIDEO)

Colin's interview continues.

                    COLIN
The love scene, as it stands now, is different than
we had originally planned, but I think it works
very nicely. I still get a lot of comments on it.

                                              CUT TO:

INT. LABORATORY—DAY (FILM)

Tammy and Jonathan enter.

                    TAMMY
Oh, Jonathan, I can't stop seeing that poor child's
face and that . . . that thing.

                    JONATHAN
Shh. Try not to think about it.

                    TAMMY
Jonathan, we may not live to see another day and
I don't want to die a woman who never knew
love. Make love to me, Jonathan.

When we cut back to Jonathan he is wearing the
different colored shirt. The scene plays through until her
shirt is unbuttoned and her back is to the camera and
then there is an awkward cut-away to a flashing light.
The scene plays through to the end in close up, a body-
double now standing in for Tammy. He removes her shirt
and the body-double has tassels glued to her nipples. The
two crawl upon the giant battery to consummate the
relationship and the camera dollies to a bubbling beaker.

                                                   CUT TO:

INT. BARREN ROOM—DAY (VIDEO)

Carl's interview continues.

                    CARL
     I've gotta be honest with you, I don't remember
     the last five or six days of the production. I've
     heard some pretty weird stuff, though. As long as
     they can't prove it, 'eh?

                                                   CUT TO:

INT./EXT. TAMMY'S CAR—DAY (FILM)

Tammy sits in the driver's seat with Jonathan next to
her. In the middle of the back seat is a mannequin
wearing a red wig.

                    TAMMY
     Okay, we know all the children were attacked in
     Irick Park, right?

                    JONATHAN
     Right.

                    TAMMY
     And, they all had red hair, right?

                    JONATHAN
     Right.

                    TAMMY
     And, since the curfew prohibits children from
     being outside alone, little Rusty here will be the
     perfect decoy.

                    JONATHAN
Let's hope the kite has the Professor's same bad
eyesight.

                                        CUT TO:

EXT. IRICK PARK—DAY (VIDEO)

Tammy and Jonathan enter the park carrying little
Rusty and two machetes. CHILDREN and PARENTS
scatter at the sight. The camera dollies beside them, only
now, instead of a dolly and track, Colin and the camera
ride atop a children's red wagon. Tammy and Jonathan
prop Rusty in the middle of the playground.

                    TAMMY
Okay, you take cover in those bushes and I'll wait
in the car.

In the background, a CHILD continues to play on the
playground, her MOM beside her.

                    LIZ
Cut.
          (to Mom)
You're supposed to be gone by now. You see these
two people with machetes and you grab your child
and leave. Got it?

Carl comes over.

                    CARL
          (to Mom)
That's it. You're off the film. Goodbye. Leave.

                    MOM
We were never in your stupid film, remember?
You told us you'd already cast everyone.

                    LIZ
Well, you'll have to leave. We can't get this shot
with you in the way here.

                    MOM
You Hollywood people are all the same.

> LIZ
> Lady, please, just leave before we call the cops.

Carl takes the machete from Jonathan's hands.

> MOM
> Why don't you go make your smutty movie
> somewhere else.

> CARL
> Look, bitch, this smutty movie has already put
> me fifty thousand in debt. I've mortgaged my
> house, my boat and my Beemer. I haven't slept
> or bathed in three days. My wife has moved out
> and I think my dog may have starved to death.
> Trust me, I'm losing my sense of humor. So, you
> can either take that ugly child and get out of
> here or I swear I'll cut your stinkin' heart
> out.

The Mom grabs the child and runs off.

> CARL
> P.R., that's all I do.

CUT TO:

INT. T.V. STUDIO—DAY (VIDEO)

> FILM REVIEWER
> It was twenty-five months ago tonight that I had
> the unimaginable burden of watching "Killer Kite"
> for the first time and, as I said at the time, "the
> film is not worthy of a serious review." So, of
> course, every child between nine and twenty has
> been to see it at least six times. It's now made
> the greatest profit of any independent film in
> history and, tonight, it begins a record 105th
> consecutive week at Los Angeles' famous Polk
> Theatre. Yes, I've been to see "Killer Kite" again
> and, no, I haven't changed my review. What
> everyone takes to be that camp, Kishman style of
> comedy is nothing more than inept filmmaking.
> The fact that these guys got a three-picture deal
> with Paramount is an inauspicious statement on
> the health of the American film system. Just take
> a look at this awful segment from an even worse
> film.

CUT TO:

EXT. IRICK PARK—DAY (FILM)

We see the segment where the kite is chasing the Young Girl. She falls and looks back at the kite.

CUT TO:

KITE'S POV

Of the Young Girl lying on the ground, screaming.

RETURN TO SCENE

Only, now, it is Liz in a red wig, wrestling with the kite. She screams and acts as badly as anyone has ever screamed and acted.

CUT TO:

INT. COLIN'S OFFICE—DAY (VIDEO)

          COLIN
Of course the critics didn't like it. None of them understood it. Not one realized that the kite is an analogy for prejudice. It only attacks red-haired children. Get it?
          (disgusted)
Critics.

CUT TO:

INT./EXT. TAMMY'S CAR, IRICK PARK—DAY (FILM)

Tammy sits behind the wheel, looking up at the sky. Slowly, the kite rises beside the car until it is looking through the window.

          TAMMY
      (startled)
Uncle Harlan, no. It's me, Tammy.

The kite backs away. Tammy grabs a machete and lunges at the kite, missing. The kite takes off. Tammy jumps out of the car and calls Jonathan.

          TAMMY
Jonathan, be careful. He knows we mean to destroy him.

ANGLE ON JONATHAN

As the kite swoops down and attacks him. He falls to the ground, bleeding. The kite then attacks the mannequin. A loud CRUNCH is heard and the kite falls to the ground, injured. Tammy and Jonathan quickly descend on the kite and stab it with their machetes. Trickles of blood come from the kite's wounds.

> TAMMY
> (sobbing)
> Oh, no. Uncle Harlan, no.

Jonathan helps her up.

> JONATHAN
> Come on. It's over. The Professor is in a better place, now.

They walk off, arm-in-arm, toward the car.

                                              CUT TO:

EXT. POLK THEATRE—NIGHT (VIDEO)

A long line of YOUNG PEOPLE extends from the front door. OTHERS wait behind barricades. Many are in costume, wearing kite suits and waving kite puppets. TWO BOYS are dressed as the Professor, ANOTHER as Jonathan and ONE as Ashley. Shrieks are heard as a stretch limo pulls up. Ashley gets out.

> ADOLESCENT BOY
> I love you, Tammy.

Ashley enters, the epitome of the Hollywood starlet. She is dressed in a low-cut gown and poses for the myriad flashbulbs. Bill Prinz gets out next, looking tan and manicured. There are more SHRIEKS from the crowd.

> TEENAGE GIRL 1
> Make love to me, Jonathan.

> TEENAGE GIRL 2
> Make love to me, Jonathan.

Another limo pulls up and Colin gets out, dressed in a tuxedo and escorting Liz who looks elegant in an evening gown. She swats away a child who asks for an autograph and hurriedly pulls Colin inside the theatre. A black motorcycle pulls up on the sidewalk and PEOPLE scatter. The rider gets off and we see it is Aspen. Next, the Young Girl arrives in a wheelchair and wearing a neck brace. She is being pushed by her Mother. They are swarmed by a pack of pre-pubescent girls and the last we see of them is the wheelchair tipping over.

CUT TO:

INT. POLK THEATRE—NIGHT (VIDEO)

We see several of the AUDIENCE MEMBERS, the light from the screen shimmering on their faces. They deliver the final lines of the film with the actors on the screen.

FEMALE CROWD
Oh, no. Uncle Harlan. No.

MALE CROWD
Come on. It's over. The Professor is in a much better place now.

CUT TO:

EXT. IRICK PARK—DAY (FILM)

After Tammy and Jonathan walk off, the camera remains on the kite. A breeze lifts it and turns it over, revealing a dozen baby killer kites below. The Crowd OOOHS and AAAHS.

FADE TO BLACK:

FADE IN:

GRAPHIC:

"This Film Is Dedicated To Shorty Logan. 'There's nothing he wouldn't do.'"

CUT TO:

INT. COLIN'S OFFICE—DAY (VIDEO)

> COLIN
> I am very busy, right now. We begin principle
> photography on "Prom Bomb" next week and I'm
> just finishing the script for "The Town That
> Couldn't Spell," which we hope to have in
> production by the time Carl gets out ... if we can
> straighten out this I.R.S. thing.

CUT TO:

INT. BARREN ROOM—DAY (VIDEO)

Carl finishes the last of a cigarette butt and looks
nervously over his shoulder. He checks his watch.

> CARL
> Do I have any advice for young filmmakers?

On the SOUND of a jail cell opening, the camera pans
over to reveal the jail bars beside Carl as the GUARD
enters.

> CARL
> Yeah, take care of the legal work first. Trust me.

The Guard leads Carl out of the cell.

FADE TO BLACK:

ROLL CREDITS.

17

SLOW DANCIN' DOWN THE AISLES OF THE QUICKCHECK

By Thomas Wade Jackson

INTRODUCTION

At the first crew meeting for *Slow Dancin' Down the Aisles of the Quickcheck*, Thomas Jackson made a brief speech:

> I told everybody the most important thing is I want everybody to have a great experience, have a good time, and learn from the experience. It was important to me that the set was pleasant and everyone felt good about it because there are so many sets you go on that suck. You hate to be there. So it was so important to me that this be a pleasant experience for all involved. Then I said, "But one of our goals is to be the first student film from Florida State to win a student Academy Award." I don't even know if the crew members remember it, but I remember it like it was yesterday because it was such a hard thing for me to say. In the South, you're taught to be self-deprecating, and when you say something like that, even humbly, it sounds like you're being pretentious, even though at the time and even when we won the regional competition I felt *we don't have a chance*. But I've learned in life you have to state things. Just verbalizing it. Putting it out there. There's something about saying it that sort of puts your ass on the line. And you have to live up to it. And if you say it, it puts you in a mindset to make it happen. But I also wanted the crew to know I was taking this seriously. I wanted them to feel they were working on something they could be proud of. And it kind of set the tone.

In May 1999, Thomas was notified that his film was a finalist for the student Academy Award. He would find out in June if he'd won first, second, or third place.

But the journey from idea to the Academy ceremony in June was a long one. In 1998, when Thomas wrote the first draft of *Slow Dancin'*, he did not have a story. *Fifteen rewrites* later, he'd found his story and a whole lot of rich significant stuff in the process:

> What's funny about writing is that I guess in some ways things come out that are somewhat your philosophy but at the same time sometimes they just develop, they just come out of nowhere, you don't know where they come from. They just kind of bubble up. In a way, I mean. I believe it. I mean, the thing is, I've been married twice and divorced twice, but you just have to take those chances, I guess. I'm a hopeless romantic. You have to believe that you can make the connection with the person. You have to look beneath the surface. See who they really are. So I'm in Georgia, and peach season came in the middle of the rewrites, and a peach came to represent this true thing in a person. So, in the screenplay, the produce manager, Jerome, says to Earl:

> JEROME
> You got to look for the peach inside of her, and see her in a way ain't nobody ever seen her. Then talk to her with your peach . . . You just look deep into her eyes, past all the flesh, blood and bone, and see that peach inside of her.

Would Earl have the courage to make this authentic connection? That became the central dramatic question of the screenplay and film. As director, Thomas didn't make a great many changes in the screenplay:

> I want to say all the scenes are there. Even in editing, we didn't cut any scenes. There was added dialogue in production, or I would give the actors lines. When you're there, you just have to see what works for you and adjust accordingly. Then there were throwaway lines like when Earl's on the floor, stuff in the background. I'd tell the actors this is what it's about, and they would adlib.

The process of filmmaking, though, like true love, did not always run smooth:

> I watched the dailies the first day and I thought, Oh my God, this is the worst thing. What am I doing? I went home and went paranoid. And I said to my girlfriend, if this film sucks, will you still love me? But you just have to walk on faith. No, it's more than just faith. You have to take action. But without the faith part, the action doesn't work. Even when

> you think it sucks, you still have to go out there and believe it will all come together and it's gonna work. It's all about just doing it. And until you have to let go of the film, it's a work in progress. That's the greatest thing about film. You have chance after chance to make it better.

But the first cut was the one he loved best.

> After that you get lost in detail. The final cut is a million times better than the rough cut, but that's the only cut that worked for me. I actually saw moments in it, but now . . . it's painful. You watch it a million times and it doesn't work for you. There are things you just cringe when you watch it. That is the saddest part about filmmaking. I don't think I'll ever be able to make a film and watch it and say, 'God, I hit the mark.' I used to listen to Woody Allen say *Annie Hall* doesn't work, and I'd think, God, how could he say that? He's just saying that. Now I totally relate.

Many others do not. *Slow Dancin' Down the Aisles of the Quickcheck* won First Place in the Student Narrative category at the 1998 Ft. Lauderdale International Film Festival; the 1999 Cine Eagle Award in Washington, D.C.; Third Place in the 1999 Student Emmy Awards for Comedy; the 1999 Grand Prize-Overall and Second Place-Fiction at the Florida Film Festival in West Palm Beach; First Place at the 1999 Palm Beach International Film Festival Student Showcase; First Place Featurette Audience Award at the 1999 Filmfest New Haven; as well as being screened nationally and internationally, including the Emerging Filmmakers series at the 1999 Cannes Film Festival. And, on June 14, 1999, in Los Angeles, California, Thomas Jackson received an Academy Award (Bronze) in the Narrative Category of the Student Academy Awards for *Slow Dancin' Down the Aisles of the Quickcheck.*

When I asked what he was up to now, he said, "As far as what I am doing—for the last year and a half I've been living in New York City and working at a small recording studio. I've just started back working on a screenplay that I began right before I moved up here and spent some time with last year. It's a Southern Gothic Romantic Comedy that at present is titled, "Rattlesnakes and Roses." Before that I spent time in Nashville teaching filmmaking at Watkins College and eight months in L.A. working at a sound post house. Mainly I've just been learning life lessons and getting my act together. Maybe one day I'll be ready to take it on the road (again)."

SLOW DANCIN' DOWN THE AISLES OF THE QUICKCHECK
By Thomas Wade Jackson

FADE IN:

EXT. QUICKCHECK—PREDAWN

The parking lot is empty and quiet, except for a green 1979 Toyota pickup, a distant train whistle, and the muffled sound of a guitar coming from inside the store.

INT. QUICKCHECK—SERIES OF SHOTS—PREDAWN

The Quickcheck sleeps as a voice lays lyrics over the music from the guitar.

The meat counter glows under the display lights, stocked with chittlins, bologna, fish roe, pork souse and the feet of both chickens and pigs.

A perfect display of peaches rests happily under a sign that reads, "Nothing's as Sweet as A Georgia Peach."

The magazine rack holds various magazines; a tabloid reads, "Ghost of Hank Williams Haunts Rush Limbaugh." DOLLY TO REVEAL:

The silhouetted back of the man, playing the guitar, sitting on one of the check out counters. CONTINUE TO DOLLY AROUND THE SIDE OF EARL, a plain-looking, 41-year-old man. He sings a troubled line and looks over at the Employee of the Month Sign:

EXTREME CLOSE UP of the Polaroid picture of Earl shaking hands with a faded beauty in a cashier's vest.

CLOSE UP of Earl as he finishes his last line and looks from the Employee of the Month sign to a newspaper in front of him.

CLOSE UP of Newspaper. CURTIS, a 38-year-old man wearing a Cowboy Hat, and a sparkling red, white and blue suit, grins at Earl from the paper. The headline reads, "Local Country Star Returns Home for Concert."

TITLE

INT. FRONT OF THE STORE—MORNING

The doors of the Quickcheck sit quiet for a second, then
MAYBELLINE, the 38-year-old Head Cashier and woman
in the picture, walks up outside, calling to someone
OFFSCREEN.

                    MAYBELLINE
    Come on, Mary Jurgeana, I want you to hear
    somethin'.

                    MARY (O.S.)
    Hold your horses.

Maybelline comes in the store and makes a bee line to
the radio. She turns it on, and a steel guitar cries out
over the music with a distinctive cheesy Nashville sound.
MARY JURGEANA, a slightly overweight black woman,
struggles through the door.

                    MAYBELLINE
    Hurry up, it's almost over.

                    MARY
            (walking towards Maybelline)
    I ain't got no hurry left in me, girl. Daryl came
    home with some Colt 45 last night, pretendin' he
    was Billie Dee Williams, again.

                    MAYBELLINE
    Let me guess, you had to be the young starlet
    who wanted a part in his next movie.

                    MARY
    No, last night, I had to be a teenage school girl
    who wanted his autograph.

                    MAYBELLINE
            (smiling)
    What did he want to write it with?

A man's twangy voice begins to sing about his Pickup
Truck, over the music.

                    MAYBELLINE
    Remember the guy I was tellin' you about
    yesterday? Curtis?

                              MARY
        You mean the old flame that ran off and became a
        Country Star?

                           MAYBELLINE
        Yeah, this is him. Listen.
                           (she listens)
        He did this on Nashville Now Tuesday.
                        (listens some more)
        They call him a star on the horizon.

                              MARY
        What horizon's that? The hillbilly horizon?

                           MAYBELLINE
        They said he had a distinct voice.

                              MARY
        Sounds like every other redneck song, to me.

                           MAYBELLINE
        And they said he'd be worth over a million dollars
        by the end of the year.

                              MARY
        You know, the more I hear it . . .

They listen some more. The deep country voice of a D.J.
speaks over the end of the song. Maybelline and Mary
turn their attention away from the radio, and clock
themselves in for the day.

                           D.J. (O.S.)
        Whew, that boy can sing it, can't he? That
        Bainbridge's own Curtis Anderson, putting the
        Country back in the Country.

Maybelline and Mary talk over the D.J.

                              MARY
        Girl, I trade my Bille Dee, for an old boyfriend
        with a million dollars, any day.

                           MAYBELLINE
        I like Daryl.

> MARY

That's 'cause you ain't ever had to pay Lando Calrissian's Jerry Curl bill.

> MAYBELLINE

Who?

Mary pulls a Lando Calrissian action figure out of her purse.

> MARY

Billie Dee played him in Star Wars. I keep findin' these in my pocketbook.

> MAYBELLINE
> (taking figure)

This don't look nothin' like Daryl.

Mary clocks in and notices the Employee of the Month sign and that the picture is missing.

> MARY

Looks like Earl's runnin' late again.

Maybelline looks at the empty slot and smiles.

INT. BATHROOM—SAME

Earl stands in front of the mirror in his brown slacks and a tank top T-shirt, his middle-age pudge hanging slightly over his belt. He pulls the wrapper off a new girdle.

> EARL
> (unsure)

Maybelline, my heart is a song.

He sucks in his gut and tightens a girdle around his waist with all his might, fastening it down. He looks at the picture and finishes the line, but has trouble due to the tightness of the girdle.

> EARL
> (groaning)

And you are its melody.

He leans towards the mirror, knocking a can of Ajax off the sink. He starts to pick it up, but the girdle keeps him from bending. He gives up, takes the Polaroid off the mirror, and puts it in his pocket.

INT. STORE FRONT—LATER

Maybelline and Mary sit in the crow's nest, counting the
money for their tills.

> MAYBELLINE
> She said that Curtis, personally, asked her to call
> me. I thought that was kind of surprisin'.

> MARY
> Why?

> MAYBELLINE
> It's just been a long time.

> MARY
> How long?

> MAYBELLINE
> At least two dress sizes ago.

Behind them Earl walks out from the end of the aisle.
He sees them, then ducks back out of their sight. He
pulls the Polaroid picture out of his breast pocket and
looks toward the Employee of the Month sign.

> MARY
> Well, what was he like?

> MAYBELLINE
> (reflecting)
> Well, back then he used to play with this band
> called East River Junction. He had long hair, and
> a tattoo on his arm of a guitar that said, "Honky
> Tonk Hero." That's how he saw himself. He always
> wore a leather jacket and black boots with silver
> tips on the toes.

As Maybelline talks, Earl sneaks up to the office,
disappearing behind the wall.

> MAYBELLINE
> And he had this '57 Harley Hydroglide with a 74-
> cubic inch overhead valve engine, one just like The
> King rode. Curtis sure loved that Harley. You ever
> do it on a motorcycle?

Earl, who is about to return the Polaroid picture to the Employee of the Month sign, misses the slot, and the picture falls to the floor and under a chewing gum machine. He starts to reach down for it, but can't bend.

MARY

No, but I did it on a lawnmower, once.

Earl struggles for the picture. He squats awkwardly, trying to reach the picture, but it's just out of his reach.

MAYBELLINE

Curtis used to drive that Harley into the bedroom, wearin' nothin' but a cowboy hat and a smile. And he'd leave it runnin' while we did it, and when things got hot, he'd rev it up. I'd feel my whole body vibrate.

MARY

I don't think that lawnmower ever ran.

MAYBELLINE

Well, let me tell you, there's just somethin' about that much horse power between your legs.

Earl loses his balance and falls over. As quick as he hits the ground, he grabs the picture and puts it in his shirt pocket. Maybelline and Mary hear Earl's fall.

MAYBELLINE

Earl, is that you?

Earl lays on the ground, looking up at the ceiling.

EARL

Yeah. Ya'll in early this morning.

He tries to sit up, but can't.

MARY

It's after eight.

MAYBELLINE

Good morning to you, too, Earl.

EARL

(still trying to get up)
Sorry, good mornin'. I guess I'm runnin' a little behind.

Earl bounces up trying to grab the time clock. His fingers almost touching it.

> MAYBELLINE (O.S.)
> Better a little behind than a big behind.

> MARY (O.S.)
> Now, don't go there.

> MAYBELLINE
> (realizing what they'd been talking about)
> How long have you been standin' there, Earl?

There is a crashing sound, and we hear Earl grunt. Maybelline and Mary react to the sound, and Maybelline leans over the top of the wall and looks down at Earl, who lays on the floor with the shell of the time clock in his hands.

> MAYBELLINE
> Earl? Are you all right?

Mary's head peers over the wall at Earl.

> EARL
> (pointing to the bottom of time clock)
> Yeah, I'm resetting the clicker.

> MARY
> Guess what, Earl, Maybelline got invited to that Country Star's welcome home party tonight. Did you know that they used to be an item? Who knows, you might be lookin' for a new employee of the month, tomorrow.

> MAYBELLINE
> You sure you're all right?

Earl nods, and Maybelline and Mary go back to work.

> MARY (O.S.)
> So, tell me more about Mr. Harley Davidson.

> MAYBELLINE
> He also had this thing about showers. For a guy with a tattoo he was always clean.

Earl can't stand to hear any more.

> EARL
> Maybelline.

Maybelline sticks her head back over the wall.

> MAYBELLINE
> What is it, Earl?

He looks at her like he had at the picture in the bathroom. He clears his throat and speaks, but the words are difficult.

> EARL
> Maybelline . . . my . . .

Mary sticks her head back over the wall.

> MARY
> Oh, yeah, he also gave her backstage passes for the concert this weekend. Ain't that something?

Earl gives up and nods.

> EARL
> Yeah, that's something.

Mary's head goes back over the wall.

> MAYBELLINE
> What was it you wanted, Earl?

> EARL
> Just wanted to remind you that we're havin' a two-for-one special on Check Cream Cola.

> MAYBELLINE
> Just like every Friday, right?

Maybelline's head goes back over the wall, and Earl puts the time clock cover over his face.

INT. GROCERY STORE—MEAT DEPARTMENT—LATER

A cleaver slams down, cutting the head off a chicken.

                          JOE (O.S.)
        Women?

        JOE, a 40-something redneck, covered in blood and
        chunks of meat and bone, turns to face Earl, who stands
        by the door.

                            JOE
          There's only two things you got to remember . . .
          Chittlin's and Mountain Oysters.

        GENE, a 30-something redneck, also covered in blood,
        laughs as he whacks open a Hog's Head.

                           GENE
          Bullshit! Mountain Oysters my ass.

                            JOE
          Go ahead and laugh, but there's just somethin'
          'bout mixin' intestines and hog balls that makes
          'em work like a African-deeshee-act.

                           GENE
                         (laughing)
          The only meat I know's gonna make a woman hot
          is some good ole USDA Tube Steak.

                            JOE
          Yeah, you must be really firin' up with that
          Vienna Sausage you're totin'.

        Gene looks at Earl, who looks out the window, down the
        aisle to a distant Maybelline.

                           GENE
          I told you, if you'd bring your ass out to Bookie's
          once in a while you could meet some women.
          Drunk Women. Women that'd be impressed you
          was the Manager of the damn Quick Check. Hell,
          most of 'em are happy if you got teeth.

        He throws the brainless hog's head in a five gallon
        bucket and grabs another head.

                           EARL
          It's too smoky and there ain't nobody like
          Maybelline out there.

Gene with hog's head in hand.

> GENE
> (mock frustration)
> Earl, that place is full of Maybellines. You just
> need to reconsider your standards. It wouldn't
> hurt you to lower 'em a notch or two.

Joe whacks off another chicken head.

> JOE
> (to Gene)
> If yours got any lower, people'ld have to start
> lockin' their dogs up at night.

Gene splits open another Hog's Head.

> GENE
> Earl, you've always been like this. In High School
> you carried around that chubby for Lou Ann
> Cullpepper for a year, but you never said a
> Goddamned word to her. And when you did finally
> say something to her, she laughed at you. Why?

Earl turns away from the window and looks at Gene.

> EARL
> This is different.

> GENE
> Because you told her some bullshit about your
> heart bein' a song.

Earl turns back to the window.

> GENE
> When you gone learn, Earl? Women don't want to
> hear poetry, they want you to buy 'em a few
> drinks, dance a couple dances with 'em, then take
> 'em home and pop your John Henry to 'em a
> couple times.

> JOE
> Boy, you talk like a man with a paper asshole.
> When it comes to women, you don't know a Dick
> Whistle from a yo-yo.

> GENE
> (to Earl)
> Ain't you heard? They want it as bad as we do.
> You just got to get 'em drunk first.

> JOE
> Look, Earl, I'll see what I can throw together by
> closin'. Maybe I can dig up a few Mountain
> Oysters for you.

Curtis's song starts to play on the radio.

> D.J. (O.S.)
> Here it is again. The new one, our very own
> Curtis Anderson.

> GENE
> (overlapping D.J.)
> I just wanta know what the big fuckin' hurry is?
> You gone this long without a woman.

Earl stands staring down the aisle at Maybelline.

> EARL
> It just has to be today.

> GENE (O.S.)
> (to himself)
> It just has to be today. The man walks around
> with a chubby for months and it has to be today.

INT. REGISTER—SAME

Maybelline is finishing checking out ROY, a heavy-set
man dressed like a cowboy.

> ROY
> They're having Oyster Night at Bookie's this
> weekend. Pay ten dollars to get in and eat all you
> want. What you think?

Maybelline smiles as she takes his money.

> MAYBELLINE
> I'll pass this time, Roy.

ROY

Okay, but Country Cruisin's gonna be playin'.

MAYBELLINE

Do you want your green stamps?

ROY

You know, you can have 'em, darlin'.

Maybelline smiles, and Roy winks at her and leaves.

MAYBELLINE

Bye, Roy.

ROY
(calling over his shoulder)

Bye, darling.

MARY

Look at you, hustlin' customers for their Green
Stamps just so you can get a set of Elvis Presley
china. If you get with Mr. Harley Davidson, you
won't have to worry about stuff like that.

MAYBELLINE

You know, I don't think I'd enjoy doin' it on a
Harley, now. I don't think I could take the noise.

MARY

So don't do it on a Harley.

MAYBELLINE

The thing is, sometimes I got the feelin' Curtis
was more into the Harley than he was me.

MARY

And that's bad? Hell, if it wasn't for Billie Dee
Williams, I don't think Daryl could do it.

MAYBELLINE

It's like when Curtis sings a song. It sounds great,
but you don't believe he means it. He's just doin'
it to be cool. You know, like when Elvis sang one,
you knew it was from his heart.

MARY

Well, girl, let me tell you, Elvis is Dead.

>   MAYBELLINE
> I know. And I'm gettin' too old to keep lookin' for
> one, right?

>   MARY
> Hell, you've already dated about every man in the
> county.
>   (pause; small laugh)
> Except Earl.

Earl marches up the aisle towards the front of the store
ready to give it another try, but when he hears Mary
mention Maybelline's dating habits, he stops and begins
to straighten a honey display, eavesdropping in on their
conversation.

>   MAYBELLINE
> Well, most of the men around here ain't good for
> nothin' but havin' a good time. Of course, I ain't
> ever been against havin' a good time.

Maybelline smiles.

>   MARY
> You know that there ain't no man around here
> gonna compare to a rich country star. You just
> need to get off your ass and go for it.

>   MAYBELLINE
> What do you want me to do? Propose to him?

>   MARY
> No, you just need to go back to that party tonight
> in a short black dress with a lot of cleavage and
> spend the evenin' wavin' it in front of his nose.

Maybelline leans forward, pushes her breasts together to
make cleavage, while considering Mary's suggestion.

>   MAYBELLINE
> What'd you think?

Earl, seeing this, turns quickly back to his work,
knocking over a bottle of honey. He sits the honey back
up right, but it spills onto his hand. He struggles with
the sticky bottle.

                          MARY
     I think, if you just give Curtis some of that
     Maybelline charm, he'll be cookin' you breakfast
     in the mornin', honey.

Earl, flustered, tries to wipe his hands on one of the toilet
tissue rolls. It sticks to his hand, and the roll rips open
as he struggles to free it. In seconds Earl's hands are
covered in tissue as he tries to gather the spilling roll.

                    MAYBELLINE (O.S.)
     You think he'd make me a back and grits omelet?

                       MARY (O.S.)
     With hash browns and gravy biscuits.

                    MAYBELLINE (O.S.)
     Stop it, girl, you're makin' me hungry.

A short elderly black woman pushes her buggy into Earl.

                         WOMAN
                 (shouting out of deafness)
     Do you know where the napkins are?

He tries to compensate for her shouting by talking real
low.

                          EARL
                    (whispering)
     They're down the aisle.

                         WOMAN
     What?

Earl tries to mime that it's down the aisle.

                         WOMAN
     You all right?

Earl rushes down the aisle and grabs a package of
napkins.

                          EARL
     Here.

> WOMAN
> No! Not the table napkins. The Menstruation
> Napkins! My grandbaby havin' her first visit.

Everyone's attention is now focused on Earl and the
Woman. His face is red. He looks down at his hands and
then up to Mary and Maybelline who are looking around
their magazine racks, laughing. Earl takes the woman to
find what she wants.

> MARY
> He's pitiful.

> MAYBELLINE
> Yeah, but he's kind of sweet.

Maybelline smiles as she watches Earl walk away,
patiently, with the Woman. Toilet tissue trailing behind
them.

> WOMAN
> Back when I had my first visit, we used rags.
> We'd just have to stop every now and then to
> wash 'em out.

INT. PRODUCE DEPARTMENT—LATER

Two shapes can be seen through the two small windows
on the stainless steel swingin' doors to the back room.

> JEROME (O.S.)
> You see, Earl, the Good Lord ain't made no fruit
> as sweet or as bitter as a woman.

JEROME, the produce manager, a 60-year-old black man,
comes through the door, pulling a cart carrying produce,
with Earl in tow. They walk through the dairy section on
their way to the Produce department.

> JEROME
> And there ain't nothing more addictive. A man
> will give a woman the last penny he's got and
> smile while he does it.

Jerome sits the peach back in the crate and starts
pulling the cart again.

> JEROME

You're missin' the point, boy. You got to look for
the peach inside of her, and see her in a way
ain't nobody ever seen her. Then talk to her with
your peach.

> EARL
> (confused)

I just want to know how to tell her how I feel.

> JEROME

That's what I'm tellin' you, boy. You just look deep
into her eyes, past all the flesh, blood and bone,
and see that peach inside of her.

He stops the cart and grabs another peach.

> JEROME

And then you speak to her from your peach.
Something like . . .
> (he looks at the peach as if a lover)
"Baby, your sugar is sweet." But don't say it. Just
think it.

> EARL

Jerome, I'm more confused now than when I came
over here.

Jerome puts the peach in Earl's hand.

> JEROME

Here, you try it.

> EARL

What?

Jerome positions Earl with the peach in front of his face.

> JEROME

Now, look into her eyes, boy, and think, "Baby,
your sugar is sweet."

> EARL

This is stupid.

> JEROME
> (insisting)

Just do it, boy. Seeee theee Peeaach.

Earl tries the most seductive look he can muster, but he looks as if he's in pain.

                    EARL
              (trying to imitate Jerome)
        Baby, your . . .

                    JEROME
        Think it. Don't say it.

Earl struggles with the thought, trying to telepathically seduce the peach. He strains.

                    JEROME
        Don't hurt yourself, boy.

Jerome laughs, shakes his head, giving up. He takes the peach out of Earl's hand and replaces it with another one.

                    JEROME
        Here, try this one. I think you scared that one.

Jerome starts pulling the cart again, leaving Earl standing there with a peach in his hand.

INT. GROCERY STORE—FRONT—LATER

Maybelline sits on her register chewing gum, smokin' a cigarette, and drinking a Dr. Pepper, while reading a magazine. Mary sweeps the floor.

                    MAYBELLINE
        There's just this thing missin' from my life.
        Somethin', I don't think no man's gonna satisfy.

                    MARY
        What's that?

Maybelline turns her magazine around to reveal a picture of a big shiny Peterbilt Truck.

                    MAYBELLINE
        A 359 Peterbilt with a 15 double over, and a Jake
        Brake.

                    MARY
        What?

Mary walks over and grabs the magazine.

> MAYBELLINE
>
> When I was nineteen I had this thing for truck drivers.

Mary gives Maybelline an "Are You Kiddin'?" look.

> MAYBELLINE
>
> You know, 'cause I ain't ever been nowhere, and they had. Anyway, it didn't take long to realize, it was the truck and not the man.
>
> MARY
> (giving her back the magazine)
>
> You're crazy.

> MAYBELLINE
>
> I'm telllin' you that if it wasn't for my speedin' tickets, I'd already have my CDL and I'd be haulin' a load of cows down some lonesome interstate.

> MARY
>
> Now I know you're crazy.

> MAYBELLINE
> (going back to Magazine)
>
> You've just never driven a Peterbilt.

> MARY
>
> Thank goodness.

> MAYBELLINE
>
> Curtis never got it, either. He kept tellin' me I'd outgrow it. The deal was if he made it, and I hadn't outgrown it, he'd have to buy me a brand new Peterbilt.

> MARY
>
> See, now you've got a reason to go to that party tonight. To get a Peter Truck.

> MAYBELLINE
>
> I guess it wouldn't hurt to go see if he's grown up any. They say anything is possible.

                         MARY
You just pretend he's got one of them Peter trucks
in his pocket, and you'll be all right.

Maybelline looks back at her magazine and turns the
page.

                      MAYBELLINE
I don't know. I might could settle for a
Freightliner, long as it had a jake brake.

She shows Mary the picture and smiles.

INT. GROCERY STORE—BACK ROOM—LATER

Earl is sitting alone in his cubby hole, staring intensely
at a peach. Maybelline walks up.

                      MAYBELLINE
    There you are.

He turns to face Maybelline, hiding the peach behind his
back.

                      MAYBELLINE
What you got behind your back, Earl?

Earl looks at Maybelline like he practiced on the peach.
He strains to send her his thought.

                      MAYBELLINE
Damn, Earl, I just asked a question. You don't
have to look at me like I pissed in your
cornflakes.

He deflates and pulls the peach from behind his back.

                         EARL
    Sorry.

He sits the peach back on the dog food bag.

                      MAYBELLINE
All that fuss over a peach? What's got into you
today, Earl?

>   EARL
> Do you like chittlins?

>   MAYBELLINE
> What? Look, Earl, I was wonderin' if I could come
> in late tomorrow. I decided I was gonna go to that
> party.

Earl tries to hide his disappointment.

>   MAYBELLINE
> Do you think I can come in after lunch? You
> never know how late these things run.

>   EARL
>   (small protest)
> Maybelline, you know Saturdays are our big day,
> and . . .

>   MAYBELLINE
>   (agitated)
> Earl, I can't believe you would be so selfish. It's
> not like I ever ask for any time off.

>   EARL
>   (reluctantly)
> Well . . . all right.

>   MAYBELLINE
> Thanks, Earl, but it wouldn't hurt you to act like
> you hoped I had a good time tonight.

>   EARL
> Yeah, I hope you have a good time.

>   MAYBELLINE
> Earl, are you sure that you're all right? I think
> you might be comin' down with somethin'. You
> been actin' stranger than usual today.

She smiles.

>   MAYBELLINE
>   (walking off)
> Earl, I thought you were allergic to peaches.

Maybelline leaves. Earl picks up the peach, looks at it,
and tosses it into a box of trash.

INT. GROCERY STORE—SERIES OF SHOTS

This is a montage of people giving Earl advice. A Bugged
Eye PEST CONTROL MAN sprays the produce section as
he speaks to the CAMERA as if to Earl. Distracted, he
sprays some of the produce that is stacked on the floor.

                   PEST CONTROL MAN
  How to get a woman's heart?
         (slimy smile)
  Try a chainsaw.

A Big Burly HUNTER stands next to the Beer cooler with
a twelve pack of Busch Beer in his hand.

                   HUNTER
  Don't bathe. It's like deer. They got to smell your
  scent. It'll drive 'em crazy.

A Middle Age GREASY TRUCK DRIVER stands at the back
entrance of his truck. He tries to tell Earl the answer, but
stutters too bad to get through what he's saying.

DARYL, a 30-something overweight black man, poorly
imitating Billy Dee Williams in both look and voice,
stands in the dairy section holding a grocery basket filled
with Colt 45.

                   DARYL
  Earl, Billie Dee don't have to worry about shit like
  that.

The Truck Driver still stutters.

An Hispanic MIGRANT WORKER stands in the Spanish
Food section of the store. He says something in Spanish.

                   MIGRANT WORKER
         (subtitles)
  You could start by takin' off that fuckin' girdle.

The Truck Driver finally gets it out.

                   DRIVER
  Axle grease.

EXT. LOADING DOCK—SUNSET

Earl sits, despondent, on the loading dock as the sun sets.

EXT. GROCERY STORE—SUNSET

Earl, downtrodden, pushes a cart of groceries out for
MR. SASSER, an old man who talks by pressing one of
those vibrating things against his neck. He has thick
glasses and chews on a cigar.

> MR. SASSER
> (subtitles)
> Now, take that Curtis fellow. He's somebody we
> can be proud of. He ain't drivin' up and down
> these streets drinkin' and doin' dope. No, he's up
> in Nashville makin' something of hisself.

Mr. Sasser gives Earl a quarter for unloading his
groceries.

> MR. SASSER
> (subtitles)
> You know why he made it, don't you?

Earl shrugs.

> MR. SASSER
> 'Cause he knew what he wanted and he went
> after it.
> (he climbs in car)
> Most people just spend their lives thinkin' and
> talkin' about shit, but never doin' nothin' about it.
> Earl, don't be a thinker, be a doer. Now, let me
> hear you say it. Come on now.

> EARL
> Don't be a thinker be a doer.

Mr. Sasser drives off, smiling.

> MR. SASSER
> Now keep that up.

Earl watches, mumbling the line. He smiles as it sinks in.

INT. FRONT OF STORE—SAME

Earl turns the OPEN side to the CLOSED side and stands
looking at his reflection in the glass door. He dabs on some
cologne and straightens the girdle. Then he turns and
walks towards the registers, mumbling Mr. Sasser's line
over and over. Mary stands alone, counting her money.

>   EARL
>   Where's Maybelline?

>   MARY
>   She's reshelving the returns. You all right?

Earl takes off in search of Maybelline. Mary sniffs the
air and makes a face about Earl's cologne.

>   CUT TO:

Maybelline takes an item out of the grocery buggy and
puts it back on the shelf.

>   CUT TO:

Earl walks quickly down the end of the Aisles looking for
Maybelline, mumbling his new mantra. He sees her at
the other end of the aisle as she's leaving. Earl rushes
quickly down the aisle. He's at the end when Joe comes
striding out of the Meat Department.

>   JOE
>   Your troubles are over, my friend.

>   EARL
>   What?

Maybelline pushes the cart out of sight down the dairy
aisle, on the other side of the store. Joe pulls Earl
towards the Meat Department, while Earl looks back in
search of a glimpse of Maybelline.

>   JOE
>   Wait 'til you see it.

Joe leads Earl, who continues to search through the
window [thinking his mantra] into the meat department.
Gene is in the corner hosing down the bloody floor.
Something lies in front of them on the table under a
dirty meat apron.

>   JOE
>   Are you ready? I call it my Lover's Surprise.

Joe pulls the apron off revealing two mountain oysters placed below a phallic-shaped pile of chittlins shrink-wrapped on a white Styrofoam tray, shaped like a heart. The chittlins are supposed to be cupid's arrow.

Earl fakes a smile and then looks back out the window, his eyes following Maybelline as she comes out the end of an aisle. He politely listens to Joe, but waits for the opportunity to leave.

> JOE
> Now, you want to make sure you mix 'em up in a skillet with scrambled eggs and Hogs Brains. Then you got all your bases covered. And don't cook 'em over five minutes or you'll cook out their potency.

> EARL
> (starting to leave)
> Thanks, Joe.

Gene steps in front of Earl and snatches the package from Earl. He looks at it with disgust and then at Joe.

> GENE
> This is just sick.
> (to Earl)
> Who you gone listen to, Earl, a pervert pushin' hog ball or your cousin who's tryin' to get your ass laid.

> EARL
> Get out of my way, Gene.

> GENE
> Look, Earl, I'll do you a favor. While you close up, I'll pick us up a fifth of OFC, and then I'll take you out to Bookie's tonight, and we'll get you a piece of ass. I guarantee it.

Earl shakes his head and tries to push past Gene.

> GENE
> I guess you think you're too good to go out to Bookie's with a lowly meat cutter, huh?

He squirts Earl with the hose.

> EARL

Now, cut it out.

> GENE

Just 'cause you Manager of the goddamn
Quickcheck, you think that you're better than the
rest of us.

He sprays Earl again.

> EARL

Stop it, or I'm gonna have to do something.

> GENE

Oh, I'm scared.

He sprays again.

Earl looks down, picks up a big tray, and chases Gene, who
continues to spray him, into the freezer. Gene pulls the
door shut, but Earl's momentum can't be stopped, and he
slips on the watery blood and bits of flesh, crashing into
the door, then falling on his ass. We hear the girdle snap
on the way down. He sits wet and panting in front of the
freezer door with his head on his knees.

> GENE (O.S.)

Let me out of here.

> EARL
> (giving up)

It's over now.

He pulls the broken girdle out from under his shirt.

> GENE (O.S.)

Damn it, Earl, it's cold in here, and my pants are
wet!

> JOE

You can't let yourself get so worked up over a
woman.

> EARL

She ain't just a woman. She's why I get up in the
morning. She's the only bright part of this
miserable job, and after tonight, she'll be gone.

Earl sits wet and defeated in watery blood and bits of flesh. He looks at the unrepairable girdle.

                    GENE (O.S.)
        I hope ya'll think this is funny.

                    JOE (O.S.)
        Gene, I ain't had this much fun since Betty Sue
        rented that Kamasutra Video.

                    GENE (O.S.)
        I'm not laughing.

Earl just sits, defeated, holding the limp girdle.

EXT. FRONT OF STORE—CLOSING TIME

Earl, still wet, opens the door to let Jerome out.

                    JEROME
        You got her all to yourself. Now's the time.

                    EARL
        I think it's a little too late for that now. Good
        night, Jerome.

Jerome walks back over to Earl and holds out a peach. Earl doesn't reach for it.

                    EARL
        Thanks anyway, but it won't do any good.

                    JEROME
             (putting the peach in Earl's hand)
        Take the peach, boy.

He turns and walks out into the night.

                    JEROME
        You can't keep your peach hid forever, Earl.

Earl watches him go, unconvinced.

INT. CROW'S NEST OFFICE—SAME

Earl stands outside the office, by the still-playing radio. Maybelline sits in the office filling out her paperwork.

                    EARL
        Do you mind if I cut this off?

> MAYBELLINE
> (not looking)
> Sure whatever.

Earl cuts off the music and climbs into the office, trying to hide his condition by putting on a coat. He puts the peach on the counter in front of him and starts making a grocery order. Maybelline notices the peach and then Earl's condition.

> MAYBELLINE
> Damn, Earl, what happened to you?

> EARL
> Gene.

> MAYBELLINE
> I don't know why you put up with him.

> EARL
> 'Cause he's my cousin.

> MAYBELLINE
> Still, Earl, you got to start standin' up for yourself.

> EARL
> (turning back to work)
> Maybe you're right.

> MAYBELLINE
> You know, a little backbone wouldn't hurt you, none.

They work in silence for a minute.

> MAYBELLINE
> Earl, I'm sorry if I got a little short with you, earlier.

> EARL
> It's all right.

> MAYBELLINE
> You just ain't been yourself today. I think you been spendin' too much time in the meat department.

> EARL
> I guess my mind's been elsewhere.

MAYBELLINE

There ain't nothin' wrong with that. My mind
spends most of its day in the front seat of a
Peterbilt.

EARL

I think it's good for a person to have dreams, like
that. It's somethin' I always like about you. I ain't
never had the courage to do much dreamin' myself.

Maybelline stops what she's doing and turns to face Earl.

MAYBELLINE

You know, you're the only person that's ever
called it that.

EARL

What?

MAYBELLINE

A dream. Most people think I'm a little crazy
'cause of wantin' to drive a truck.

Earl, nervous by Maybelline's attention, turns back to
work.

EARL

Everybody's got to want something.

MAYBELLINE

What is it you want, Earl?

He didn't expect this.

EARL

I can't say.

MAYBELLINE

Come on, Earl. I know there's got to be something
you've always wanted.

Earl pauses, looks at Maybelline, then he turns back
towards his work. Trying to think of something to say.

EARL

Well, nobody knows it, but I'm kind of a closet
songwriter.

MAYBELLINE

I didn't know you were musical, Earl.

                              EARL
                    (he goes back to work)
          Yeah.

                           MAYBELLINE
          What'd you play?

                              EARL
          The guitar.

                           MAYBELLINE
          What kind?

                              EARL
          I got a couple. I got a Gibson J-45 flattop at home,
          and I keep an old Yamaha FG-460 at the store, for
          times when I'm here alone.

                           MAYBELLINE
          You mean you come here on your time off? You
          need a life, honey.

                              EARL
                         (explaining)
          I come here because it's quiet, except for the hum a
          sleepin' store makes. I write my best songs here.

                           MAYBELLINE
                       (looking around)
          It's kind of sleepin' now, ain't it? Why don't you
          get that guitar and play me one of them songs.

                              EARL
          Well, I really need to change the strings.

                           MAYBELLINE
          Come on, Earl. I'd really like to hear one of your
          songs.

                              EARL
          I couldn't. You're use to hearin' people like Curtis.

                           MAYBELLINE
          I'll have you know, I used to be queen of the
          karaoke down at the Charter House. And you
          can't be no worse than any of us were.

          Earl hesitates and lets out a small sigh.

> EARL

Well . . . Okay, I guess.

Earl gets up, climbs out of the office, and opens his
secret compartment in the hollow under the crow's nest.

> EARL

Just don't laugh.

> MAYBELLINE

I might throw tomatoes, but I'd never laugh.

Earl gets the guitar out. He puts his leg on the steps and
the guitar on his knee, and makes a few tuning
adjustments and starts strumming.

> EARL

I'm not used to playing with somebody listenin'.

> MAYBELLINE

Don't be nervous, honey. It's just ole Maybelline.
I'm an easy audience.

Earl sees the peach and decides to play a different song.

> EARL

This one I've been workin' on. It's not quite
finished.

> MAYBELLINE

Okay, Earl, sing the song before we get old.

With his head looking down at the guitar, Earl stands
below Maybelline and serenades her with a song that
expresses the things he hasn't been able to tell her.*
Maybelline sees a side of Earl she never knew existed.
As he sings, he finally gets the courage to look up, and
Maybelline smiles.

> CUT TO:

LATER

As the song continues to play, Earl and Maybelline dance
down the aisles of the Quickcheck. We PULL BACK
through the register and PAN to the peach.

FADE OUT

* Earl's song:

I've often wondered if this moment came

Would I have the courage to call out your name

And could I look in your eyes without going insane

Darling, I'm calling you now

I've often wondered if I had the chance

Would I find the courage to ask you to dance

And could we waltz into some sweet romance

Darling, I'm asking you now

18

CONCLUSION

What's left to say? Only this: Having stressed the importance of craft in screenwriting, I have to be honest: Craft can only take you so far.

"The rest," as William Gibson so wisely said, "is art and up to God."

"Young screenwriters forget they're writers," Mark Spragg told me. "They believe too much in craft—form—and not enough in the art of the piece. It is organic."

Messy. Mysterious. Ultimately, creating a screenplay and film that connect is a mysterious process. And the act of connecting with others, Peter Weir suggests, may be more unconscious than conscious:

> You have to remember that the audience is sitting in their seats dreaming and if you can connect with their unconscious, you really have a powerful connection between viewer and screen. You want them to let the stuff come up from their unconscious, provoked by your energies with just enough logic to feel like you know what you're doing and the picture is under control. That's the challenge, to have enough logic without inhibiting the unconscious.[1]

Enough logic, yes, but not *rules*, as Academy Award winner, Nicholas Kazan, says in *American Screenwriters*:

> In essence, there are *no rules* with film. It's like a dream: it can take many different forms. The important thing is that what happens should be continually surprising and in retrospect seem inevitable. If you have that it doesn't matter what your structure is.[2]

Learn the craft, then give yourself permission to go beyond it.

"Research, think," as Mark Spragg says, "then turn the dogs loose and see where they go."

So the last thing I'd like to say is what I've been saying all along: *Play*. Or, as Seamus Heaney says in "Station Island":

> *You are fasted now, light-headed, dangerous.*
> *Take off from here. And don't be so earnest,*
> *so ready for the sackcloth and the ashes.*
> *Let go, let fly, forget.*
> *You've listened long enough. Now strike your note.*[3]

NOTES

1. Linda Seger and Edward Jay Whetmore, *From Script to Screen: The Collaborative Art of Filmmaking*, Henry Holt, New York, 1994, p. 145.
2. Karl Schanzer and Thomas Lee Wright, *American Screenwriters: The Insider's Look at the Art, the Craft, and the Business of Writing Movies*, Avon Books, New York, 1993, p. 248.
3. Seamus Heaney, *Selected Poems 1966–1987*, Farrar, Straus & Giroux, New York, 1990, pp. 211–212.

AVAILABLE SCREENWRITING SOFTWARE

Software	E-Mail or Web Site	Phone
Final Draft	info@finaldraft.com	1-800-231-4055
Movie Magic Screenwriter 2000	screenplay.com	1-800-847-8679
Scriptware	http://scriptware.com	1-800-788-7090
SideBySide	sidebyside@simon1.com	1-888-234-6789

APPENDIX B
FILMS REFERENCED

Title	Availability (DVD unless otherwise indicated)
Romeo and Juliet (1968)	amazon.com ASIN# 0792165055
Death of a Salesman (1985)	amazon.com ASIN# B00007ELDP
The Fugitive	amazon.com ASIN# B00005ATZT
Red (Trois Coleurs: Rouge)	amazon.com ASIN# B000083C5F
Lost in Translation	amazon.com ASIN# B00005JMJ4
Apollo 13	amazon.com ASIN# 0783225733
Pulp Fiction	amazon.com ASIN# 1558908242
Metropolis	amazon.com ASIN# B00007L4MJ
M	amazon.com ASIN# 0780021150
The Big Heat	amazon.com ASIN# B00005RDRL
The Full Monty	amazon.com ASIN# 6305622914
Star Wars (Star Wars Trilogy)	amazon.com ASIN# B00003CXCT
Babe	amazon.com ASIN# B0000AK7AB
Marty	amazon.com ASIN# B00005AUKB
The Hospital	amazon.com ASIN# B00009Y3QE
City Lights	amazon.com ASIN# B00017LVN2
Citizen Kane	amazon.com ASIN# B00003CX9E
Tootsie	amazon.com ASIN# B0000CXD0
Ed Wood	amazon.com ASIN# B0000VD04M
People vs. Larry Flynt	amazon.com ASIN# 0800141865
crazy/beautiful	amazon.com ASIN# B00003CY5P
The Tuxedo	amazon.com ASIN# B00005JL8Z
My Beautiful Laundrette	amazon.com ASIN# B00008R9KF
Animal House	amazon.com ASIN# B0000A02T2
Analyze This/Analyze That	amazon.com ASIN# B00008NJFT
Election	amazon.com ASIN# B00001MXXJ
About Schmidt	amazon.com ASIN# B00005JLSK
Teacher's Pet (VHS)	amazon.com ASIN# 6302287448
The Opposite Sex (VHS)	amazon.com ASIN# 6301980727
Batman Forever	amazon.com ASIN# 0790731002

The Adventures of Felix	amazon.com ASIN# B00005U2FI
Jeanne and the Perfect Guy	amazon.com ASIN# B00004W55WP
Matilda	amazon.com ASIN# 0800130227
Life	amazon.com ASIN# 0783237367
Big Trouble	amazon.com ASIN# 0783237367
Intolerable Cruelty	amazon.com ASIN# B00005JMET
Bedazzled (2000)	amazon.com ASIN# B00003CXKJ
Manhattan	amazon.com ASIN# 0792846109
Citizen Ruth	amazon.com ASIN# B00007K028
Dr. Strangelove	amazon.com ASIN# B000055Y0X
As Good as it Gets	amazon.com ASIN# 767811100
Courage Under Fire	amazon.com ASIN# B00005221J
Nick of Time	amazon.com ASIN# B0000IRE6
Ulee's Gold	amazon.com ASIN# 0792842189
Butch Cassidy and the Sundance Kid	amazon.com ASIN# B00003RQNJ
The Princess Bride	amazon.com ASIN# B00005LOKQ
Everything That Rises (VHS)	amazon.com ASIN# 0780624130
Poison Ivy	amazon.com ASIN# 0780627776
Shine	amazon.com ASIN# 0780619587
Marnie	amazon.com ASIN# 6305839395
When Harry Met Sally	amazon.com ASIN# B00003CXDC
Bull Durham	amazon.com ASIN# B00005V9HG
Grosse Point Blanke	amazon.com ASIN# 1558908382
Shawshank Redemption	amazon.com ASIN# B0000399WI
Rain Man	amazon.com ASIN# B0000YEEGM
Annie Hall	amazon.com ASIN# 6304907729
Hannah and Her Sisters	amazon.com ASIN# B00005O06J
Philadelphia	amazon.com ASIN# 0800141806
sex, lies, and videotape	amazon.com ASIN# 0767812158
Say Anything	amazon.com ASIN# B00008G7UK

FURTHER READING

You have a great many books on writing in general and screenwriting in particular to choose from, but if I could only take a dozen to a desert island for the rest of my writing life, I would choose these for instruction and inspiration:

Dancyger, Ken and Jeff Rush. *Alternative Scriptwriting: Writing Beyond the Rules.* Boston: Focal Press, 1995.

Dannenbaum, Jed, Carroll Hodge, and Doe Mayer. *Creative Filmmaking From the Inside Out.* New York: Simon & Schuster, 2003

Egri, Lajos. *The Art of Dramatic Writing.* New York: Simon and Schuster, 1960.

Gibson, William. *Shakespeare's Game.* New York: Atheneum, 1978.

Goldman, William. *Adventures In the Screen Trade: A Personal View of Hollywood and Scriptwriting.* New York: Warner Books, 1983.

Lamott, Anne. *Bird By Bird: Some Instructions On Writing and Life.* New York: Pantheon, 1994.

Rodale, J.I. *The Synonym Finder.* New York: Warner Books, 1978.

Seger, Linda. *Making a Good Script Great,* 2nd ed. Hollywood: Samuel French, 1994.

Smiley, Sam. *Playwriting: The Structure of Action.* Englewood Cliffs, New Jersey: Prentice-Hall, 1971.

Stern, Jerome. *Making Shapely Fiction.* New York: Norton, 1991.

Strunk, William C. and E.B. White. *The Elements of Style,* 3rd ed. New York: Macmillan, 1979.

REFERENCES

Aristotle. *The Poetics.* Translated by Gerald F. Else. Ann Arbor: University of Michigan Press, 1978.

Atchity, Kenneth. *A Writer's Time.* New York: Norton, 1995.

Baker, George Pierce. *Dramatic Technique.* Boston: Houghton Mifflin, 1919.

Benton, Robert. *Kramer versus Kramer.* Screenplay manuscript, revised 3rd draft, July 14, 1978.

Bettelheim, Bruno. *Surviving.* New York: Knopf, 1979.

Bradbury, Ray. *Zen in the Art of Writing: Releasing the Creative Genius Within You.* New York: Bantam Books, 1992.

Burroway, Janet. *Writing Fiction: A Guide to Narrative Craft,* 4th ed. New York: Harper-Collins, 1996.

Cameron, Julia. *The Artist's Way: A Spiritual Path to Creativity.* New York: G.P. Putnam's Sons, 1992.

Capra, Fritjof. *The Tao of Physics,* 3rd ed. Boston: Shambhala, 1991.

Cooper, Dona. *Writing Great Screenplays for Film and TV,* New York: Prentice Hall, 1994.

Cowgill, Linda. *Writing Short Films: Structure and Content for Screenwriters.* Los Angeles: Lone Eagle Press, 1997.

Csikszentmihalyi, Mihaly. *Creativity: Flow and the Psychology of Discovery and Invention.* New York: HarperPerennial, 1996.

Dancyger, Ken and Jeff Rush. *Alternative Scriptwriting: Writing Beyond the Rules.* Boston: Focal Press, 1995.

Dannenbaum, Jed, Carroll Hodge, and Doe Mayer. *Creative Filmmaking From the Inside Out.* New York: Simon & Schuster, 2003.

Egri, Lajos. *The Art of Dramatic Writing.* New York: Simon & Schuster, 1960.

Ephron, Nora. *When Harry Met Sally.* New York: Knopf, 1992.

Field, Syd. *Screenplay: The Foundations of Screenwriting.* New York: Dell, 1982.

Friedan, Betty. *The Fountain of Age.* New York: Simon & Schuster, 1993.

Froug, William. *Screenwriting Tricks of the Trade.* Los Angeles: Silman-James Press, 1992.

Gibson, William. *Shakespeare's Game.* New York: Atheneum, 1978.

Gilligan, Carol. *In a Different Voice.* Cambridge: Harvard University Press, 1982.

Goldman, William. *Adventures in the Screen Trade: A Personal View of Hollywood and Screenwriting.* New York: Warner Books, 1983.

Goldman, William. *Butch Cassidy and the Sundance Kid.* New York: Bantam Books, 1969.

Gould, Stephen Jay. "Counters and Cable Cars." *The Best American Essays 1991.* New York: Ticknor & Fields, 1991, pp. 78–86.

House, Humphrey. *Aristotle's Poetics.* London: Madeline House, 1956.

Hyde, Lewis. *The Gift: Imagination and the Erotic Life of Property.* New York: Vintage Books, 1979.

Johnson, Claudia & Matt Stevens. *Script Partners: What Makes Film and TV Writing Teams Work.* Studio City, California: Michael Wiese Productions, 2003.

Keane, Chris. *How to Write a Selling Screenplay.* New York: Broadway Books, 1998.

Lamott, Anne. *Bird By Bird: Some Instructions on Writing and Life.* New York: Pantheon Books, 1994.

Lerner, Harriet. *The Dance of Anger: A Woman's Guide to Changing the Patterns of Intimate Relationships.* New York: HarperCollins, 1989.

Lindgren, Ernest. *The Art of the Film.* New York: Collier Books, 1970.

Lucas, George, Gloria Katz, and Willard Huyck. *American Grafitti.* New York: Grove Press, 1973.

McKee, Robert. *Story: Substance, Structure, Style, and the Principles of Screenwriting.* New York: HarperCollins, 1997.

Miller, Jean Baker. *Toward a New Psychology of Women,* 2nd ed. Boston: Beacon Press, 1986.

Olds, Linda. *Metaphors of Interrelatedness: Toward a Systems Theory of Psychology.* Albany: State University of New York Press, 1992.

Raphaelson, Samson. *The Human Nature of Playwriting*. New York: Macmillan, 1949.

Rich, R. Ruby. "Choose One Memory to Take With You, He Asks." *The New York Times*, Sunday, May 16, 1999, p. 268.

Schanzer, Karl and Thomas Lee Wright. *American Screenwriters: The Insider's Look at the Art, the Craft, and the Business of Writing Movies*. New York: Avon Books, 1993.

Seger, Linda. *Making a Good Script Great*. Hollywood: Samuel French, 1994.

Seger, Linda and Edward Jay Whetmore. *From Script to Screen: The Collaborative Art of Filmmaking*. New York: Henry Holt, 1994.

Shelton, Robert. *Bull Durham*, Screenplay manuscript, May 1, 1987.

Sherman, Eric. *Directing the Film: Film Directors on Their Art*. Los Angeles: Acrobat Books, 1996.

Smiley, Sam. *Playwriting: The Structure of Action*. Englewood Cliffs, New Jersey: Prentice-Hall, 1971.

Stern, Jerome. *Making Shapely Fiction*. New York: Norton, 1991.

Sweet, Jeffrey. "An Object Lesson for Playwrights." *The Writer*, December 1989, pp. 18–20.

Tarantino, Quentin. *Pulp Fiction*, screenplay manuscript.

Wade, Nicholas. "Play Fair: Your Life May Depend On It," *The New York Times*, Sunday, September 21, 2003.

INDEX